INTRODUCTIO

MANAGERIAL ECC

GU00792462

Economics

Editor

SIR ROY HARROD
F.B.A.

Hon. Student of Christ Church, Oxford,
and Hon. Fellow of Nuffield College

INTRODUCTION TO
MANAGERIAL ECONOMICS

Christopher I. Savage
Professor of Economics in
the University of Leicester

&

John R. Small
Professor of Accountancy and Finance
at the Heriot-Watt University, Edinburgh

HUTCHINSON UNIVERSITY LIBRARY
LONDON

HUTCHINSON & CO (*Publishers*) LTD
178–202 Great Portland Street, London W1

London Melbourne Sydney
Auckland Bombay Toronto
Johannesburg New York

First published 1967
Reprinted 1968

*This book has been set in Times, printed in Great Britain
on Smooth Wove paper by Anchor Press, and
bound by Wm. Brendon, both of Tiptree, Essex*
09 084092 5 (cased)
09 084093 4 (paper)

CONTENTS

Preface   7

1 THE ECONOMIC BACKGROUND TO MANAGEMENT   9

2 THE BUSINESS FIRM AND ITS OBJECTIVES   13

3 PROFIT

    1. The nature of profit   22
    2. The measurement of profit   26
    3. Profit policy   33

4 INVESTMENT POLICY

    1. Investment decisions   36
    2. Measuring investment opportunities   39
    3. Cash movement over the period of investment   50
    4. The investment life   55
    5. The cost of capital   59
    6. Uncertainty   72

5 COMPETITION

    1. The rationale of competition   81
    2. Exchange and market categories   83
    3. Competitive behaviour   85
    4. Understanding competition   92

6 COST

    1. Long-run influences on cost: location, scope, size 94
    2. Production and costs   103
    3. Operational research   124

7 COST CONTROL

    1. Aims and purposes of cost control   134
    2 The management problems of a cost control
        system   141
    3 The level of achievement incorporated into budgets 143

8 DEMAND ANALYSIS AND FORECASTING

    1. The elementary economics of demand   153
    2. A digression on the socio-economic analysis of
        demand   160
    3. Demand forecasting   163

9 PRICING POLICY

    1. Introduction   185
    2. The elementary economics of price   186
    3. Innovation: pricing over the life cycle of a product 194
    4. Prescriptive: alternative pricing conventions 197
    5. Descriptive: how firms actually price their
        products   202

10 PRODUCT POLICY, SALES PROMOTION AND
    MARKET STRATEGY

    1. Introduction   210
    2. Product policy   212
    3. Advertising and sales promotion   218
    4. Market strategy—the decision theory approach 223

    Index   227

PREFACE

This is intended as an elementary introduction to managerial economics. It does not pretend to be a comprehensive treatise. It is hoped that this book will be of use to the general reader, to the student working for a degree or diploma in management, business studies or economics, as well as to the practising manager interested in the relevance of economic concepts and analysis to business problems and decisions.

Modern management needs both knowledge of techniques and skill in judgement. We have tried to keep a balance between the two. Some modern quantitative techniques are introduced and discussed, though we have not tried to provide a comprehensive manual of such techniques. What we would stress is that *intelligent application of quantitative techniques to business presupposes considered judgement and hard and careful thinking about the nature of the particular problem to be solved*. We believe that the economist, schooled to recognize relevant objectives and criteria, to understand problems of choice and to recognize the difficulties attaching to such concepts as value, cost, efficiency, profit, etc., is well equipped to provide a basis for the considered judgement and careful thinking needed in making business decisions. In his pioneer work on *Managerial Economics* in 1951, Professor Joel Dean described its role as 'conceptual rather than metrical'. Recent advances suggest that managerial economics should be both conceptual *and* metrical; for while measurement without theory can only lead to false precision, theory without measurement can rarely be operationally useful.

It is hoped that this book will serve as an introduction to the more advanced works available in the field of managerial economics, operational research and management accounting. No advanced knowledge of economics, accounting or mathematics is assumed here, though prior or concurrent study of these disciplines is obviously helpful.

Inevitably, an introductory work of this kind must draw heavily on the ideas of others, for which, we hope, due acknowledgment has been made in the text and footnotes. We would also like to thank all those academic colleagues who have read and given advice on various chapters of this book in the course of completion. We are particularly grateful to Sir Roy Harrod for his detailed comments and valuable suggestions on our final draft. Responsibility for all defects and shortcomings that remain is, of course, entirely that of the authors.

Acknowledgement is due to Gerald Duckworth & Co. Ltd for permission to quote from 'The Microbe' by Hilaire Belloc; Faber & Faber Ltd for permission to quote from 'The Love Song of J. Alfred Prufrock' by T. S. Eliot; and John Murray (Publishers) Ltd for permission to quote from *Collected Poems* by John Betjeman.

C. I. S.
J. R. S.

September 1966

I

THE ECONOMIC BACKGROUND
TO MANAGEMENT

This book is about the use of economics in management decisions.
The main concern of political economists has usually been the
grand design of the economic system: its form, its functioning and
its regulation. We, however, are concerned, not with the national
economy, but with the business firm and the economic problems
that every business management must somehow solve. *Micro*-
economic decision-making by the firm has nevertheless to be made
within the broader *macro*-economic environment,* so that it is
appropriate to begin by mentioning briefly the characteristics of
the economic system in which the business of today has to operate.

Social and political arrangements of different countries vary
enormously, but civilized societies, whether capitalist, socialist or
communist, have certain fundamental economic problems to solve.
Despite the recent debate about 'the affluent society', the hard fact
is that most resources are scarce. Consequently, choices have to be
made by individuals, by businesses and by society. What goods and
services shall be produced and in what quantities? How shall goods
and services be produced—by what technological processes? For
whom shall goods be produced—who is to get the fruits of production? Textbooks on general economic principles show how, in
a mixed-enterprise economy like our own, these fundamental
decisions are largely settled through the price system rather than
by centralized planning. Consumer demand expressing itself
through prices and the market and the response of business firms
to profitable opportunities in conditions of competitive free
enterprise largely settle what is to be produced and how, and also
determine the incomes of those who supply the necessary produc-
ive services or inputs.

*Macro-economics is concerned with the economic system as a whole; *micro*-
conomics with the individual components—e.g. firms—within that system.

This thumbnail sketch is a gross over-simplification of reality for several reasons. One is that there are many obstacles to the free working of the price system and competition in practice does not conform to the 'perfect' conditions postulated by economic theories of the pricing mechanism. This probably matters less than some economists appear to think, since change, innovation and the exploitation of new products and opportunities are more characteristic of modern business behaviour in a dynamic economy than routine adjustments of price or output. Indeed, the most important single fact about the economic background in which modern business operates is the tremendous pace of technological, economic and social change. Modern society is committed to the idea of 'rapid and cumulative economic progress' and no industry or business firm can isolate itself from the consequences. In such an environment, as Professor G. C. Allen has written:

Established producers are under frequent pressure to adapt themselves to new demands and technical methods. The way lies open to the innovator and the business of the routineer becomes insecure.[1]

Dunning and Thomas, in describing 'the new technological revolution' that has occurred in British industry since the war, have shown how in twenty years the whole balance of industrial power has shifted with the advent of new technologies and innovations such as in oil refining, nuclear energy, chemicals and electronics. An important result has been the closer dependence between different branches of industry and between science and technology. Many of the new 'science based' industries are hybrids and the specialist producer is less common than formerly.[2]

Our quick sketch of the economy also over-simplifies in another important respect: it ignores the state. Free competitive enterprise and the price system can only function within a framework of state regulation. Perhaps surprisingly, this has always been so. In the past, that framework was mainly confined to the laws of contract and the sale of goods and to statutes governing the incorporation of joint-stock companies. Today, the state intervenes in many other ways. The regulation of wages and working conditions, pricing and production of agricultural commodities, the location of industry and regulation of monopoly power are only a few of the areas in which the freedom of private business is limited. Moreover, since the Second World War, the British Government, like Governments of many other countries, has intervened actively through monetary and fiscal policies of the kind advocated by the late Lord Keynes[3] to maintain full employment and to lessen inequalities in the distribution of incomes. In the post-war years, monetary policy has also been applied, sometimes quite severely, to protect the British balance of payments. Recently, Governments have been experimenting with ways of achieving more rapid economic growth and combining it with an incomes policy. This does not exhaust the possible ways in which the modern state can intervene in economic affairs, but it is sufficient to indicate the kind of environment in which the business firm must operate.[4] Government policies which expand or contract bank credit, vary rates of taxation, influence wages and their regulation or limit freedom in pricing policy impose important restraints on managerial discretion.

The Government intervenes in such matters because, in a modern democratic 'welfare state', the public expects the state to assume an active rather than a passive role in looking after society's needs. Many people in the 1960's might, for example, consider the following as reasonable economic objectives for the Government to pursue:

(1) high and stable level of employment;

(2) the avoidance of inflation;

(3) rising standards of living, i.e. economic growth;

(4) satisfactory balance of payments situation and maintenance of the external value of the currency;

(5) avoidance of inequalities in the distribution of income;

(6) freedom of choice for the consumer and removal of monopoly.

These are only some possible objectives and obviously they cannot all be pursued simultaneously. An attempt at too rapid economic growth could easily lead to inflation and serious balance of payments problems. Taxation aimed at narrowing unequal income distribution might prove a disincentive to economic growth. It is easy to list economic and social objectives, but often difficult to reconcile them. The difficult task of reconciliation is the province of macro-economic analysis and policy. What must be stressed here, however, is that, while the British economy works mainly according to free enterprise principles, Government intervention today is considerable and is probably here to stay.

In surveying the economic background to management, we have stressed three points. First, the economy in which business operates is predominantly a free enterprise economy using prices and markets. Secondly, it is an economy undergoing rapid technological and economic change. Thirdly, the intervention of Government in economic affairs has increased in recent decades and is likely to remain considerable. These facts set the constraints within which modern business management must operate. Management can ignore neither the workings of the market; nor the pace of economic change; nor the activities of Government in the economic sphere. It must work within an economic system which has these characteristics. And it hardly needs to be pointed out that a progressive management must keep itself well and continuously informed of changes in Government economic policies and also be alert to changes in the main trends in the national and international economy.[5]*

NOTES

1. G. C. Allen, *The Structure of Industry in Britain*, p. 5.

2. Dunning and Thomas, *British Industry—Change and Development in the Twentieth Century*, pp. 31–38.

3. J. M. Keynes, *General Theory of Employment, Interest and Money* (1936).

4. See Dunning and Thomas, op. cit., ch. 6 for a discussion of other aspects of Government intervention.

5. See, for example, HMSO, *Economic Trends* and *Monthly Digest of Statistics*.

*See Chapter 8 below for a list of important economic indicators.

THE BUSINESS FIRM AND ITS OBJECTIVES

'Would you tell me please, which way I ought to go from here?'
'That depends a good deal on where you want to get to,' said the
Cat.
'I don't much care where. . . .' said Alice.
'Then it doesn't much matter which way you go,' said the Cat.
'. . . so long as I get somewhere' *Alice added as an explanation.*
ALICE'S ADVENTURES IN WONDERLAND

Economics is a social science concerned with the efficient allocation of scarce resources. The function of *management* is the efficient direction of a business organization—'to make a productive enterprise out of human and material resources'.[1] Problems of scarcity and choice are an important part of managerial decision-making. For example, a firm with limited floor space might have to choose between making car bodies or refrigerators. Clearly, rational choice could only be made in such a situation if the firm's objectives were first clearly defined.

Managerial economics is concerned with business efficiency. *Efficiency* is an elusive concept and we must resist the temptation to be lured into a philosophical debate about its meaning. A useful distinction for our present purpose is between technological and economic efficiency. The former assumes that resources are available and that production is carried out to the best possible technological specifications. Economic efficiency, however, recognizes the limitations of cost and consumer preferences. First, in the choice of inputs to produce a given output, economic efficiency requires that the proportions of alternative resources used should achieve the required result at minimum cost—'an economic decision taken within a technical framework'.[2] Secondly, in choosing between alternative outputs, prices and consumer preferences determine the quantities and types produced. These principles are important. Businesses have failed because they placed too much emphasis on technical perfection and ignored costs and market requirements.

The business organization, like the larger national economy, engages in production, consumption and exchange and both may be conceived as moving efficiently towards their respective goals or objectives.

Within the business, scarce resources have to be allocated among alternative uses. The expected *return* from employing resources for one purpose must be balanced against their opportunity costs— what they might have earned in alternative uses—and the most profitable alternative must be chosen. The internal goals of the business organization in a free enterprise system are, however, different from those of the economy of which it forms a part. The firm is not primarily concerned, as is Government, with the welfare of society; it is usually concerned with such things as profits or related matters such as cost reduction. Profits are commonly taken as the criterion of business efficiency, maximum profits being attained when the difference between Total Receipts of the firm and its Total Costs is maximized. Simon in his *Administrative Behaviour* states:

The criterion of efficiency is most easily understood in its application to commercial organizations that are largely guided by profit objectives. In such organizations the criterion of efficiency dictates the selection of that alternative of all those available to the individual which will yield the greatest net (money) return to the organization. This 'balance sheet' efficiency involves on the one hand the maximization of income if costs are considered as fixed, and on the other hand the minimization of costs if income is considered as fixed. In practice, of course, the maximization of income and the minimization of cost must be considered simultaneously—that is what is really to be maximized is the difference between the two. The simplicity of the efficiency criterion in commercial organizations is due in large part to the fact that money provides a common denominator for the measurement of both output and income and permits them to be directly compared.[3]

Economists have developed a theory of the firm which is based on the assumption of profit maximization in the face of a given market environment and technical conditions of production. There are different versions of the theory of the firm. In particular, the goal of profit maximization has frequently been criticized and rejected by some economists, though no completely adequate alternative theory has replaced it. Without entering on elaborate refinements, the economist's theory of the firm may be summed up in the following propositions:

(1) The firm has goals or objectives towards which it strives, usually defined as to maximize long-run profits or net revenue (leaving aside for the moment the question of defining 'profit').

(2) The firm moves towards its objectives in a rational manner, implying (a) that no action will be taken by the firm which will move it away from its goal of maximum profit; (b) that when confronted with a choice between alternatives, the firm will invariably select that alternative which will tend to move it closer to profit maximization. Rational action is normally understood by economists to mean action in which relevant variables are weighed at the margin. Businesses weigh the expected costs of producing additional units of output (marginal cost) against expected revenue from the sale of additional units of output (marginal revenue), profits being maximized where marginal cost equals marginal revenue.[4]

(3) The firm is conceived as a transformation unit, transforming valued inputs into outputs of a higher order of value. This involves (a) knowledge of the relevant 'production function', which summarizes the relationships between rates of input and rates of output, given the state of technological knowledge; (b) the 'minimum cost mix'—the least costly combination of inputs capable of producing a given output.

(4) The market environment in which the firm operates is given. There is a continuum of such environments (each one of which, however, is discrete) ranging from perfect competition to monopoly. Markets are defined by (a) the number of competitive firms; (b) the nature of their product—whether homogeneous or differentiated.[5]

(5) The theory of the firm concentrates primarily on changes in the prices and quantities of inputs and outputs.[6]

The economist's theory of the firm can be carried to varying degrees of elaboration. Fundamentally it centres on the assumption of profit maximization and the assumption that the firm acts rationally in pursuit of this objective. Rationality is usually taken as implying that the firm has perfect knowledge of all relevant variables when making decisions. Criticism of the theory has been directed from many standpoints: its lack of realism and unsuitability for predictive purposes; its narrow concentration on economic objectives, leaving out of account variables other than profit; its assumption that knowledge is given to the firm and that maximization is not only possible but that firms do in fact maximize profits. Literature criticizing the economist's theory of the firm is extensive and much of it is of considerable economic and philosophical subtlety. The main areas of criticism seem, however, to be as follows:

(1) That profit is only one of the many objectives and variables that businesses consider.

(2) That maximization does not adequately describe what firms do about profits.

These criticisms are directed against the *motivational* assumptions of the theory of the firm, and

(3) That perfect knowledge cannot reasonably be assumed.
This criticism is directed at the *cognitive* assumptions of the theory.

The following are some of the more important criticisms made by economists under the first head:

(a) A. Papandreou[7] argues that organizational objectives grow out of interaction among the various participants in the organization—this interaction produces a 'general preference function'. It is questionable whether this is any better than profit maximization theory. It raises serious difficulties of measurement.

(b) K. Rothschild[8] has suggested that the primary motive of enterprise is long-run survival. Decisions therefore aim to maximize the security of the organization. The desire for secure profit is a dominant motive in oligopolistic industries. W. Fellner has similarly argued that firms are interested in 'safety margins'.

(c) W. J. Baumol argues that firms seek to maximize *sales* (total revenue) subject to a profit constraint.[9]

(d) T. Scitovsky introduces leisure as a variable.[10] The entrepreneur, depending on his character, may elect to maximize his profits and forego leisure, or to choose total leisure and give up all profit, or may decide on some combination of the two.

(e) M. Reder has argued that an entrepreneur may have two objectives: (i) to maximize profits and (ii) to maintain financial control of the firm.[11] In these circumstances he may not maximize profits, making some profit sacrifice to finance the firm's expansion from private funds or retained earnings.

(f) W. W. Cooper introduces another variable—liquidity.[12] A commercial bank which operates within a profit maximization framework is limited by certain liquidity restraints. Businesses, it is argued, attempt to maintain liquidity sufficient to assure the firm's financial position and retention of control.

(g) Other economists emphasize the importance of the maintenance of the firm's share of the market as a dominant business objective—a notion not unrelated to the sales maximization hypothesis.

(h) Another possible goal may be payment of good wages and the welfare of employees. Social psychologists commonly stress such factors.

This list of alternative goals is by no means exhaustive. Others have stressed such things as growth, the excellence of a product— e.g. a Rolls-Royce car—the maintenance of good public relations or variables emphasizing the human qualities of the entrepreneur such as the desire for economic power as exemplified by size, or empire building tendencies, which interfere with profit maximization.

These alternative theories emphasize other goals than profits, though most do not exclude profit as constraint within which firms pursue these other goals.

Looking now at the second area of criticism, that maximization does not adequately describe what firms do about profits, this is clearly consistent with some of the theories already mentioned, for instance that of Rothschild which states that firms aim at secure profits. It is assumed that firms have a profit goal, but that they do not attempt to maximize profits. This view has been based on empirical studies such as those of Hall and Hitch[13] and Lester,[14] which suggested that firms did not follow the economists' marginal rules, but used conventions and rules of thumb in their pricing policies and were not generally interested in maximum profits. Accounting procedures and the use of standard costs may suggest that firms rarely use anything approaching the economist's marginal calculation of cost.* It has also been pointed out that standard business procedures, 'short cuts' or guides to policy in fact dominate most short-run business decisions.

The third criticism of the theory of the firm concerns the cognitive assumption. It is argued that, since the significant period in

*Contrast this, however, with Earley's interpretation, p. 18 below and Chapter 9.

making business decisions is the future, it is hardly reasonable to assume perfect knowledge. Most business decisions are taken in a fog of uncertainty. It is unlikely that businesses even know the probability that certain outcomes will occur.* Given such uncertainty, it would seem impossible for a business to know how to maximize its profits as a long-run goal and it seems almost as doubtful if *ex post* it could know whether profits have been maximized or not. Business does not operate in total ignorance and modern management techniques may help to reduce uncertainty. But uncertainty is still a dominant fact of economic life, which makes the notion of maximization seem meaningless.

Since the 'entrepreneur' in the business firm does not have all the information necessary for maximization, since he does not know all the alternative courses open to the firm, it has been suggested that the firm is 'deliberative' in its actions rather than 'maximizing'. R. A. Gordon, H. A. Simon and J. Margolis[15] have put forward a theory that the firm will attempt only to 'satisfice'— to make satisfactory profits. 'Satisfaction' is defined with reference to some aspiration level. This must be related to some time period; it must be sufficient to keep the firm viable and will be just as great as, and probably greater than, the level which it is now earning. Simon and others have also argued that information is not given to the firm but must be obtained; that alternatives are searched for and discovered sequentially. The theory of choice and the theory of search thus become part of a general theory of business decision making.[16]

The various criticisms of the conventional economic theory of the firm have not gone unanswered. Friedman[17] has argued that the test of a theory is its predictive power and not the relevance of its assumptions. Machlup[18] has defended orthodox marginal theory as reasonable, costs, revenues and profits being subjective or perceived by the businessman rather than objective. Earley,[19] in his study of 110 American corporations rated as 'excellently managed', believed that these did use 'marginal' accounting principles, which resembled the marginal principles of the economist's theory of the firm.

It would be easy to conclude from this welter of different theories that it is impossible to formulate an acceptable theory of the firm or to define business objectives. This, however, is far from the truth.

---

*At best one can assume that firms maximise the discounted value of future profits and that firms have perfect knowledge only up to a probability distribution of all possible future states of the world.

First, the economist's theory of the firm is an abstract model which has the virtues of neatness and simplicity. It evolved as part of the larger theory of markets to explain at a general level how resources are allocated by the price system. Since the theory was not strictly developed to answer internal questions of resource allocation, it cannot therefore be expected to answer these questions completely. But it can provide a useful basis for the further development of a theory applicable to a different set of questions appropriate to managerial decisions.

Secondly, from the array of alternative goals suggested by those who dispense with the profit motive, no single one has gained wide acceptance. It would be truer to say that these alternative goals are not so much intended to replace the profit maximization hypothesis as to deny its primary importance. Business goals are probably multiple. Some are mutually exclusive, but others are not necessarily inconsistent, so that like the Dodo we can perhaps say that 'everyone has won and all must have prizes'. No simple generalization about business behaviour could hope to describe the complexity of business decision making. There is a tremendous variety in the size and character of businesses and it would be surprising if their objectives did not differ. In small businesses, carried on as a source of livelihood, the owners may be content if they get enough to live on and are ready to forego the risks attendant on expansion. Security may be preferred to risk though it is as well to point out that many small businesses may not enjoy the luxury of choice between the two. Leaders of large business organizations, on the other hand, are generally fired by more ambitious objectives and time becomes an important factor in their decisions. Financial and other objectives are embodied in budgets relating to both short and long periods. Profits enter into the calculations of every business though they need not necessarily be its most important goal.

Thirdly, it is more difficult to sustain the view that firms do 'maximize' profits. In a complex environment, where information is lacking and uncertainty prevails, maximization is an unattainable procedure and theories that substitute rules of thumb or 'satisficing' may provide us with a more acceptable generalization.

Fourthly, economics alone can probably not provide a single theory of business behaviour or decision making. In the last resort, what is actually best for a business can only be decided by the policy makers in the business itself. Economics and other social sciences can, however, indicate relevant variables and modern quantitative techniques can systematically explore the implications of choice between alternative objectives.

It may therefore be concluded that there is no universally acceptable objective for business policy and therefore no simple or obvious criterion of business efficiency. Each business must define its own objectives, which may have to satisfy the needs of those groups whose co-operation makes the continued existence of the business possible: the shareholders, management, employees and, above all, customers. Businesses have multiple goals and the needs of survival, goodwill, security or growth commonly call for some sacrifice of short-term profits. Management does not exploit every opportunity of short-term gain and, to quote Professor T. Wilson, 'students should not be taught to believe that manufacturers have the mentality of barrow boys exploiting a temporary shortage of bananas'.[20] Most businesses do, however, rate profitability consistently high among their long-term objectives and it could be argued that short-term goals such as security and growth are in fact subordinate to long-term profitability. The view taken in this book is that while profit is not the only goal of the business, it is an extremely important one and that, where choice has to be made between profit and some alternative goal, profit is usually dominant because the firm's survival depends on it.* While profit 'maximization' may be impossible so that it may be more realistic to speak of 'satisficing', profit, reasonably defined, must always be an important indicator of business efficiency. It is to problems of definition and analysis of profit that we now turn.

NOTES

1. Drucker, *The Practice of Management*, p. 9.

2. Carter, *The Science of Wealth*, p. 15.

3. Simon, *Administrative Behaviour*, pp. 172–173. For some further discussion of efficiency and of productivity, see Florence, *Logic of British and American Industry*, p. 49, and Salter, *Productivity and Technical Change*.

4. Explanation of the marginal analysis may be found in most economic textbooks, e.g. Stigler, *The Theory of Price*, Stonier and Hague, *A Textbook of Economic Theory*. Also in Dowsett, *Elementary Mathematics in Economics*. It is briefly discussed below, Chapter 9.

5. See further below, Chapter 5.

6. This summary is largely based on McGuire, *Theories of Business Behaviour*, ch. 3, and Cyert and March, *A Behavioural Theory of the Firm*, ch. 2.

7. A. Papandreou, 'Some Basic Problems of the Theory of the Firm' in *A Survey of Contemporary Economics*, ed. Haley (1952).

*Profit also provides a yardstick of comparison where multiple objectives of the firm are in conflict. See below, Chapter 4.

8. K. W. Rothschild, 'Price Theory and Oligopoly', *Economic Journal*, 1947.

9. Baumol, 'On a Theory of Oligopoly', *Economica*, 1958.

10. 'A Note on Profit Maximisation and its Implications', *Review of Economic Studies*, 1943.

11. Reder, 'A Re-consideration of the Marginal Productivity Theory', *Journal of Political Economy*, 1947.

12. Cooper, 'Theory of the Firm: Some Suggestions for Revision', *American Economic Review*, 1949.

13. Hall and Hitch, *Price Theory and Business Behaviour*, discussed below, Chapter 9.

14. R. A. Lester, 'Shortcomings of Marginal Analysis for Wage-Employment Problems', *American Economic Review*, 1947.

15. See, for example, Simon, 'A Behavioural Model of Rational Choice'. *Quarterly Journal of Economics*, 1952; also March and Simon, *Organizations*, 1958,

16. One of the most recent and fully-developed theories of how decisions are made within the firm is that of Cyert and March. Their model incorporates the following: (1) The business firm is a coalition with multiple, changing and acceptable level goals—implying 'satisficing' behaviour. (2) Sequential examination of alternatives, with acceptance of the first satisfactory one—this implies further a theory of problem-directed search activity and of organizational learning. (3) Uncertainty is a feature of organizational decision making, but organizations try to avoid it through the use of routine procedures. In particular, they tend to solve each problem as it arises, thereby reacting to feedback rather than trying to forecast the environment. (4) The organization uses standard operating procedures and rules of thumb in the short run.
See Cyert and March, *A Behavioural Theory of The Firm*, esp. Chs. 5 and 6.

17. Friedman, *Essays in Positive Economics*.

18. Machlup, 'Marginal Analysis and Empirical Research', *American Economic Review*, 1956.

19. Earley, 'Marginal Policies of "Excellently Managed" Companies', *American Economic Review*, 1956, discussed below, Chapter 9.

20. Burn, *Structure of British Industry*, vol. 2, p. 171.

3

PROFIT

1. THE NATURE OF PROFIT

Profit is but one form of income. The economic theory of income distribution analyses the nature and size of the payments made for productive inputs. Such inputs may be classified in a number of ways, and so may the income each receives for its share in the productive process. The traditional classification of incomes distinguished wages, interest, rent and profit. Wages are the income received in return for a worker's labour. Interest is received as the payment for a money loan. Rent is the excess income received by a productive input (e.g. land) over and above the minimum needed to keep it in its present employment. Profit is what remains—the difference between the business's total receipts and total costs (incomes of other productive inputs being counted as costs to the firm). Profit may be clearly distinguished from interest: while interest is paid for the use of borrowed money (e.g. to a debenture holder), profit is paid for the use of ownership money. It is the non-interest part of the return on equity.

For an economist the most important point about profit is that it is a residual. Wages, interest and rents are contractual costs, agreed in advance between the business and the receivers. Profit is what remains of the firm's revenues after all inputs have been paid. Its amount, however, is neither determined nor contracted in advance since profit is uncertain, variable and unpredictable. We can discover from published accounts and the financial press the apparent rate of 'profit' on capital invested for say Marks & Spencer or Imperial Chemical Industries for past years. What we cannot now know is their rates of profit in future years and we could not know even if we had access to all present available data about those companies. What distinguishes pure economic profit from payments made to productive inputs is its variability and unpredictability. Business operates in an environment of uncertainty. Much of what is ordinarily called profit, however, is really nothing but interest, wages and rent under a different name. The difference between book profit and pure economic profit may be illustrated. A garage run by its owner-mechanic has a gross income of £20,000 a year. Expenses amount to £17,500 a year, leaving £2,500 a year 'profit'. The building and equipment represent an investment of £8,000. Is the £2,500 a year which we have called profit an adequate return for the proprietor? His apparent costs were £17,500. However, if we apply the concept of *opportunity cost* to the firm's operations: i.e. if we ask what earning opportunities were foregone by using the resources of the business in their present way, a different picture of true costs and hence true economic profit emerges.* Capital sunk in buildings and equipment might have earned 5 per cent interest on a government security, or £400 a year. The site rent saved had the business not been carried on might amount to another £200 a year, while the owner might have earned £1,800 a year from his managerial and engineering skills by working for the main car distributor for his area. The sum of these opportunity costs is £400+£200+£1,800=£2,400, leaving only £100 pure economic profit from running his own garage rather than working for and lending to others.

Thus the true economic profit of an owner-operated garage, grocer's shop, farm or small business ought to be determined after proper allowance has been made for these implicit interest, rent, and wage payments. Indeed, whatever the type of business, profit is what remains after the opportunity costs of all productive inputs have been paid. The question now to be answered is why does anything remain at all.

If we lived in a stationary economy, where the future could be perfectly predicted and where no change or innovation occurred, there would be no profits. All incomes would take the form of wages, interest and rents and these costs—including all implicit costs—would be precisely known to the business beforehand. In practice the future cannot be predicted and expectations are rarely if ever fulfilled. A business may turn out successfully or it may fail; it may get an unexpected surplus or profit or it may make a loss. The explanation of profit and of loss (negative profit) has to be sought in the dynamic nature of our modern economy and the fact that business decisions are made against a background of uncertainty.

*The concept of opportunity cost is discussed below, p. 30.

Profit theories

We may distinguish several broad groups of profit theories:
(1) entrepreneurial compensation; (2) risk and uncertainty; (3)
innovation; (4) market imperfection and monopoly.

(1) *Entrepreneurial compensation.* Enterprise, according to this
view, is the fourth factor of production, the other three being land,
labour and capital. Profit is regarded as the reward for enterprise
and accrues to the *entrepreneur* who both manages the business
and assumes the risk of enterprise. Such a view may have had
relevance half a century ago when the typical business was owner-
managed. It is much less relevant today when the typical pattern is
for ownership and control to be divorced. Shareholders and
salaried managers are two distinct groups.

(2) *Risk and uncertainty.* Gamblers like taking risks, but most
people do not. Yet in a world characterized by economic change
and imperfect knowledge, businesses have to make their decisions
in the face of risk and uncertainty. Firms try to forecast the future,
but with limited success and, in producing to meet future market
requirements, there is always the risk of loss. Profit, according to
this line of reasoning is necessary to induce the businessman to
take risks rather than to play safe. No sane person who could get
6 per cent per annum interest on government stock would think
of investing in a gold mining company for the same meagre return.
He would expect a much higher rate because of the greater risk
of total loss.

Economists distinguish between risk and uncertainty. Risk is,
in principle, insurable whereas uncertainty cannot be insured
against. The former is a calculable actuarial probability, whereas
the latter is not. An insurance company, by dealing in large
numbers, can cancel one risk against another. It can calculate with
considerable accuracy what percentage of houses will suffer
damage by fire in the course of the coming year, though it cannot
say whether Jones's or Smith's house will be damaged. There is,
however, no way of insuring against uncertainty, because there is
no way of calculating the probability of particular events occurring.* An insurance company would not consider insuring a manu-

*Decision theory distinguishes between certainty, risk and uncertainty. Under
certainty there exists only one state of nature; under risk the decision maker knows
the probability with which two or more states of nature will occur; under uncertainty it is impossible to assign objective rational probability to the states of nature,
though an arbitrary assumption may be made as, for example, in the Bayes
(Laplace) criterion that events are equi-probable.

facturer of washing machines or a gold mine prospector against the possibility of loss. While therefore risks may be regarded as a 'measurable uncertainty', there is always a large area of uncertainty that is not measurable. The investor or speculator expects to be paid a higher premium on his risky investment to compensate for his greater risk of loss. F. H. Knight has advanced the well-known theory that pure economic profit (whether positive or negative) is related to uncertainty. The speculator who outguesses the market makes a profit, because the market could not have known future prices with certainty. Another speculator might make a loss because his guess turned out worse than that of the market.

(3) *Innovation theories.* Innovation means a fundamental cost-reducing technological change in production methods and usually a complete change in the nature of the product itself. It is a dominant characteristic of our modern dynamic economy in which a substantial proportion of every business's resources are devoted to research and the development of new products. Innovation is, however, something more than invention, for it implies not only scientific discovery but successful commercial exploitation of the new product. Many products that are now taken for granted were innovations when they were first introduced and revolutionized existing ways of doing things: electric lighting, television, the jet airliner, the ball point pen and a host of others. What has this got to do with profit?

The innovation theory of profit is associated with J. A. Schumpeter. The entrepreneur or innovator is the one who turns a new idea or invention into a commercial proposition. Many try to do this, but only a few succeed. Those who do earn high profits from bringing their new, revolutionary product into the market do so because the public is attracted by the new and apparently superior product and is willing to pay the innovator a high price for it. The opportunity costs of the firm's inputs—labour and capital—however will be no higher than those of business generally. If indeed by technical improvements they are combined more efficiently, costs will be reduced. The innovator thus reaps the profits of innovation. Following a successful innovation comes a period of adjustment. New firms imitate the successful innovator, labour and capital move into the new industry and obsolete products die out. This 'herd like' movement of followers attracted by tempting profit possibilities sooner or later compete away his innovational profits. Meanwhile, in a dynamic economy, other innovations are hitting the market. The process of innovation is a realistic explanation of the rise and decline of many businesses and may be one of the most satisfactory explanations of the business cycle.

(4) *Market imperfection and monopoly.* This view attributes profits to monopoly exploitation. It is, however, important not to confuse an emotional attitude with a careful scientific explanation. Where a firm possesses monopoly power, or more correctly where the market in which it sells is not 'perfect' in the economist's sense, a producer can restrict output and obtain a higher 'profit' than he could under competitive conditions. Such 'profit' is usually compounded of wages, interest and rent as well as some pure profit. Sometimes it is the result of contrived scarcity. It can only exist in an imperfect market where output is, for various reasons, restricted and consumers are denied the opportunity of alternative sources of supply. Sources of such power are usually found in legal restrictions, sole ownerships of raw materials or sole access to particular markets. Even some degree of uniqueness in a firm's product confers some monopoly power, though it may not be very strong or lasting. This is a different thing from natural scarcity. Natural scarcity exists in the supply of central urban building sites or high grade farm land. These earn *rents*—in the economist's sense—rather than monopoly profits, since practically nothing can be done to alter their supply.

No one of the several theories discussed is necessarily 'correct'. All are, in some sense, complementary, since uncertainty, innovation, change and monopoly power are factors which affect every business in its policy decisions.

2. THE MEASUREMENT OF PROFIT

Measurement of profit for different business purposes is not a straightforward matter. Financial accounting conventions and legal requirements call for a different definition of profit from that used by economists. In particular the question of what is included in the costs to be subtracted from revenues to obtain profits has to be decided. It is necessary to outline the nature of the problem.

The first difference between accounting practice and economic concepts may be dealt with briefly. We saw that our garage proprietor with an apparent 'profit' of £2,500 a year, was in fact only making £100 pure economic profit, when all opportunit costs had been counted. When ownership and management is separate, as in a large organization, management is paid a salary. Where the owner himself manages the business, he may not pay himself a salary adequate for his management function. In the latter case, accounting profit or income will overstate true profit; in the former the accountant's profit, though not the same as the economist's conception, will be much closer to true economic profit.* More generally, financial accounting involves an orderly process by which the transactions of the firm are recorded, classified and summarized. Its concern is to record the past transactions of the business so that a variety of interested parties—the owners (shareholders); the tax authorities; the Registrar of Companies and others—can know its financial results and assess its financial position. A basic accounting principle is that the assets of a business are subject to the claims of two parties: owners (proprietorship) and creditors.

Thus: Assets=Liabilities+Proprietorship.
Therefore: Assets−Liabilities=Proprietorship=Net Assets.

The balance sheet indicates the 'value of the firm's assets and the corresponding claims of creditors and owners at some given time. *The income statement* or profit and loss account records the changes in these amounts resulting from the business transactions over the course of a year. Income or profit is the difference between net assets at the beginning of the year and at the end of the year.† The shareholders' claim on the company may be defined as Total Assets minus Financial Obligations to non-owners, the year to year change in this amount being business income. *The funds statement* is a report on changes in the financial position (assets and liabilities) resulting from, among other things, the operations covered by the profit and loss statement. It is concerned with a record of funds available and the manner in which funds are employed.

In preparing these statements the accountant must report historically verifiable facts with the minimum of speculation about the future. Thus the balance sheet usually shows assets valued at original cost rather than realizable values; the assumption is normally made that the £ represents a stable unit of value and a conservative approach is followed in measuring changes in assets,

*In the converse case, an owner manager may pay himself too much and accounting profits would under-state true profits.

†Strictly, while this statement is historically correct, with current accounting conventions, the net asset value at the end of the period is the result of measuring profit and not a factor which determines it.

liabilities and equity, and consistency observed in making valuations; the assumption is made that business income is determined by matching the revenue *earned* in a period of time with expenses *incurred* in earning that revenue.

The economist's approach to the valuation of a business's assets is different. Instead of relying on historically recorded cost data, he may value assets on a replacement cost* basis, or ideally he attempts to assess the present worth of the future earnings or cash flows which existing assets will bring to the business. This is a theoretical concept and is difficult to compute in practice, since sufficiently accurate forecasts of markets, technological changes and costs are not available. Each asset, however, may be assumed to have a present worth, equal to the expected stream of earnings over its working life discounted at an appropriate rate of interest.† The value of a firm's combined assets would normally be greater than the sum of the asset values computed separately, since a firm's earning power may be enhanced by established market connections, brand loyalties, and know how, etc. This 'goodwill' is not necessarily the same as the accountant's goodwill.

The economist's approach to valuation of assets thus derives from income expectations. Orthodox financial accounting finds it unsatisfactory because it is essentially speculative: the future cannot be predicted accurately. But in economics it is often 'better to be vaguely right than precisely wrong', and the apparent precision of orthodox accounting must be rejected when it is inappropriate for decision-making purposes. There are three specific aspects of profit measurement where accounting conventions and the application of economic concepts give different results: (i) depreciation; (ii) inventory valuation; (iii) unaccounted value changes in assets and liabilities.

Depreciation

Depreciation of industrial assets occurs through use and with the passage of time. Assets may also become obsolete as a result of new technology or innovation. For example, a machine will deteriorate with normal wear and tear, or from continual exposure to the elements; or it may become obsolete because a new, automated process enables it to be dispensed with. The economist may view depreciation as a periodic reduction in the value of a fixed asset, arising from a change in the asset's expected earning power.

*Replacement cost defined below, p. 31.

†Variations of this concept are applied to investment decisions in Chapter 4, below.

The expected stream of future earnings at any point of time is expressed as a discounted value at that point of time, depreciation between any two points of time being measured by the difference between the discounted values of future earnings at those points of time.[1] Alternatively, for many purposes, the concept of opportunity cost may be appropriate, the earnings foregone over a period of time by employing an asset for one purpose rather than its most profitable alternative use. Both of these concepts differ from normal accounting procedures which usually regard the full depreciation cost to be charged as an expense against revenue earned over the expected working life of the asset as being equal to its original cost less its prospective salvage value—a convention which only approaches economic realism in the simplest conditions of stable prices and money values. There are several alternative methods of computing depreciation. Among those most used in industry are (1) straight line; (2) diminishing balance method; (3) annuity method; (4) service unit method.

(1) Straight line depreciation is the simplest method of calculating time depreciation. A fixed percentage of original value is deducted annually over the working life of the asset to leave only salvage value at the end of working life. Thus if P is the cost of the asset and L is salvage value and N the number of years of expected life,

$$\text{annual depreciation charge} = \frac{P-L}{N}.$$

(2) Diminishing balance depreciation provides larger depreciation charges or fast write-off in the early years, since the annual depreciation charge is a constant percentage of an annually diminishing written down asset value. Such a method could never depreciate the asset to zero and some salvage value must be assumed. In which case the constant depreciation rate

$$D = 1 - \left(\frac{L}{P}\right)^{1/N}.$$

(3) The annuity method requires that the cost to be recovered equals the original installed cost of the asset plus an interest rate equal to the cost of capital. Depreciation is allocated in fixed instalments, the amount of which represents an annuity of fixed amount over the estimated life of the asset.[2]

(4) Service unit method of depreciation is appropriate where the life of an asset depends on its use rather than time. In its simplest form, the difference between original cost and salvage value is

divided by the lifetime capacity of the asset, according to the formula $\dfrac{P-L}{\text{lifetime capacity}}$. Thus a truck with a life of 100,000 miles, a cost of £1,100 and a salvage value of £100 would be depreciated at a rate of £10 every 1,000 miles.

These and other conventions for measuring depreciation are primarily of interest to financial accountants. From the point of view of the economist concerned either with a management decision relating to the future use of assets or with the economic measurement of profit, the year to year depreciation figure produced by these conventions is usually irrelevant. The economist is concerned with differences in discounted values if enough is known about future earnings to enable these to be computed, or the opportunity cost of using an asset and its ultimate replacement cost and not a conventional depreciation formula based on original cost.

For management decisions, opportunity cost is usually the relevant criterion. The opportunity cost of using an asset is the most profitable alternative foregone because the asset is employed in its present use rather than for something else. For example, if a building has a profitable use as office premises then the opportunity cost of using it as a retail store for a year is the net return that could have been obtained had it been rented out for offices. For many assets the alternative to using is to sell. A machine may be used for one year as an alternative to selling and the opportunity cost of using it for one year is the difference between its market value at the beginning of the year and its market value at the end of the year. Opportunity cost is measured by the fall in disposal value over the year from keeping and using the asset and may bear no relation to depreciation calculated on straight line or on other conventional bases.

In other cases, the only alternative to using an asset may be to keep it idle, in which case the opportunity costs of using it will be negligible. Some types of asset, a dock, canal, hydro-electric dam —or any type of specialized sunk investment—may have no alternative uses; moreover their *user costs*[3] may be zero and so may their opportunity costs. An annual depreciation charge calculated for accounting purposes on original cost clearly has little or no relevance to the opportunity cost of employing such assets.

From the point of view of income measurement, it must be realized that all assets have a limited useful life even though use costs may be negligible. Sooner or later every asset, whether it be a motor van or dock installation, reaches the end of its useful life and the question of replacement arises. Replacement cost, not original cost, is the appropriate criterion to be used for calculating depreciation in such cases; replacement cost being the sum required to purchase at the time of expected replacement another asset with the same earning power as the original asset had at the beginning—assuming that the business still needs such an asset and that technology has not changed, otherwise appropriate adjustments would have to be made. In the case of a machine with a ten-year life, its replacement cost would equal the cost of a similar new machine (or one with equivalent earning capacity) *minus* the salvage value of the old one. Except in conditions of stable prices, any depreciation formula based on original costs either fails to maintain capital intact or makes excess provision. In times of rising price level, replacement cost will exceed original cost. In times of falling price level original cost will exceed replacement cost. If the expected stream of future earnings from a machine could be determined with reasonable accuracy, measuring the difference between the discounted value of future earnings at various points of time over the life of the asset, including as one item the expected salvage value at the end of its life, would provide appropriate depreciation charges over its working life. Accounting conventions employing original cost would almost inevitably result in inappropriate profit measurement.

Inventory valuation

There would be no problem of measuring inventory if the price level were stable and the cost of materials never changed. The problem of valuing physical inventory is in practice complicated by the fact that different prices are paid for various lots of the same material over a period of time. Two well-known methods of valuation are FIFO and LIFO. (1) With FIFO (first-in-first-out), materials are assumed to be withdrawn from stock in the order in which they are received, so that current manufacturing costs are based on costs of the oldest material in stock. (2) With LIFO (last-in-first-out) the most recently purchased materials are assumed to be withdrawn from stock first, so that current manufacturing costs are based on costs of more recent acquisitions.*[4]

*Another method, the weighted average cost method of stock valuation takes into account the costs of the different lots purchased in each time period and values them by taking a weighted average of the different costs: other methods, e.g. NIFO base stock, cost price of last bulk receipt, etc., are not discussed here.

The choice of methods of inventory valuation can make a substantial difference to recorded value of business income in periods of rising or falling prices. FIFO will show unrealistically high profits during inflation and low profits during deflation, since manufacturing costs will be based on past acquisitions and inventory valuations on the most recent. LIFO will show more accurate manufacturing costs and hence profits during inflation or deflation since the most recent costs of acquiring inventory will be recorded and used in the computation of income. Both of these methods are assumptions made for the accounting purpose of reporting profit; a business's behaviour is unlikely to correspond to either assumption. While LIFO is the better choice for profit measurement purposes neither FIFO nor LIFO provide the basis for a true measure of business income at current market prices, since they offer a choice between historical accounting methods. LIFO, for example, may provide quite misleading out of date information about inventory values when inventories are being run down. Moreover, the realistic measurement of business income in times of changing price levels, must take some account of the changing purchasing power of the business's cash assets. Essentially the problem is to express all costs in terms of money of constant purchasing power, whereas the crude cost and profit data available from the business's books of account may for example include this week's cash, inventory valued in last year's pounds and machines valued in pounds of some years ago. A correct measure of business income can only be computed if the financial accounts of the firm are first adjusted to constant prices.

Unaccounted value changes

The profits and net worth of a business may also be incorrectly stated because of unrecorded values of certain assets and liabilities. Expenditure on research and development may be creating intangible assets by increasing the company's future earning power. Advertising expenditures may be creating brand loyalties and increasing goodwill. The quality of the management in terms of training and experience may be another intangible asset, unrecorded in the firm's accounts. Accountants normally ignore 'goodwill' unless the firm has changed hands and 'goodwill' in the balance sheet may relate to some time in the past. The firm's financial accounts may therefore underestimate the real future earning power of the company and hence the value of its assets.

A relevant measurement of business profit is of major impo

tance for correct management decisions and we have shown in this brief discussion that the profits recorded in orthodox financial accounts are not usually relevant for this purpose. Firstly, costs and profits must be adjusted to constant prices. This affects depreciation policy and calls for adjustments to inventory valuation. All assets should, as far as possible, be valued in terms of the future earning power of the company. Secondly, relevant economic concepts, such as opportunity costs, are more appropriate for decisions relating to the future use of assets than orthodox accounting conventions and valuations. Management accounting techniques may enable these concepts to be quantified for decision-making purposes. But accounting data and techniques must always be appraised critically and be adapted as necessary to the purpose in hand.

3. PROFIT POLICY

While a business may pursue other goals besides profit, businesses do budget in the expectation of achieving a planned rate of profit and seek to improve their profit performance over time. 'Low profit realization is very seldom explainable by multiple management goals. It is probably more consistent with poor management, failing to achieve the profit which it would like to achieve.'[5] How much freedom a firm has in its profit policy clearly depends on its market environment. But given this, economics can throw some light on two sets of problems which the firm faces in its profit policy: (1) what rate of profit should the business aim to earn? (2) how far do external opinions and other factors call for some limitation on profits?

Setting profit standards

Profit can be measured in aggregate money terms or as a ratio. There are several such ratios, the two commonest being gross (or net) operating margin which is the gross (or net) operating profit as a percentage of sales; and return on capital which is net operating profit after tax as a percentage of net worth. The choice of an appropriate ratio and its interpretation must be made with care. For many purposes, including inter-firm comparison, rate of return on capital is perhaps the most meaningful.

Various criteria may be applied in deciding what is an acceptable rate of profit:

(1) Rate necessary to attract equity capital. A company likely to want to issue new shares must earn sufficient to support a high enough average level of prices for its ordinary shares to 'protect the equity' of present shareholders when the new capital issue is made.

(2) Rate earned by other companies in the same industry or of selected companies in other industries working in similar conditions.

(3) Normal or historical profit rate of the company and/or of the industry. A comparison with the firm's own past earnings in 'normal' times may be useful if such rates have been sufficient to attract capital, provide adequate return to shareholders and have not encouraged excessive competition in the past.

(4) Rate sufficient to finance growth from internal sources. Such a 'plough back rate' may be an appropriate standard to adopt where a firm's planned expansion is to be financed from internal sources (net profits and depreciation) without recourse to the capital market. However, mis-allocation of resources could occur if retained earnings were invested in low earning projects within the company when they could have obtained better returns outside. The converse also holds.

Limitation of profits

Confining our attention to the external influences which may cause a business to limit its profits, we may note the following reasons:

(1) To maintain good labour relations and restrain the demands of organized labour for wage increases. Under full employment industry is in a weak position vis à vis organized labour. High profits may be taken as evidence of ability to pay higher wages.

(2) To discourage new competition. Imitators follow innovators and competitors tend to invade a market once they discover its high profitability, unless there are substantial barriers to entry. Limitation of profits in the short run may be practised by a firm in the hope of preventing such competition, though it seems unlikely that potential competitors would be easily deceived for long by artificially contrived profit levels.

(3) To maintain goodwill with customers. Customers have their own ideas of 'fair' profits and a firm which exploits a short-term scarcity may seriously damage its long-term goodwill. Consumers' ideas of fairness may be inconsistent and may not accord with the

views of economists. A business should, however, respect its consumers' views if it wishes to retain their goodwill.

(4) To maintain good public relations. Political factors nowadays enter into many business decisions. The public and the Government have, at any time, attitudes to profits which may differ sharply from those of economists or of business management. High profits may attract price regulation or even focus public attention on the industry as being suitable for nationalization or for proceedings before the Restrictive Practices Court or the Monopolies Commission. A firm engaged on Government contracts is not likely to be viewed favourably if it pursues a commercial policy of maximizing profits.[6]

The choice of a profit policy is never easy. Each business must determine its own profit policy in the light of its general objectives and within its particular market environment.[7]

NOTES

1. This simple statement ignores problems of jointness and choice of appropriate discount rate. For a description of this method see H. R. Hudson and Russell Mathews, 'An Aspect of Depreciation', *Economic Record*, June 1963, pp. 232–236.

2. See Fitzgerald, *Accounting* (4th ed.), p. 182, for a discussion and the appropriate formula.

3. The reduction in the value of equipment due to using it as compared with not using it. This idea underlies the concept of user cost first analysed by Keynes in *The General Theory of Employment, Interest and Money*, appendix to ch. 6.

4. On weighted average cost, see R. Mathews, *Accounting for Economists*, p. 123.

5. Neil Chamberlain, *The Firm: Micro-economic Planning and Action*, p. 75.

6. See *The Economist*, 18 April 1964, p. 296, for a comment on the Ferranti affair.

7. Besides the books already mentioned, the following are relevant to the matters discussed in this chapter: Paish, *Business Finance*; H. B. Rose, *The Economic Background to Investment*; Baxter and Davidson, *Studies in Accounting Theory*; J. Fred Weston, *Managerial Finance*.

4

INVESTMENT POLICY

Do I dare
Disturb the universe?
In a minute there is time
For decisions and revisions which a minute will reverse.
                                                    T. S. ELIOT

1. INVESTMENT DECISIONS

Probably the most important decision which any management has
to take is the decision to invest, i.e. to incur expenditure now which
it is anticipated will produce a stream of benefits which will result
in the firm being in a more favourable position than it would have
been had the original expenditure been directed towards another
use. Investment decisions are distinguished from operating
decisions by reference to the time period within which the full
effect of the decision is felt. It is assumed for decision-making
purposes that management views the future as a series of discrete
time periods and if the full effect of a decision takes place completely within one of these time periods and its acceptance or
rejection does not affect the course of events in future time periods
then this is not an investment decision. The assessment of capital
investment projects, or capital budgeting, differs from macro-
economic investment in that it is not restricted to the creation of
something new and transfers such as the purchase of existing stocks
and securities and the return to shareholders of funds higher than
the normal or expected dividend distribution, come under the
definition of investment.

There are three main reasons why investment decisions are
among the most important as far as the managers and the owners
of capital are concerned. First, because the effect of the decision
extends beyond the current accounting period its result is not

immediately reported in the Profit and Loss Account and, there-fore, its apparent rightness or wrongness cannot be quickly diagnosed. Secondly, it broadens the base on which profit will be earned, and probably measured, through return on capital employed and, in so far as this is regarded as the main yardstick of company achievement, it is an important factor in the assessment of managerial efficiency. Finally, because the decision extends into the future there is more uncertainty attached to it and as profit is a residual reward closely linked to the existence of uncertainty, the success or otherwise of investment decisions will determine the amount of this residue.

As the number of time periods over which the effect of the decision will be felt increases the less certain becomes the information on which the decision will be based. The very nature of this uncertainty seems to have resulted in an unwillingness on the part of management to approach this type of problem in a logical and consistent fashion, e.g.

They show widespread failure to measure the investment worth of individual proposals directly. Lack of defensible objective standards of an acceptable investment and distorted dedication to procedures and paper work with an inadequate understanding of the economic content of the concepts used.[1]

Above all they shy away from any capital expenditure that may increase the invested capital base against which profits are measured.[2]

Lack of awareness of the true economics of intensive investment has been, I believe, largely responsible for the slow rate of modernization of British Industry.[3]

Many of the criticisms which Dean and others have made have their roots in the relationship between qualitative factors and investment decisions. Apparent sophisms have arisen because of the inability to quantify all of the relevant factors.* Business is too complex an organism to allow of a simple figure presentation which would depict the complete effect of a change in capital structure and, therefore, it cannot be disputed that any quantitative analysis must be interpreted in light of the qualitative factors not depicted thereto. However, it does appear that this can allow fallacious reasoning to determine which line of action should be followed, e.g. it can be contended that strategy is sufficient justification

---

*Even where factors are quantifiable there is a limit to their accuracy beyond which they can be regarded as qualitative.

for capital expenditure in that while a project cannot apparently pass the test of economics it has some incalculable benefit which cannot be measured but which will undoubtedly lead to a position of great advantage. Similar to this is what Dean[4] calls 'the must investment'—the situation where the benefits are so obvious that there is no need to submit a decision to the normal scrutiny mechanism. What constitutes a 'must' is likely to be a function of the objectives of the person making the application and these need not necessarily coincide with the objectives of the organization as a whole. It is most important that economic criteria are applied, because while qualitative factors cannot be measured they must be judged and judgment requires a yardstick of comparison which in most cases will be the opportunity cost of the investment. The cost of spending £X on preserving the long-run image of the company cannot be decided in isolation. Even if it is impossible to quantify the results of this it is still necessary to measure the alternative uses to which the funds can be put, e.g. if this can produce a benefit of £Y per annum over the next N years then the loss of image must be evaluated and compared to the loss of £NY. Possibly a more serious affect of the existence of non-quantifiable factors can be found in the use of these to justify the application of statistical techniques of evaluation whose usefulness in this area is open to doubt. It is quite legitimate to argue that irrespective of the sophistication of the technique used if the original data is uncertain then the answer must be uncertain. However, it is not valid to use this as a justification for the use of dubious techniques. To do this is simply to add to the uncertainty, not to leave it in the position of the *status quo* as is sometimes implied. As with all decisions the uncertainty of input data qualifies the interpretation of the output, not the method of processing.

Although the subject matter of investment appraisal covers the search for new investment opportunities, the search for finance to carry out these opportunities, and the selection of those which should be carried out, the main interest here is with the methods of selection. Before these can be discussed, however, it is essential that the objective of the organization be quite explicit. Techniques of selection cannot be determined in isolation, they must be based on a predetermined goal or goals. For example, if a decision maker must choose between the following mutually exclusive proposals:*

*The question of timing and uncertainty have been purposely avoided as they are irrelevant for this particular illustration.

Proposal	Factory	Invest-ment	Quantity	Sales revenue	Produc-tion cost	Other cost	Profit
A	W	£10,000	20,000 units	£20,000	£13,000	£6,425	£575
B	X	£10,000	30,000 ,,	£18,000	£12,000	£5,300	£700
C	Y	£10,000	25,000 ,,	£17,000	£11,000	£5,450	£550
D	Z	£10,000	35,000 ,,	£18,000	£14,000	£3,350	£650

then dependent on the goal or the organization the goal order of satisfaction could be as in the table on the following page.

Different goals will therefore lead to different choices so that it is essential before any technique of selection is applied or indeed devised, that the goals be made quite clear, i.e. they should be defined, alternative uses for the funds clearly specified and any limit or constraint on a particular goal indicated. In a multi-goal organization, individual goals will often be contradictory. In the illustration above it is impossible to maximize sales revenue and also maximize profits. There may be a limit on the amount of capital expenditure which the firm is going to undertake in a specific period so that the objective may well have to be expressed in terms of 'maximize profits subject to a limit of capital expenditure of £X'. The prime purpose of economics in investment decisions is to provide a financial measure of the worthwhileness of the acceptance or rejection of a proposal, i.e. to provide a yardstick which can be used as a measure of sacrifice so that the strength of conflicting demands with different results, in terms of objectives achieved, can be judged.

2. MEASURING INVESTMENT OPPORTUNITIES

The first decision which has to be made is the choice of technique to be used for measuring the worthwhileness of the investment opportunity. The measure should be one which will give a consistent answer irrespective of the nature of the variables which are fed into it. It should indicate the degree of profitability of the proposal and it should provide a viable measure of comparison with alternative opportunities.

Return on original investment
An obvious relationship exists between the investment and the

Goal / Order of satisfaction	Maximize profits	Maximize sales revenue	Maximize profit per unit of sale	Maximize sales quantity	Maximize profit per £ of turnover	Maximize selling price per unit	Minimize factory cost of production	Minimize production cost per unit	Minimize total cost per unit
1	B	A	A	D	B	A	C	B/D	D
2	D	B/D	B	B	D	C	B	C	B
3	A	C	C	C	C	B	A	A	C
4	C	—	D	A	A	D	D	—	A

income which it produces and perhaps the most popular method of expressing this is the return on original investment. This is the average annual profit expressed as a percentage of the original capital outlay, e.g. if an investment of £100,000 will result in cash inflows of £40,000 per annum over the next five years the return on original investment is 20 per cent calculated as follows:

PROFIT   = Cash inflows less cash outflows
                                = £200,000 less £100,000
                                = £100,000

∴ AVERAGE $$\frac{£100,000}{5}$$
ANNUAL PROFIT
                                = £20,000
                                = 20 per cent of original capital outlay

However, this technique does not take account of the recovery of the capital outlay over the life of the project. To overcome this problem, a variation is adopted whereby the average profit of £20,000 is compared with half of the original capital outlay of £100,000, on the assumption that the original capital outlay is recovered evenly over the life of the project. Under these circumstances the return now becomes 40 per cent. This only overcomes the problem of capital recovery provided the assumption of even capital recovery is correct which in most situations is unlikely to be true. In addition, like the return on original investment, it is subject to the following criticisms. It ignores the earning life of the investment and tends to discriminate against projects of a short life. Neither does it give any weight to the timing of cash inflows. One pound today is given the same value as one pound n years hence, e.g. in the illustration, provided the total cash flows over the five years sum to £200,000, a 20 per cent return is given. This will discriminate against projects which have high cash flows in the early years and low cash flows in the later years. Finally, the rate of return achieved by this method is not comparable with either a borrowing or a lending rate. The 20 per cent return does not mean that if the firm has to borrow at a rate higher than 20 per cent to finance the project it will not be profitable. If it can borrow at less than $28\frac{1}{2}$ per cent, on the capital sum outstanding at the beginning of each year, then this is a profitable proposition. Return on original or average investment is not, therefore, a valid yardstick for measuring the opportunity cost of an investment.

Pay-off

A popular screening device for investment proposals is the pay-off, i.e. a definite period of time during which the original capital outlay must be covered by the cash inflows, and unless a proposal can satisfy this particular requirement then it is not considered, e.g. in the previous illustration the pay-off period is $2\frac{1}{2}$ years. The apparent simplicity of this technique has led to its widespread usage.[5] However, it does not satisfy the criteria which have been stipulated. There is no method for determining what is the exact pay-off period to use. It ignores profitability, e.g. two proposals may have the same pay-off period but both may require different capital outlays, have different cash inflows over a different number of years and while, as a result, there may be great difference in the profitability of each as far as pay-off is concerned they are identical. Neither does it take account of variations in the timing of the cash inflows, i.e. within the prescribed pay-off period one pound today is given the same weight as one pound in two years' time. Although these criticisms have led to this technique being rejected as far as theorists are concerned some recent studies have indicated that under certain circumstances it provides an answer consistent with that obtained by more sophisticated methods.[6,7]

To overcome the weakness of these methods a technique which takes account of variations in the earning life of the project, fluctuating cash flows, the recovery of capital over the life of the project and presents a rate which can be compared with external opportunities is required. The techniques which most comply with these requirements go under the heading of discounted cash flow.

Discounted cash flow techniques

Although there are many variations of this technique the two most popular are the yield and the excess present value, and although the yield receives much support it has certain limitations which make it an inferior method for determining investment opportunities.

The Yield method (or as it is sometimes called 'the internal rate of return') is the rate of interest which when applied to the capital sum outstanding at the beginning of each period will enable the cash inflows to exactly cover the total interest charge and repay the capital outlays. It is the solution to r in the following equation:

$$Co + \sum_{t=1}^{n} \frac{Ct}{(1+r)^t} = 0*$$

where Co=cash movement at the commencement of the investment period (usually negative)

Ct =subsequent cash movements in period t (positive or negative)

r =yield rate of return (in decimal form)

If by investing £300 cash inflows of £114 per annum can be achieved over a three year period then the rate of return achieved is 7 per cent, viz.

$$Co + \sum_{t=1}^{n} \frac{Ct}{(1+r)^t} = 0$$

$$-300 + \frac{114}{(1\cdot07)^1} + \frac{114}{(1\cdot07)^2} + \frac{114}{(1\cdot07)^3} = 0$$

and provided the cost of capital to the business is less than 7 per cent then this is a worthwhile proposition.

An alternative presentation of this is

	1 *Capital outstanding at commencement of period*	2 *7 per cent interest*	3 *Total*	4 *Cash flow*	5 *Capital outstanding at close of period*
	£	£	£	£	£
Year 1	300	21	321	114	207
Year 2	207	14	221	114	107
Year 3	107	7	114	114	0

The Excess Present Value (EPV) introduces directly into the computation the concept of a rate of interest that has to be paid on capital, called hereafter the 'cost of capital'. It discounts at this cost of capital all cash outflows and inflows down to a present value which if it is positive indicates that the project is showing a higher return than the cost of capital required to achieve it. Using the above notation this means that if i=the cost of capital

*In most situations the solution of this equation has to be determined by trial and error.

and Co $+\displaystyle\sum_{t=1}^{n}\dfrac{Ct}{(1+i)^t}$ =0 then the rate of return achieved by the project equals the cost of capital required to finance it.

 ,,   ,, >0 then the rate of return is greater than the cost of capital.

 ,,   ,, <0 then the rate of return is lower than the cost of capital.

e.g. if in the previous illustration the cost of capital is 5 per cent there is an excess present value, i.e.

$$-300+\frac{114}{(1\cdot05)^1}+\frac{114}{(1\cdot05)^2}+\frac{114}{(1\cdot05)^3}=10\cdot5>0$$

Both of the above methods set out to provide a yardstick which takes into consideration the time factor and the repayment of capital over the life of the project but here the similarity ends. Only if the task of management is to make an accept or reject decision on the basis of profitability will both techniques lead to the same decision and can be used indiscriminately. However, in few cases is this likely to be the situation as appraisal techniques in addition to indicating whether or not any particular project

	1 Capital outstanding at commencement of period	2 10 per cent interest	3 Total	4 Cash flow	5 Capital outstanding at close of period
	£	£	£	£	£
Year 1	100	10	110	500	−390
Year 2	−390	−39	−429	−429	0
Year 3	0				
	1	2 290 per cent	3	4	5
Year 1	100	290	390	500	110
Year 2	−110	−319	−429	−429	0
Year 3	0				

satisfies the minimum financial requirements which are imposed by the organization, should also indicate which of several proposals is most likely to achieve the profitability goal imposed by management, here assumed to be the maximization of present value.

The yield can produce more than one answer and in certain situations management will not be faced with a single return. An initial investment of £100 results in net positive cash flows of £500 at the end of year 1 and in negative cash outflows of £429 at the end of year 2. Here the yield method provides returns of both 10 per cent and 290 per cent. (See the table on p. 44.)

If in the organization the cost of capital was 15 per cent the yield would signal that this proposal did and also did not satisfy this requirement! The yield method is, therefore, capable of multiple solutions, e.g. in the following illustration

	Cash flow
	£
Year .0	−10,000
Year 1	33,700
Year 2	−37,850
Year 3	14,168

the rate of return using the yield method is 10 per cent, 12 per cent and 15 per cent. It is also possible to produce illustrations which are incapable of solution. While it can be argued that rarely after the initial capital outlay is there likely to be a negative cash flow and in any event, even if this situation does arise then further calculations can be used to determine which is the rate of return to adopt, this does not detract from the principle that this method cannot under all situations provide a single solution to be used as a measure of the worthwhileness of a particular project in relation to the cost of capital required to finance it.

Other criticisms can be levied against the yield when selecting from alternative investment opportunities is considered. It does not take into account the possibility of borrowing and lending on the open market at the market rate, and therefore, it is not an all-embracing measure of foregone opportunities. Consider the following example. A firm must decide between two mutually exclusive proposals which require an initial capital investment of

£1,000. The first, proposal A, produces net cash inflows of £1,000 at the end of year 1 and £6,000 at the end of year 2; the second, proposal B, produces £2,800 at the end of year 1 and £1,000 at the end of year 2. The yield method indicates that proposal B, 212 per cent against 200 per cent, should be chosen whereas the EPV at 8 per cent selects proposal A. In the choice process the implicit assumption underlying the yield method is that the firm will choose the project which affords the highest return whereas under the EPV it is that the firm will choose the proposal which shows the highest EPV.

YIELD

A

	1 Capital outstanding at commencement of period	2 200 per cent interest	3 Total	4 Cash flow	5 Capital outstanding at close of period
	£	£	£	£	£
Year 1	1,000	2,000	3,000	1,000	2,000
Year 2	2,000	4,000	6,000	6,000	0
Year 3	0				

B

	1	2 212 per cent	3	4	5
	£	£	£	£	£
Year 1	1,000	2,120	3,120	2,800	320
Year 2	320	680	1,000	1,000	0
Year 3	0				

Therefore, B is best choice.

EXCESS PRESENT VALUE AT 8 PER CENT

A		Present value	B		Present value
Year 0	−£1,000	−£1,000	Year 0	−£1,000	−£1,000
Year 1	£1,000	926	Year 1	£2,800	2,593
Year 2	£6,000	5,144	Year 2	£1,000	857
		EPV £5,070			EPV £2,450

Therefore, A is best choice.

If the cost of capital to the firm is 8 per cent by utilizing borrowing opportunities the cash flow under proposal A of £1,000 at the end of year 1 and £6,000 at the end of year 2 can be converted into a cash flow of £5,630 at the end of year 1 and £1,000 at the end of year 2, i.e. at the beginning of year 2 the firm can borrow £4,630 at 8 per cent, repay this capital sum plus the accrued interest of £370 and still leave itself with a net cash flow inflow of £1,000 at the end of year 2. The situation now becomes:

	Original proposal A	Adjusted proposal A	Proposal B
Year 0	−£1,000	−£1,000	−£1,000
Year 1	£1,000	£5,630	£2,800
Year 2	£1,000	£1,000	£1,000

By inspection A is now obviously the best choice.

In these circumstances it would only be advisable to use the yield without further computation if it were assumed that any net cash inflows could be reinvested in other projects which offered the same rate, or very close to it, as that earned on the original project. This is not a reasonable assumption as it implies that the firm is faced with an endless stream of investment opportunities offering the same return as the proposal under consideration which is at variance with the traditional view of the firm with many opportunities offering different returns, accepting those until the marginal efficiency of capital equals its marginal cost, i.e. until the return achieved from the investment equals the cost of financing it.

Another weakness of the yield is that it does not satisfactorily distinguish between projects which have different lives. If X and Y are two mutually exclusive proposals which each require an initial investment of £1,000 and X produces one cash inflow at the end of year 1 of £1,200 whereas Y has net cash inflows of £453 at the end of each year for three years, which proposal should be accepted? The yield indicates that Y should be chosen—20 per cent against 17 per cent where at 8 per cent Y has the highest EPV £167 against £111. Which is the most appropriate choice can only be determined by the assumption which is made about the use of the funds which are generated by each proposal. The yield method is only indicative of the best opportunity provided that it is assumed that there are other opportunities available offering a return higher than the firm's cost of capital. The exact return required will depend on the relative difference between the return given on the higher project compared to the lower. If it is assumed that the opportunities available give a return equal to the firm's cost of capital then the EPV gives the best choice.

The techniques also differ where a choice has to be made between proposals which require different capital outlays. A choice has to be made between two proposals. Proposal I with initial capital expenditure of £2,000 and cash inflows of £1,309 for each of two succeeding years and Proposal II expenditure of £20,000 and cash inflows of £12,302 for each of two succeeding years. The yield will indicate a preference for Proposal I because of its 20 per cent return compared with the 15 per cent of Proposal II. Whereas again at 8 per cent, II is the best choice with a net excess present value of £1,936 against £334.

YIELD

I

	1 Capital outstanding at commencement of period	2 20 per cent interest	3 Total	4 Cash flow	5 Capital outstanding at close of period
	£	£	£	£	£
Year 1	2,000	400	2,400	1,309	1,091
Year 2	1,091	218	1,309	1,309	0
Year 3	0				

II

	1	2 15 per cent	3	4	5
	£	£	£	£	£
Year 1	20,000	3,000	23,000	12,302	10,698
Year 2	10,698	1,604	12,302	12,302	0

Therefore, I is the best choice.

EXCESS PRESENT VALUE AT 8 PER CENT

	I		Present value		II		Present value
Year 0	−£2,000		−£2,000	Year 0	−£20,000		−£20,000
Year 1	£1,309		£1,212	Year 1	£12,302		£11,390
Year 2	£1,309		£1,122	Year 2	£12,302		£10,546
		EPV	£ 334			EPV	£ 1,936

Therefore, II is best choice.

The yield method cannot distinguish, satisfactorily, without further processing, between projects with different capital outlays. If, for example, there is a limit of £20,000 available for capital expenditure then the comparison of Proposal I and II is dependent on the return which can be achieved on the £18,000 (Proposal III) which is available if I is undertaken. For example, if only 10 per cent can be achieved on this £18,000 because of the following situation then by inspection II is obviously the best choice.

| | Capital outlay | Cash inflows | |
		Year 1	Year 2
	£	£	£
Proposal I	2,000	1,309	1,309
Proposal III	18,000	10,000	10,780
	20,000	11,309	12,089
Proposal II	20,000	12,302	12,302

It is impossible to state what the remaining £18,000 should earn for I to be superior to II without deciding in advance which technique, the yield or EPV, is the most suitable.

It is suggested, therefore, that because of the weaknesses in the yield method, i.e. its inability to distinguish between projects with different lives, different capital outlays and to take account of borrowing or lending at market rates and the possibility of multiple solutions along with its reliance on certain assumptions about alternative uses which do not seem to fit into a rational framework for a theory of decision making within a firm, it is an unsuitable yardstick for investment appraisals and that management is in the long run more likely to reach its goal or goals by adopting the excess present value technique.[8]*

3. CASH MOVEMENT OVER THE PERIOD OF INVESTMENT

It is convenient to assume that a decision to invest results in an immediate cash outflow followed by a series of net positive inflows.† The number of operating periods over which there will be a cash movement will be determined by the investment life of the project which will be discussed in a later section. Here we are concerned with the pattern of these, i.e. their timing and amount. The immediate outflow should be the least uncertain of the cash movement because it takes place more closely to the present than any of the others and, with forecasting, the accuracy of the forecast bears a functional relationship to the horizon of the time period. The introduction by many firms of cost accounting systems designed primarily for the control of cost[9] has considerably improved the accuracy of estimates in that they can be based on relevant past knowledge on which mathematical forecasting is dependent.

However most accounting systems have been designed to produce data for the control function and it is not necessary that the figures will be relevant for planning. The classification of costs assumes that the cost centre, e.g. a factory or department, will continue in operation and this continuity is a relevant factor in the allocation of expenses to a fixed or variable category. However

---

*Most writers who favour the yield method accept these deficiencies and have indicated what further analyses would be required to overcome them. The basic weakness of the yield remains, however—it is not a unique yardstick applicable in all circumstances.

†Although assumptions different from this will not invalidate the excess present value of technique.

this assumption need not be present in a planning decision and, therefore, the classification may be irrelevant. In full costing systems joint costs will have been allocated to products on a basis which contains a degree of arbitrariness. This does not mean, however, that new projects should be burdened with a fair share of the new total joint costs. It is only the additional joint costs which are relevant and which should be included. Neither can it be concluded that no additional overheads will be incurred. It is perhaps wiser to assume that while differential joint costs may be less than an overall average cost they will probably be greater than immediate marginal costs.

One important factor in the timing and amount of cash flows is the system of taxation which exists in the particular country where the investment will take place. In the United Kingdom most depreciation allowances for tax purposes have been constructed on the acceleration principle, i.e. greater allowances are given in the early years and are proportionately reduced over the life of the assets. The most recent Government proposals[10] envisage for qualifying expenditure a system of cash grants which will vary according to the locality and type of investment. The following illustration indicates how the net cash flow after tax differs from the pre-tax position. The data are as follows:

Investment	= £25,000 plant equipment £25,000 working capital
Life	= 7 years
Scrap value	= £1,000
Corporation tax	= 40 per cent
Cash inflows	= years 1 £10,000 5 £11,000
	2 £10,000 6 £12,000
	3 £14,000 7 £36,000
	4 £13,000

One of the most common measures of the achievement of a company is the ratio of its profit earned to capital employed. When the word profit is used it usually refers to profit computed according to accounting principles and conventions. Certain of the differences between the accountant's measurement of profit and the economist's measure have already been mentioned. However, in investment appraisal, the accounting concept of profit has been abandoned and replaced by net cash movement over time. Over the investment life of the project there is no dichotomy in that the summation of profits should equal the summation of the net positive cash inflows. However, the dichotomy does arise when the profit earned over the investment life has to be allocated to the accounting periods which dissect this. The accountancy profession has formulated a set of principles to deal with the problems which

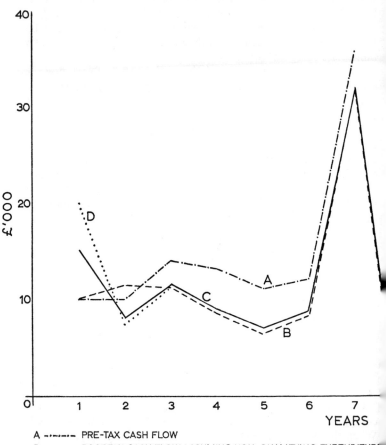

A ⏤·⏤·⏤ PRE-TAX CASH FLOW
B ⏤ ⏤ ⏤ POST TAX CASH FLOW ASSUMING NON-QUALIFYING EXPENDITURE
C ⏤⏤⏤⏤ POST TAX CASH FLOW ASSUMING QUALIFYING EXPENDITURE
D · · · · · · POST TAX CASH FLOW ASSUMING QUALIFYING EXPENDITURE IN A
        DEVELOPMENT AREA   N.B. FOR YEARS 3-8 IDENTICAL TO B

Impact of taxation on amount and timing of cash inflows

arise with this allocation. But these are flexible in that their interpretation and application can be varied according to the circumstances of the individual firm. By substituting net cash movement
for profit many of these problems can be by-passed. This is
advantageous in that with any decision while *a priori* subjective
factors exist it is reasonable to assume that all other things being
equal a measurement which requires less of these is superior to one
which requires more. Net cash movement does not require a
decision to be made as to whether expenditure is capital or revenue,
i.e. whether it is a cost to be charged against profits or the acquisi-
tion of a service which will produce benefits in a future period.
This distinction is not something which can be easily decided, e.g.
the treatment of research cost always creates problems in the
measurement of profit. However, in an investment decision it is
irrelevant whether the charge should be made to an asset account
or to an expenditure account. What is significant is when the charge
will be eliminated by an outflow of cash. Neither need it be debated
as to whether, and, if so how much, certain expenditure should be
capitalized and carried forward as part of the value of stock.
Other valuation problems are also overcome in that net cash movement is not affected if the usage of materials is priced on a FIFO,
LIFO, Average, Replacement or any other basis.

The matching of benefits with cost through the accruing of
expenditure, the benefit of which has been received in an accounting
period but which has not yet been paid for is an important factor
in determining the amount of profit which will be reported in the
accounts for a period but it does not enter into an investment
decision.

Cash movement is not dependent like profit on the method of
depreciation which is used to amortize the cost of the original
capital outlay. Neither is it concerned with whether the cost to be
amortized is historical, or a replacement cost which will allow for
both technical improvements and changes in the value of money.
To say that depreciation is not relevant is only true if we define
depreciation as the system of allocating capital costs to accounting
periods. If, on the other hand, it is regarded as a technique which
either determines the investment life or is a by-product of it then
it is, of course, highly relevant and is dealt with in a later section.

By adopting cash movement many of the inherent problems in
the measurement of profit are by-passed. However, it does raise the
question as to whether or not a management system which for-
mulates actions on the basis of one set of principles but reports the

results of this action on another can provide an operational framework for decision theory. If, for example, the method of depreciation is ignored, is it right that the results of this decision as displayed in successive accounting reports should be materially affected by it? The following example highlights the problem and although the effects are no doubt magnified because of the short life and the techniques adopted, the general principles remain valid.

Investment   = £100,000
Cash inflows   = £40,000 per annum for 5 years
Method of depreciation A = Straight line
Method of depreciation B = Diminishing balance

	Profit statements	
	A	B
Year 1	£20,000 Profit	£50,000 Loss
Year 2	£20,000 ,,	£31,000 Profit
Year 3	£20,000 ,,	£39,100 ,,
Year 4	£20,000 ,,	£39,910 ,,
Year 5	£20,000 ,,	£39,990 ,,

The investment decision and the profitability rate is the same in either case but as far as management is concerned is it the same decision? The answer to this problem would seem to be that the reporting function should be based on the same set of principles as the planning function. However, this would create communication problems if the conventional method of reporting events was abandoned. Some adjustment would always have to be made to set a limit in any case on the amount of profit available for distribution to shareholders. An important factor in human behaviour is not what is true or significant but what is seen to be true and significant, and one can hypothesize that the accounting year is regarded by businessmen as highly significant particularly in public companies where the published results of the period are the only indices of managerial performance which are disclosed to the owners and to the general public. A statement by Drucker that '. . . the greatest weakness of conventional accounting; its superstitious belief that the calendar year has any economic meaning or reality'[11] is not true in that the decisions of businessmen may be affected by it and if they are affected there is then the problem of its impact on a management greatly influenced by profit as the ultimate yardstick of success apparently forsaking this by ignoring the conventions which determine how this profit will be measured and reported. Despite the difficulties which would arise in the development of an accounting system to cope with this problem, it may well be that it is a necessary base for the construction of a framework of organization decision theory.

4. THE INVESTMENT LIFE

This section is concerned with the depreciation of the capital investment. There has been considerable controversy over what is the correct depreciation charge, how should it be valued, on what should it be based, etc., and to date, the many different opinions still seem incapable of reconciliation. Depreciation performs many functions and the differences of opinion can be traced to conflicting beliefs as to which of these is the most important, and the one which depreciation should therefore serve. However, it is quite impossible to produce a single depreciation figure which can perform satisfactorily all of these various functions, and as long as attempts are made to provide this all-embracing touchstone then controversy will persist.

Many quite distinct functions of depreciation can be identified; for example, to determine the reportable and legally distributable profit of a discrete accounting period, to arrive at a net income figure for taxation, to charge against profits a sum sufficient to replace the asset at the end of its useful life, to compute unit production costs, to value a business for purchase or sale, to indicate the investment life of the asset.

It is with this final function and how it is determined that we are concerned.

Most capital assets have a definite life. This may be physical in that factors such as metal fatigue will destroy it. Even if repairs can keep the asset serviceable, at some point the cost of these will be greater than the cost of a replacement. The asset may also have a technical life. This is the period during which valuable services are provided and obsolescence can discontinue these if a technically superior asset becomes available. Another limiting factor may be the product's market life, i.e. the number of years that the service produced has a value.

Any of these can determine the investment life and a usual assumption is that the physical life is the least likely factor to determine this and that more likely reasons are the loss of market,

or technical obsolescence. The life cycle of the capital asset would
be as follows:

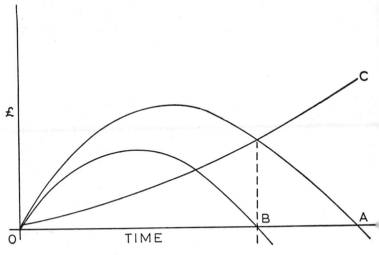

OC = COMPLEMENTARY COST CURVE
OA = SERVICE LIFE CURVE
OB = NET SERVICE LIFE CURVE
DISTANCE ON X-AXIS   OA = ABSOLUTE LIFE (PHYSICAL)
DISTANCE ON X-AXIS   OB = INVESTMENT LIFE

Investment life diagram

In the above diagram the life of the asset is restricted by a
combination of technical and market factors. These can be subdivided into two types:

(1) Internal factors which are a consequence of the qualities of
the asset itself, e.g. a reduction in quantity produced, an increase
in costs of production through additional waste and scrap, the
definite physical life of any component contained therein;

(2) External factors which are beyond the apparent control of
the organization and are due not to the quality of the asset but
to external circumstances, e.g. a new machine coming on to the
market which produces the same quantity at a lower cost, a
greater quantity at the same cost or a product of a different quality
a reduction in demand due to increased competition or a change
in consumer tastes and habits, etc.

In assessing the investment life of a project, therefore, attention must be paid to these, both from an internal and an external viewpoint, and an attempt made to forecast the effect of the interplay of these on the investment life. How important a particular factor is will depend on the impact it has—whether the decline in quantity and/or quality means that the equipment must be scrapped immediately or whether it merely indicates that it will have to be scrapped sooner than was anticipated in that the complementary cost curve will meet the service life curve nearer to the point of origin than originally forecast.

Replacement

Most business decisions assume that the firm will continue in existence and this requires substitution of new equipment for old. Although when the equipment was originally installed a forecast would have been made of its investment life it cannot be assumed that the end of this estimated life is the correct moment to replace. Traditionally it has been assumed that a distinction must be drawn between a decision to invest and a decision to replace although both are investment decisions. An investment which merely replaces a piece of equipment to maintain current production capacity is regarded as replacement investment, whereas, investment which extends productive capacity is defined as net investment or new investment. It can be questioned whether or not this distinction between replacement and net investment is valid. Both involve the same economic factors; the outlay of cash now which it is anticipated will produce a stream of income benefits the present value of which should more than cover the capital outlay of the project. The distinction is even more difficult to make if a business is operating in a fluctuating economy because it has been shown that under these circumstances[12] it cannot be assumed there is a zero lead time between the scrapping of a particular asset and its replacement. The two do not take place simultaneously and the firm is involved not in one but two decisions—the decision to scrap and the decision to buy.

If it is accepted that conceptually there is no distinction between replacement and net investment, a machine will be replaced by another provided the present value of the excess cash flows which is anticipated its replacement will bring, discounted down at the company's cost of capital exceeds the capital outlay for the replacement, e.g. if it is assumed that a machine which currently has a book value of £5,000 but which requires exceptional repair costs immediately of £2,000 as a result of which it will have a life of ten years, can be replaced by a machine which will cost £20,000 and which will also have a life of ten years, but will reduce costs by £3,000 per annum; and if the scrap value now of the existing machine is £1,000 and the cost of capital 10 per cent then, ignoring taxation, the arithmetic of the decision is as follows:

Cash outlay   Year 0   = Cost of new machine—(scrap
                                 value of old machine and re-
                                 pair costs avoided)
                               = £20,000—(£1,000+£2,000)
                               = £17,000

Cash inflows Year 1–Year 10 = £3,000 per annum

Present value of cash inflows
at 10 per cent   = £18,432

Cash outlay of £17,000 and, therefore, replacement should take place.

Part of the problem with replacement is to decide whether or not it is more profitable to delay replacement for one year rather than replace now. One method would be to compare the present value now compared to the present if replacement was delayed for n years and the year to replace would be that which gives the highest present value. This is the line of reasoning which has been followed by the Lutzes,[13] when they suggest that the optimum period of use is that which maximizes goodwill, goodwill being defined as the difference between the discounted value of a series of *quasi-rents* (i.e. the difference between the complementary costs and the income received from the flow of services which is generated by the asset) and the original cost of the asset. This is identical to the cash inflow and outflow logic which has been used in the preceding sections.

This approach has been criticized on the grounds that while this is a viable method for new investment it is not so easy to apply in terms of replacement. The objections against it are usually on the grounds of administrative expediency rather than theoretical weaknesses, e.g. that often machines produce goods for use in a later process and, therefore, there are no proceeds from these or that the method imputes to an individual capital good the whole profit which is earned by a combination of factors of production including other assets. These objections can be challenged. An investment decision about a machine which produces goods for use in a later process is no different from any other decision. If the new machine does not produce additional cash inflows through cost savings, increased sales income, etc., which give a profitable return compared to the cost of the machine then it should not be installed. The fact that the machine to be replaced is one cog in a big wheel is irrelevant. To decide whether or not another cog will do a more economical job does not depend upon applying the whole of the profit which is earned by the wheel to this new cog. It is sometimes suggested that the present value technique is really only worthwhile for important problems and that for the day to day routine replacement of small items of plant the administrative inconvenience of applying present value techniques outweighs its advantages. For example, in *Business Week*[14] when this particular problem was discussed the author, referring to the discounted cash flow technique, says:

. . . isn't likely to be used for any but important investment problems where the hoped for gain in accuracy is likely to exceed the cost of the analysis.

This can be challenged on two grounds; first, it is basically an argument not for a different technique of appraisal but for the substitution of standard values for variables in place of a realistic forecast of these because the advantages in accuracy will not outweigh the cost of obtaining them. This cannot be used as a criticism of a technique, it is simply a factor which must be taken into account with all measurements. Secondly, if replacement is to be based on a figure assessment of the situation then irrespective of how these figures have been determined it is difficult to visualize circumstances where these cannot be fitted as easily into a present value formalization as any other.[15]

12-7-70

5. THE COST OF CAPITAL

In assessing investment opportunity an essential factor is the cost of capital, i.e. the cost of financing the capital required for the particular venture. This cost serves two purposes. It acts as a screening device or cut-off point for projects. If the yield technique is used the return will have to be greater than this cost and if the net excess present value is used then this is the cost which indicates the amount of surplus or deficit net present value. In addition, it gives an indication of, at the particular moment of time, the profitability margin which apparently can be achieved. In a perfectly competitive market with no uncertainty there would only be a single rate of interest at which a business could borrow or lend and, therefore, there would be no problem in determining this rate as it would emerge from the interplay of market forces. However, in most, if not all, business situations there are neither perfectly competitive conditions nor is there the absence of uncertainty. A decision must also be made as to the source of funds, each with a different cost both superficial and imputed, out of which the investment opportunities can be financed, e.g. long-term loans, fixed interest shares, residual equity shares, retained profits and non cash charges in the profit and loss acount of which depreciation is by far the most important. In most organizations little attempt is made to identify the use of funds with their source. The funds are fed into a reservoir, become intermixed and from this mixture the various requirements are drawn off as and when they are required. Further there is the problem that many of the sources do not have an obvious cost in that there is no legal contract between borrower and lender which indicates a rate of interest which must be paid. This applies to shares on which a dividend will only be paid if there are profits available, and if the directors of the company feel that such a dividend should be paid. It may be that, in order to attract new equity funds while there is not a legal rate, there is an implied rate in that if there is no indication as to the likely return which shareholders will receive then the company will not be able to raise the necessary funds. The problem is even more complicated with retained earnings and depreciation provisions because there is neither an immediate payment determined by the market nor the necessity to imply a rate in order to raise them because they are already at the company's disposal.

It is convenient to summarize the sources of long-term finance under the following headings:

(1) Fixed interest loans, e.g. Debentures

(2) Fixed interest shares, e.g. Preference shares

(3) Residual equity shares, e.g. Rights and other issues of ordinary shares

(4) Retained cash flows—retained profits and depreciation provisions.

It is quite impossible to lay down a formula which will give the exact cost for the above, however, there is general agreement that

for fixed interest loans and fixed interest shares, the cost to the
company is the rate of interest it must pay to raise this finance plus
an allowance for the internal costs to the firm less taxation.

Long-term loans = (rate of interest+service charge) less
company tax rate

for example = (7 per cent+$\frac{1}{2}$ per cent) less 40 per cent
corporation tax
= 4·5 per cent

Fixed interest shares = rate of interest+(service charge less
company tax rate)*

for example = 7 per cent+($\frac{1}{2}$ per cent−40 per cent)
= 7·3 per cent.

The above is essentially a simplification, ignoring such problems as
issue of shares at a discount or a premium, convertible debentures,
redeemable shares, and also how the service charge assumed at
$\frac{1}{2}$ per cent above is computed.

Although new issues of residual shares do not require to indicate
a predetermined rate of interest, nevertheless, there must be an
imputed rate or the issue will not be successful. In trying to determine what this is it is essential to restate the basis assumptions of
the aims of the organization because if these vary so will the
determination of the cost of capital. If the motivating force for
managerial decision is the maximization of the present worth of
the company the cost of capital will be that which achieves this
desired position at the lowest cost. The shareholders will have
certain expectations, the minimum of which will be that the company will at least maintain its present value and, therefore, if the
current position is as follows:

Number of shares outstanding = 100,000
Current annual earnings after tax = £20,000
Current market value per share = £2

If a firm wishes to raise £25,000 for a new project and it decides
to do this out of equity shares, the net proceeds from each share
being £1.18.0,† what rate of earnings must be achieved for this to
be an acceptable proposition?

*The different tax treatment is because interest on loans is an allowance deduction
for tax purposes but dividends on shares are not.

†The difference between the £1.18.0 and the market value of £2 is due to issue
costs, etc.

$$\text{Current earnings per share} \quad = \frac{£20,000}{100,000} = 4/\text{-}$$

$$\text{Number of shares to be issued} = \frac{£25,000}{£1.18.0} = 13,158$$

$$\therefore \text{Total earnings required} \quad = 4/\text{-} \times 13,158 = £2,632$$

$$\therefore \text{Return required} \quad = \frac{£2,632}{£25,000} = 10 \cdot 5 \text{ per cent*}$$

Unless the new equity shares can earn a return of 10·5 per cent there will be a reduction in value as far as investors are concerned.

The cost of equity issues, ignoring issue costs, will, therefore, be the percentage which current earnings bears to the value of the shares. This again is a simplification which assumes that current earnings are of the same quality as expected future earnings and that the company has no other form of finance other than equity shares, that the only difference between the cost of rights issues as opposed to general issues is one of internal cost and that expectation of growth and earnings is not a material factor. Nevertheless, it is from this simplified model that the more sophisticated models have been developed[16] and it does provide a 'first attempt' for the computation of the cost of issue of new equity shares, i.e. the rate which must be earned if the company is to maintain its present position.

The computation of the cost of retained earnings and depreciation provisions (hereafter both will be referred to as retained earnings) is perhaps the most immediate problem as far as management is concerned. Do these cost anything at all? They flow by operation into the firm and there is no legal requirement that they should be distributed, the control over the level of these which will be forthcoming in the future, in so far as it is under the control of those associated with the firm, lies with management and not existing or prospective shareholders. To the shareholders the cost of retained earnings is essentially one of opportunity and is what could be earned by investing elsewhere. In order that the value of an individual share should not be decreased, the retention of £1 of earnings is only reasonable if it added £1 to the present value of the company. If the questions of growth and the impact of

*If it was expected that the proceeds would be £2 per share—the current market price—then the cost of capital would be 10 per cent, i.e. the percentage of current earnings to market value.

taxation are ignored and if it can be assumed that present earnings coincide with future expectations of earning then the cost of retained earnings is similar to the cost of a new equity issue, which is the ratio of current earnings to market value. However, once these rather rigid assumptions, particularly in relation to growth, are relaxed the construction of a model for the calculation of the cost of capital becomes more complex.

In assessing the cost of capital for retained earnings in a growth model it is essential to distinguish between growth of earnings which is the result of past investment decisions and is not dependent on reinvestment and growth which is dependent on such reinvestment. The calculation of the cost of capital for the former is still that rate of interest which discounts that growing stream of earnings down to a present value equal to the present worth to the company. This is no different from the static model except that the arithmetic is slightly more difficult and necessitates the adoption of trial and error techniques. Instead of the simple relationship of current earnings and market value a rate of interest is found which when applied to the different annual earnings produces a present value equal to the market value.

The introduction of real growth prevents the deduction of a unique formula for calculating the cost to a company of retained earnings. Instead the cost of capital will vary according to the assumptions which are made about both the quality of reinvestment and the factors which determine market values. Perhaps the most common debate revolves round the issue as to whether the market value of a company is a function of earnings or a function of dividends, and which, therefore, should be included in a theoretical framework of a cost of capital model. However, such arguments are largely pointless as Solomons has indicated:

The debate is an empty one. When dividends are equal to earnings no problem exists; when dividends are not equal to earnings the firm is expanding through the use of retained earnings and in this case neither dividends *per se* nor earnings *per se* can provide an adequate basis for measuring the returns which investors capitalize when arriving at a market price.[17]

Perhaps the best known growth model was that originally developed by Gordon and Shapiro[18] and which has been modified by other writers.[19] The cost of capital is computed from the viewpoint of a pre-established ratio of dividends to earnings so that reinvestment of earnings must earn a return which will still maintain this ratio and will also enable growing dividends.

Let y   = discount rate (cost of capital)

Do = dividends (net of tax) in year 0

Dn = dividends (net of tax) in year n

Eo = earnings (net of tax) in year 0

En = earnings (net of tax) in year n

MV = market value of company

b   = fraction of earnings retained in the company

r   = expected rate of return on reinvestment of retained earnings

g   = expected growth rate of earnings, dividends and market value

It can be shown that the growth rate g will be equal to br, for example, if a company has a market value of £1,000 and annual earnings of £100 one half of which are distributed as dividends, then next year's earnings will be £100+10 per cent of £50 which is £105, i.e. a growth of 5 per cent, which is equal to the earnings rate of 10 per cent times the proportion of re-investment $-\frac{1}{2}$.

Under the circumstances, where earnings, dividends and market values are growing at a constant rate, then the cost of capital is

$$y = \frac{Do}{MV} + g^*$$

*MV is assumed to be the present value of future dividends capitalized at the cost of capital,

$$\therefore MV = \sum_{n=1}^{\infty} \frac{Dn}{(1+y)^n}$$

this is the discrete case but to simplify the mathematics we take the continuous case where

$$MV = \int_{0}^{\infty} Dne^{-y} \, dn$$

However, if dividends grow at the continued rate of g

$$Dn = Doe^{gn}$$

$$\therefore MV = \int_{0}^{\infty} Do \, e^{gn} e^{-yn} \, dn$$

i.e. the cost of capital is the current dividend yield plus the anticipated growth rate. The growth rate must be less than the cost of
capital otherwise the company will have an infinite value:

$$\text{a company with MV} = £100$$
$$\text{E} = £10$$
$$\text{D} = £5$$
$$\therefore \text{ b (retention factor)} = 0 \cdot 5$$

if it is anticipated that the growth will be 6 per cent the cost of
capital is

$$\frac{5}{100} + 6 \text{ per cent}$$

$$= 11 \text{ per cent}$$

This is the rate which discounts the future anticipated cash flows
down to £100, the current market value, viz.:

in the first year the dividends will be £5

in the second year the dividends will be £5·3 (6 per cent inc.)

in the third year the dividends will be £5·618 (6 per cent inc.)

in the third year the MV will be £119·1016 (6 per cent
growth over three years)

the present value of these cash flows at 11 per cent will be

$$\frac{£5}{(1 \cdot 11)^1} + \frac{£5 \cdot 3}{(1 \cdot 11)^2} + \frac{£5 \cdot 618 + £119 \cdot 1016}{(1 \cdot 11)^3} = £100$$

In this situation the re-investment rate r is 12 per cent and is
greater than the current earnings rate of 10 per cent. When the
re-investment rate is equal to the current earnings rate then we
have expansion, and growth is the result of retention at normal
rather than superior rates. For example, with the previous illustration if 10 per cent will be achieved on re-investment, then

$$= Do \int_{0}^{\infty} e^{-n(y-g)}\, dn$$

$$= \frac{Do}{y-g}$$

$$\therefore y = \frac{Do}{MV} + g$$

$$g = br$$
$$= 0.5 \times 10 \text{ per cent}$$
$$= 5 \text{ per cent}$$
$$y = \frac{5}{100} + 5 \text{ per cent}$$
$$= 10 \text{ per cent} = \text{current earnings rate}$$

Finally if the rate of re-investment is less than the current rate the re-investment should not take place.[20]

It is, of course, possible to construct other frameworks, based on different assumptions, for estimating the cost of retained earnings.[21]

All that any formula can do is provide a starting point, highlighting the important factors contained therein and the relationship which exists between them.

A major source of finance is the retention of depreciation provisions and it has been assumed that their cost is identical to the cost of retained earnings.

The average cost of capital

Having determined the cost of each individual source of capital the next step is to extract from them a unique cost which can be applied to any project irrespective of the source of its finance. The most common procedure is to take a weighted average of the costs of the different types of finance. In determining this there are two approaches. The first is to take the present position of the company and to weight the cost of capital according to the relative value which the specific type of capital bears to the company's total financial structure, e.g. if the total market value of the company is £1,400,000 and of this £400,000 is fixed interest or loan stock and £1,000,000 equity stock and if the cost of loan stock is 3 per cent and that of equity 10 per cent, then the cost of capital is as follows:

Source		Net cost	Net annual cost
Loan stock	£ 400,000	3 per cent	£ 12,000
Equity	£1,000,000	10 per cent	£100,000
	£1,400,000	8 per cent	£112,000

and, therefore, the average cost of capital and the cut-off rate fo accepting investment opportunities is 8 per cent. This would seem to be a logical approach when the desire is to maintain the present value of the company and if it is assumed there will not be a significant change in the balance between the various types of capital.

An alternative is to project the long-run optimum capital structure which the firm wishes to achieve, the optimum capital structure being that which gives the firm the lowest cost of capital consistent with the maximization of its present worth. It assumes that there is a financial structure of the various types of capital so that although sources are available whose apparent cost is lower than the return which could be achieved within the organization the introduction of these would so upset the balance between the types of finance that the impact of the increased profitability on market value would be more than offset by the reduction which the non-optimum financial balance would bring. It is this projected optimum financial relationship between the various types of capital which is used as a weight. For example, if the optimum structure consists of the following:

	Optimum proportion	Net cost	Contribution to average cost
Loan stock	30 per cent	3·0 per cent	0·9 per cent
Equity	30 ,,	10·0 ,,	3·0 ,,
Retained earnings	40 ,,	9·5 ,,	3·8 ,,
			7·7 per cent

the average cost of capital will be 7·7 per cent.

The above reasoning has accepted the traditional view that the degree of gearing in a company affects its market value and consequently its cost of capital. That for most companies which start off debt free as the proportion of fixed income capital is increased, the cost of capital falls and the market value increases (provided, of course, that this additional finance is invested at a rate equal to the company's cost of capital) up to a certain point, and, thereafter, the reverse takes place, i.e. the market value falls with subsequent increases in gearing. The cost of capital curve is U-shaped. This traditional view has been challenged by Modigliani and Miller[22] who have put forward the thesis that two firms with asset structures of roughly the same size and quality of earnings and in the same

risk class will have the same total market value irrespective of their
financial structure and that their cost of capital will not be affected
by the degree of gearing. Although initially their proposition is
developed under the assumption of perfect markets and of rational
behaviour on the part of the investors, they then proceed to argue
that many situations correspond sufficiently well with this to
validate their proposition on a much wider front. The crux of
their argument is that individual investors engage in home-made
'gearing' which is adjusted to coincide with the gearing of the firms
in which they have invested. They withdraw from one and move
into another until the *status quo* is established. Their argument can
be illustrated by the simple example in the table on p. 69.

Under these circumstances then a rational investor will sell his
shares in B—say he holds 10 per cent which have a market value of
£1,800 and which produce an income of £270—for £1,800, borrow
£600 at 6 per cent and invest the resultant £2,400 in Company A
from which investment he will receive £360. After paying the loan
interest of £36 on the £600 he has borrowed, he still has an income
of £324, which is better than the original £270. In addition, it is
more attractive because it is less risky through the relatively low
level of gearing providing a greater margin of safety for his income.
   This view has been challenged on many issues, some of which are
as follows:

   (1) It does not distinguish between personal debt and company
debt in that it assumes that an individual utilizes gearing in his own
personal stockholding in the same way as a company does and
that this cannot be substantiated because individuals do not have
limited liability such as companies and certain institutional
investors are restricted in the degree of personal gearing in which
they can indulge.[23, 24, 25]

   (2) It does not take account of the different tax treatments
which are afforded to the various types of capital; e.g. payments on
loan capital are deductible for tax payment whereas payments to
ordinary shareholders are not.

   (3) That the empirical evidence to date does not justify the
Modigliani and Miller contention and that what little evidence is
available is not sufficiently detailed to permit refined interpretation
i.e. variations of $\frac{1}{2}$ per cent to $\frac{1}{4}$ per cent cannot be distinguished
and these are significant in the finances of large companies. Of
course, the lack of evidence, while not proving the Modigliani and
Miller theory, does not disprove it either.

	Company A	Company B
CAPITAL	All Equity £20,000—20,000 shares	LOAN STOCK £5,000 at 6 per cent—5,000 shares
		EQUITY £15,000—15,000 shares
GROSS OPERATING INCOME (Ignore tax)	= £3,000	= £3,000
NET OPERATING INCOME	= £3,000	= £2,700
EARNINGS PER £ EQUITY SHARE	= £3,000 20,000	= £2,700 15,000
	= 3/-	= 3/7
MARKET VALUE AT CAPITALISATION, RATE OF 15 per cent	Equity £20,000 Loan stock — £20,000	£18,000 5,000 £23,000
MARKET VALUE PER SHARE	Equity 20/- Loan stock —	24/- £100

Much more detailed investigation is required in this particular area. However, the majority view is still of a U-shaped cost of capital curve whether or not the traditional reasons for justifying this are, in fact, correct. It would also seem that the flat bottom extends over a wider range of financial structures than was previously thought and that within these limits there would be no significant variation in the company's market value and its cost of capital because of different financial structures.

Having constructed a weighted average cost of capital what importance can be attached to this figure? It is only a norm which has been based on many estimates of dividends, earnings and growth possibilities and which cannot be imputed with absolute accuracy. It will only be used as a preliminary screening device By altering the assumptions a range of costs can be provided. It is likely, however, that if the company does this it will provide a spectrum within which its own true capital costs will be found and conservatism would seem to dictate that as a first step unless projects satisfy the highest capital cost so computed, a rigorou reappraisal of them would be required.

Many businesses do not formally stipulate a cost of capital particularly where a high proportion of investment is through retained earnings and depreciation provisions. Instead, management sets a target rate of return. Conceptually, this target return would appear to be similar to the opportunity cost concept in that it appears to be the rate which the firm believes it can earn by diverting the funds to alternative uses either internal or external to the firm. If this opportunity cost of capital coincides with the real cost then the results are the same. However, if the opportunity cost is greater or less than the company's real cost, the company will fail to achieve its theoretically possible maximum present worth. There is no real dichotomy here between the two approaches because they are both based on different assumptions about the market situation. The opportunity cost technique assumes that firm is faced with a continual stream of investment opportunities for which there is a definite limit of funds available at any particular time irrespective of cost. If a project with a lower opportunity cost is accepted now it means that in the foreseeable future, if a higher return project appears it will have to be rejected and, therefore, this is not an optimum decision. Under conditions of capital rationing this is likely to be the case where the firm has a budgeting system within which the capital budget provides an overall restraint on the total amount to be invested in any particular period.

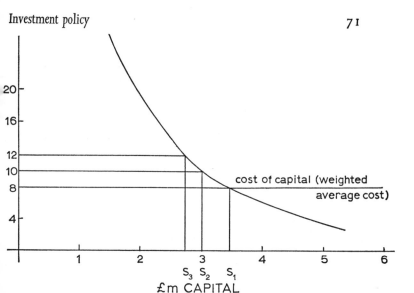

Opportunity cost can be viewed either as the result or cause of capital rationing.

In normal circumstances £3½m., i.e. S1 worth of projects, would be undertaken because they can all satisfy the test of the cost of capital Y1, i.e. 8 per cent. However, if the company imposes an opportunity cost of 10 per cent by assuming that if it accepts projects below this now they will have to reject projects above it in the future, the capital requirements are now S2, i.e. £3m. The opportunity cost has imposed capital rationing on the organization. On the other hand, the company may impose a restraint on capital expenditure of £2¾m. which will result in an opportunity cost of Y3—12 per cent—as the cut off point for investment: here the opportunity cost rate has been determined by the level of capital rationing.

Although within the context of most investment theory, 'the common use of capital budgets as administrative control devices without economic significance is irrelevant for this discussion',[26] nevertheless, if a firm accepts the existence of capital rationing and controls its operations accordingly by using opportunity costs as a screening device although it will not reach its theoretically achievable maximum present worth, it will come as close to this as it possibly can given the conditions under which it believes it is working.

6. UNCERTAINTY

When discussing the techniques for selecting investment opportunities the implicit assumption was of a comparison and assessment between projects with a like degree of uncertainty. Any difference in uncertainty between different investment opportunities had been adjusted in the amount and timing of the cash inflows and inflows. However, one of the central characteristics of an investment decision is that it is accompanied by uncertainty and it is the measurement of this and its introduction into a viable decision rule with which this section is concerned.

There are many factors which make for uncertainty in business decisions, for example, factors which can determine investment life. Some of these factors can be insured against, for example, the loss of profit which arises as a result of a fire disrupting production and sales. When this can be done these events cease to be uncertainties but become costs but this cannot be extended to cover all of the possible eventualities.[27] Profit is a reward associated with uncertainty and the desire for a monopoly situation can be regarded as simply one method of reducing the uncertainty attached to business decisions. Uncertainty is closely associated with the desire to survive which according to the behavioural scientists is the dominant factor in the minds of all decision makers. In many ways there is an analogy between the biological world of Darwin and the business world. To survive, a business must mutate and adapt to its changing environment. However, a business cannot rely on accidental mutation, it must adapt through innovation and innovation presupposes investment. Yet empirical studies of investment decisions in action would seem to indicate that the combined effect of survival and uncertainty works against this.

Uncertainty is probably the main reason for a reluctance to commit resources to fixed investment in advance of the known need, and for the effort to maintain a more liquid position in bad times than in good. Uncertainty is the basis of many of the rules of thumb a firm uses for appraising investment opportunities such as the short pay-off criterion which place great emphasis on quick turnover and approximate profits and discount the more distant future nearly or wholly to the vanishing point.[28]

It is uncertainty which underlies the cautious approach which characterizes decisions in this field. An extension of plant facilities is always regarded as a last resort decision, and other improvizations such as shift working, overtime working, etc., irrespective of their economic worth are always utilized first before expansion is contemplated,[29] and even when such plans are made a measure of escapability is built into them as a hedge against uncertainty.[30] The economic factors such as payoff and liquidity which receive the greatest attention also seem typical of a survival attitude in a world of uncertainty.

It is obvious, therefore, that if uncertainty is ignored in a theory of decision making that theory can have only a limited value. Because of this much attention has been devoted to this particular problem in the literature over the last twenty years, but despite this there has been little success in formulating a theory which is universally acceptable at both a conceptual and, possibly more important, an operational level. There have been many approaches to the problem and although we can distinguish broad areas where the methodology is unique, the dividing line between these is not clear and the one overlaps the other.

One approach seeks to apply the deductive reasoning of game theory to investment decisions. If survival is the dominant objective of the businessman then it is likely that this will prohibit decisions which involve the possibility of extreme losses. It is more likely that a basic criterion for a decision will be 'what course of action is likely to minimize or lessen losses due to the uncertainty inherent in the decision?' From this basic assumption about attitudes a series of decision rules have been developed. Most of these assume that the outcome of a series of events cannot be predicted in probabilistic terms in the sense that the actual outcome of a series of possible actions is determined by nature.

The maximin criterion is an extremely conservative rule where the 'player' determines the worst possible outcome for each line of action and chooses that which shows the least unattractive position, assuming the worst happens. For example, in the following matrix:

	R1	R2	R3
S1	96	8	6
S2	95	92	5

(Strategy one (S1) has three possible results—R1, R2 or R3)

the player will adopt strategy S1 because its worst payoff is 6 whereas with S2 it is 5; S1 has the largest of the worst payoffs and is the maximin choice.

A basic objection to this method is that because it is influenced by extreme values it can lead to a choice which intuitively does not appear to be rational. S1 is chosen while observation would seem to indicate that of the two S2 is superior because it has almost identical maximum and minimum payoffs, 95 to 96 and 5 to 6, to which most people would be indifferent whereas it has a much better intermediate position, 92 to 8.

L. J. Savage[31] has developed another rule known as the minimax regret criterion. Regret is a formulation of the supposition that uncertainty and survival lead to a decision rule which measures the cost of mistakes, i.e. the difference between the return under one set of circumstances and the possible return had the more favourable outcome resulted. Using the previous matrix if S1 is chosen and R1 results then there is zero regret as this is the best outcome of the two payoffs. However, if S2 is chosen and R1 results then the player is in an inferior position because by not choosing S1 he has incurred a regret of 1—(96 less 95) and this is entered in the regret matrix which will appear in final form as follows:

	R1	R2	R3
S1	0	84	0
S2	1	0	1

The maximum regret in each column is then compared, i.e. 84 for S1 and 1 for S2. The action which has the smallest maximum regret, i.e. S2, is chosen. This criterion also suffers from an extreme approach in that it only considers maximum regrets and like the maximin ignores intermediate positions. In addition, where there are more than two strategies it is quite easy to show that the best choice of the set is not necessarily the best choice of the sub-set which at first sight would appear to be illogical for a decision rule based on preferences. For example, in the following:

	Original matrix			Regret	
	R1	R2		R1	R2
S1	58	70	S1	7	0
S2	65	58	S2	0	12
S3	60	65	S3	5	5

S3 is chosen. However, if S2 is not considered a possibility, the position becomes:

	Revised matrix				*Revised regret*	
	R1	**R2**			**R1**	**R2**
S1	58	70		S1	2	0
S3	60	65		S3	0	5

and S1 is chosen although S3 is still an alternative choice. In an attempt to overcome the problem of a dependence on extremes, other decision rules have been developed.

The Hurwicz criterion employs a weighted average of the minimum and maximum payoffs. If the maximum payoff is given a weight of $\frac{1}{8}$, and the minimum payoff a weight of $\frac{7}{8}$,

	Original matrix		
	R1	**R2**	**R3**
S1	96	8	6
S2	95	92	5

applying the weights

$$S1 = \tfrac{1}{8} \times 96 + \tfrac{7}{8} \times 6 = 17{\cdot}25$$
$$S2 = \tfrac{1}{8} \times 95 + \tfrac{7}{8} \times 5 = 16{\cdot}26$$

and, therefore, S1 is chosen because the sum of the weighted maximum and minimum payoff is the greater. The Bayes approach on the other hand assigns equal probability to each and accepts that which ensures the highest resultant payoff. The logic being that if there is no knowledge of the possible outcome of a series of events then equal probabilities must be assigned to each.

$$S1 = \frac{96+8+6}{3} = 36\tfrac{2}{3}$$

$$S2 = \frac{95+92+5}{3} = 64$$

and therefore, S2 is chosen.

Although to some extent these criteria do get over the weaknesses of dependence on extreme values, they leave unanswered such questions as how are the weights which are given to the possible outcomes determined and is not the allocation of probabilities in the Bayes criterion ambiguous in the sense that until a decision about the number of possible outcomes of a strategy has been made the probability factor cannot be stipulated? If the number of outcomes vary then the probabilities vary and, if this is so, it seems only reasonable to allow a subjective probability factor to be assigned to the various states. Once this is allowed then another approach to the treatment of uncertainty by the allocation of subjective probability weights to the variables involved in the decision can be developed. Before examining this it can be concluded that the current situation of game and statistical decision theory has little to offer as an operational tool for business decisions in the investment area. The assumption that the outcome of a particular decision is dependent completely on factors which are external to the firm—states of nature over which the firm has no subsequent control—does not appear to coincide with the environment within which business decisions are made. Rather, decisions are sequential in that they are part of a chain, each decision being determined to a greater or lesser degree by the current outcome of decisions which were taken in the past,[32] many of these current decisions being in the nature of appendices to the original decision, taking account of the reappraised situation. Which criterion will be adopted by a firm will depend on the psychological make up of the person responsible for the decision and it is not certain whether in this respect we can speak about the corporate personality of the firm as reflecting the strategy which will be adopted under all circumstances. In addition, psychological make up is not static but is a dynamic factor which will vary from time to time, being probably a function of the financial situation of the firm when the decision is made.

Another approach for dealing with uncertainty is the numerical weighting by a probability factor of the range of possible outcomes of a decision to arrive at the anticipated outcome. It is this anticipated outcome which is then subjected to statistical appraisal techniques to determine whether or not it should be undertaken. Determining the likely cash flows which will result from a particular project could be as follows:

PROBABILITY CALCULATION OF CASH FLOWS

Cash flow	Year 1		Year 2		Year 3	
	Proba-bility	Expecta-tion	Proba-bility	Expecta-tion	Proba-bility	Expecta-tion
£		£		£		£
8,000	0·0	—	0·0	—	0·3	2,400
9,000	0·0	—	0·1	900	0·3	2,700
10,000	0·1	1,000	0·1	1,000	0·2	2,000
11,000	0·2	2,200	0·3	3,300	0·1	1,100
12,000	0·3	3,600	0·3	3,600	0·05	600
13,000	0·2	2,600	0·1	1,300	0·05	650
14,000	0·1	1,400	0·1	1,400	0·0	—
15,000	0·1	1,500	0·0	—	0·0	—
		12,300		11,500		9,450

The cash flows for years 1, 2 and 3 will therefore be £12,300, £11,500 and £9,450 respectively.

At first sight this would appear to be a method which coincides with the business situation. The survival factor will mean that a higher probability rating is given to those opportunities which have short payoffs, and a strong overall liquidity. Undoubtedly, in appraising future projects, businessmen do assess the likely outcome in the light of their experience of similar activities in the past and their judgment of the current and future situation. Provided it can be assumed that the forecast of an outcome of a series of events can be expressed in probabilistic terms then the investment decision under uncertainty simply becomes a restatement of the excess present value equation except that the variables are now represented by the means of the probability distribution.

Objections to the use of probabilities have been made on two grounds. It is unlikely that the event under consideration is one which has been repeated so often in independent but identical circumstances in the past that an objective probability rating can be obtained; therefore, the probability must be subjective and doubts have been thrown on the validity of using subjective probabilities. These may invalidate any external assessment of the probabilities which a particular decision maker or company will choose in all circumstances but as a conceptual tool the measurements for which can only be assessed internally, subjective probability is still useful. An examination of the nature of probability theory indicates that it is 'essentially an appeal to experience for the primary data to which mathematical reasoning is then applied'[33] and it cannot be denied that in the assessment of the effect of policy decisions, experience is a most important factor.

The assumption that human behaviour can be expressed in probabilistic terms has also been challenged. There are circumstances where it would not be reasonable to assume that expected value would be relevant for determining choice. For example, the St. Petersburg paradox when a game offers a reward of $£2^n$ where n is the number of tosses of a fair coin before a head is obtained, then the expectation is infinite but it is unlikely that any of us would risk more than £2 or £3 on a wager of this sort. Experiments in utility theory have shown people do not make decisions in accordance with the true probability but they are motivated by their subjective belief that one outcome is more likely than another, and although attempts have been made to overcome this problem of probability by substituting utility for money, the basic problem still remains.[34] It would appear, however, that this also is more a problem of measurement and the creation of preference scales rather than a weakness of the conceptual notion itself.[35] Nevertheless, it would appear that to treat uncertainty by obtaining subjective numerical estimates about an individual's thoughts on a certain factor and then to assume that he will make future decisions accordingly is not completely satisfactory, particularly from the viewpoint of introducing this into an effective decision rule.

To date, therefore, there is no method for treatment of uncertainty which is not open to doubt either on its conceptual significance or its operational usefulness.[36] The existence of uncertainty, however, cannot be ignored and it is essential that some attempt, even if it is subjective, should be made to measure this; otherwise it is unlikely that a capital sanctioning procedure based on sound economic reasoning can be introduced into an organization. As more evidence about human behaviour becomes available and as recording systems become more sophisticated and produce more relevant data, then the introduction of uncertainty into a theoretical framework for investment decisions may become easier. However, that there are areas about which currently little is known makes it even more important that those factors which can be quantified are subjected to a rigorous statistical processing, so that a confidence limit can be given to them and their real economic effect expressed in a manner which has some operational significance.

NOTES

1. Joel Dean, 'Measuring the Productivity of Capital', *Harvard Business Review*, XXXII, 1954.

2. Drucker, *The Practice of Management*.

3. A. M. Alfred, 'Discounted Cash Flow and Corporate Planning', *Woolwich Economic Papers*, no. 3.

4. Dean, op. cit.

5. D. F. Istvan, *Capital Expenditure Decisions: how they are made in large corporations*.

6. M. M. Dryden, 'The MAPI Urgency Rating as an Investment Ranking Criterion', *Journal of Business*, October 1960.

7. M. J. Gordon, 'The Pay-off Period and the Rate of Profit', *Journal of Business*, October 1955.

8. It has been shown that utility is likely to be maximized more often with the EPV than with the Yield. M. M. Dryden, 'Capital Budgeting: treatment of uncertainty and investment criteria', *Scottish Journal of Political Economy*, vol. XI.

9. See Chapter 7.

10. '*Investment Incentives*', Cmnd. 2874.

11. Drucker, *The Practice of Management*.

12. Meij, *Depreciation and Replacement Policy*.

13. Lutz, F. and V. L., *The Theory of Investment of the Firm*.

14. *Business Week*, September 1958.

15. For alternative approaches to the replacement problem see:

(1) J. S. Taylor, 'A Statistical Theory of Depreciation', *Journal of the American Statistical Association*, December 1923.

(2) H. Hotelling, 'A General Mathematical Theory of Depreciation', *Journal of the American Statistical Association*, September 1925.

(3) Meij, op. cit.

(4) G. Terborgh, *Dynamic Equipment Policy*
　　　　　　　　 MAPI Replacement Manual
　　　　　　　　 Realistic Depreciation Policy

Terborgh's approach has been the most successful, in terms of practical application, replacement model developed to date. He has formulated a 'do it yourself' replacement kit which is based on the yield technique. It assumes standard values for the main variables such as the rate at which earnings decline; the service life of new equipment; the depreciation system; cost of capital and financial structure.

All of the approaches make it quite clear that book value is an irrelevant factor when considering replacement.

16. For a complete treatment of this see Solomons, *The Theory of Financial Management*.

17. Solomons, op. cit.

18. Gordon and Shapiro, 'Capital Equipment Analysis: the required rate of profit', *Management Science*, III.

19. Solomons, op. cit.

20. With the current taxation position in the UK this statement might have to be amended to take account of tax saved by not distributing.

21. Solomons, op. cit.

22. Modigliani and Miller, 'The Cost of Capital, Corporation Finance, and the Theory of Investment', *American Economic Review*, XLVIII, June 1958.

23. Durand, 'The Cost of Capital on an Imperfect Market', *American Economic Review*, June 1959.

24. Weston, *Journal of Business*, April 1961, Review Article.

25. Merrett and Sykes, *The Finance and Analysis of Capital Projects*, accept the theoretical possibility that institutional as opposed to individual investors can indulge in home-made gearing although they can see no evidence in the United Kingdom that they do.

26. Weingarten, 'The Excess Present Value Index', *Journal of Accounting Research*, vol. I, no. 2, Autumn 1963.

27. Freidman and Savage have shown that businessmen may pay more for insurance cover than it is apparently worth in order to minimize the uncertainty attached to their decisions. 'The Utility Analysis of Choices Involving Risk', *Journal of Political Economy*, vol. LVI, 1948.

28. E. M. Hoover, commenting on Joel Dean's contribution to the National Bureau of Economic Research Report on the 'Regularization of Business Investment'.

29. P. W. S. Andrews, *Manufacturing Business*.

30. Gort, 'Planning of Investment', *Journal of Business*, 1951.

31. L. J. Savage, 'The Theory of Statistical Decisions', *Journal of the American Statistical Association*, no. 4, 1951.

32. Massé, *Optimal Investment Decisions. Rules for Action and Criteria for Choice*.

33. Klein, *Mathematics and Western Culture*.

34. K. J. Arrow, 'Alternative Approaches to the Theory of Choice in Risk Taking Situations', *Econometrica*, October 1951.

35. For the most comprehensive discussion on the establishment of values for decision making see Churchman, *Prediction and Optimal Decision*.

36. Other treatments have been tried. See, for example, Shackle, *Time in Economics*.

5

COMPETITION

It is possible to take the tough-minded line that Schumpeter derived from Marx. The system is cruel, unjust, turbulent, but it does deliver the goods, and, damn it all, it's the goods that you want.   JOAN ROBINSON, *Economic Philosophy*

1. THE RATIONALE OF COMPETITION

Competition exists if the party with whom a business or an individual wants to trade has alternative opportunities of exchange, the people who offer these alternative opportunities being the competitors. Since exchange involves two parties, competition can be among the buyers, among the sellers or both. Most firms sell to many customers, though occasionally a business may face a sole buyer and its bargaining power will be consequently reduced. Customers usually have a choice of suppliers. Occasionally, however, as in the case of domestic water supply, the customer has only one source of supply and is consequently in a weak bargaining position. Where the numbers of customers on the one hand or suppliers on the other are substantially reduced, competition is restricted and monopoly power can develop.

Essentially, competition is a process by which alternative opportunities are made available to customers. A business competes with its rivals by (1) offering the consumer the same product at a lower price; (2) offering a slightly different product, for example a different type of ball-point pen or a piece of furniture of improved design; (3) offering a radically-improved product or innovation, for example jet air travel in place of travel by ocean liner, television for sound radio, motor scooters for conventional pedal bicycles; (4) by successful sales promotion, by which a firm tries to make consumers buy its product rather than a rival's or to create a wholly new scheme of wants in the mind of the consumer.*[1] Such actions are what the competitive process consists of. Each business seeks to offer its customers something unique: through price advantage, differentiated and improved products, or by creating a successful 'image' for its products. By contrast, a business possesses monopoly power when other firms are denied the opportunity of offering alternatives to the consumer or are prevented from responding to a firm's competitive bid for increased custom. Such power is rarely, if ever, absolute. It usually arises through: (1) financial or technical barriers to entry into costly and complex technological processes; (2) government intervention and legal restrictions; (3) collusion among producers on prices, market shares, tendering, etc.[2]

In taking this preliminary look at competition and monopoly, it is particularly necessary to stress that competition is a dynamic process by which alternative opportunities are made available to potential customers and information about them is disseminated. This is a flexible concept of competition. Modern economists often define the term more rigorously in terms of market categories.† In doing so, they are really defining the conditions under which competition takes place as a basis for analysing its results in terms of equilibrium situations. This is not the same thing as the actual day-to-day *process* of competition, which is what most businesses have to live with.

Economists have devoted much time to defining and analysing competition, largely because common attitudes to competition vary greatly. Adam Smith, the founder of modern economics, saw competition as an aspect of 'the obvious and simple system of natural liberty' in which 'every man, as long as he does not violate the laws of justice, is left perfectly free to pursue his own interest in his own way, and to bring both his industry and capital into competition with those of any other man or order of men'.[3] Other economists have taken a more pragmatic view, seeing competition as promoting industrial efficiency and economic welfare and enabling economic resources to be employed to the best advantage in accordance with consumer preferences. Businessmen, however, possibly from bitter experience, sometimes speak

*The cosmetic manufacturer, who advertises 'the limitless tints, and the almost bodiless textures of these gossamer powders, nutrient foundations and lipsticks' provides an appeal which can hardly fail to create new wants in the minds of female buyers!

†See below, p. 84.

of 'ruinous', 'cut-throat', 'wasteful' and 'unfair' competition and consequently seek to limit it. Economists nowadays judge competition on its practical merits rather than by appeal to abstract philosophical principles. Their underlying presumption is usually that free competition generally operates in the social interest unless the contrary can be proved, since it provides an effective check on the power of a seller to make or fix the terms (usually the price) on which he will sell. Competition, by providing the buyer with alternatives and by compelling the producer to be a price taker, safeguards the consumer against exploitation and makes it unnecessary for the State to intervene by regulating prices and production in order to protect him.[4]

2. EXCHANGE AND MARKET CATEGORIES

While a few prices are fixed by law or custom, such as telephone charges or legal fees, most are not. Marketing arrangements of varying degrees of sophistication exist for most competitive commodities, ranging from the simplest exchange—horse trading or higgling—to more complex markets involving competition among buyers and sellers on both sides of the market.

Custom, convenience, location of the markets and the nature of the commodity being dealt in largely decide how exchanges are conducted and the institutions created for the purpose.

The economist distinguishes market situations according to the degree of monopoly found in each. The categories summarized in the following table are used by economists to analyse the pricing and output policies of the firm as the market situation varies by number of firms and nature of product.[5]

Such analysis is not our main concern in this book, but it is relevant since management should clearly understand the markets it operates in and the limitations on its freedom of action imposed by different market environments. It must also be alert and recognize when market conditions change. A successful innovation may give a firm a real monopoly today, but the situation may quickly change to one of monopolistic competition once a host of imitators enter and compete. A railway must pursue a different marketing policy when faced with air competition from the one it followed in earlier days when it had monopoly power.

MARKET CATEGORIES

NUMBER OF PRODUCERS / NATURE OF PRODUCT	LARGE NUMBER	FEW	ONE
HOMOGENEOUS	*Pure (perfect) competition* Includes agricultural products, raw materials and commodities traded on organized markets. Producer has no control over price, which is set impersonally by the market.	*Pure (homogeneous) oligopoly* Exists where there are only a few producers of a raw material or of identical commodities. Producers have control over their own price, but their pricing policy must take serious account of rivals' probable reactions. Pricing interdependence. Tendency to rigid prices and price leadership schemes.	*Isolated (industry-wide) monopoly* Rarely found, but examples include telephone service, water supply and some public utilities. Producer has considerable control over price (or output) usually limited in practice by Government regulation or fear of public opinion. Such monopoly power tends to be eroded in the long run as a result of innovation and technological change, e.g. railways and nationalized coal.
DIFFERENTIATED	*Monopolistic competition* Widespread and includes many firms producing similar, but differentiated goods or services: e.g. branded foods, retail establishments, electrical goods, etc. Firm has some small degree of control over price because of differentiation, which confers slight monopoly power. Competition takes the form of branded products and adver-	*Differentiated oligopoly* Includes many manufactured and other products: e.g. motor vehicles, detergents, gramophone records, air services. Suppliers have control over their own price, but because of interdependence, prefer price rigidity (or agreements) to price wars. Competition tends to take the form of differentiation (branding) and advertising	

3. COMPETITIVE BEHAVIOUR

Market categories describe the conditions in which competition operates. They do not describe competitive behaviour. Theories have been advanced which try to explain the process of competition. J. Downie has done so in terms of a 'transfer mechanism' and an 'innovation mechanism'. The transfer mechanism is the process by which shares of the market are transferred from less efficient firms to the more efficient. The more efficient grow mainly by using their high profits for investment. The innovation mechanism is the process by which firms change in efficiency by innovating, since pressure of competition forces the less efficient firms to innovate in order to survive. Thus new leaders are produced and different firms are expanding at different times.[6] This is an ingenious if controversial theory, which still leaves a good deal to be explained about the means and the process by which a particular firm encroaches on the market of its rivals. The process by which a business competes with its rivals is indeed complex. Professor Joan Robinson has pointed out:

Competition between sellers is not confined to offering an identical commodity at a lower price but enters into the design of the commodity itself as well as into all the multifarious forms of enticements to buy with which it is surrounded. The conditions of supply and demand are never, and are never expected to be, unchanging from week to week and from year to year, but are in a continuing state of flux.[7]

The same author has shown, in another connection, that the assumption that price is the main vehicle for competition is an over-simplification. Competition may take many forms:

(1) imitation of products;

(2) differentiation of products—these may be in respect of qualities which affect practical usefulness or pleasure to the consumer, qualities which appeal to snobbishness or to pseudo-scientific notions, or simply methods of packing and labelling articles;

(3) services of all kinds, prompt delivery, long credit;

(4) advertisement;

(5) pure salesmanship, in the sense of the persuasiveness of travellers, etc.;

(6) a higher price—giving the impression of better quality;

(7) lower price.[8]

This summary of the multi-dimensional nature of competition could no doubt be further elaborated and an alert management must consider every avenue by which competition may be carried on. Most competitive behaviour may, however, be broadly viewed as taking the form of (a) pricing, (b) product differentiation, (c) innovation, (d) promotional activity.

(a) Pricing

Pricing decisions have been more thoroughly analysed in economics than other types of competitive behaviour and the general problem of pricing policy will be discussed later.[9] Several observations may, however, be made about pricing as an aspect of competitive behaviour, assuming that the business does not operate in perfect markets and therefore has some discretion in its pricing policy. First, pricing decisions are not taken in isolation, but are treated as one of several factors contributing to the utility of the product in the eyes of the consumer. Pricing cannot be considered independently of quality variations or promotional activity. Secondly, manufactured products are not simply taken to a market and sold for what they will fetch. Prices have to be quoted and varied from time to time to meet changing competitive conditions. Further, prices may be quoted competitively either in *response* to the market or in situations where the business itself is taking the *initiative* in an effort to control or modify market forces. Examples of the first are (i) pricing in response to a growth in sales volume, which calls for careful assessment of the trend in demand and full knowledge of capacity output; (ii) pricing in response to increased competition, which may take a wide variety of forms depending on the nature of competition, the shrewdness of the competing parties and the existing relationship between price and costs; (iii) pricing in response to increased direct cost—e.g. labour or materials—which also depends on how rival firms react, whether cost increases can be absorbed in lower profit margins and on the elasticity of final consumer demand. Examples of the second are (iv) pricing a new product introduced into the market, such prices being often crudely fixed in practice to cover costs (full costs) including a margin for profit. Such pricing should, however, always take full account of market demand; (v) pricing to accelerate an expansion of demand, which involves getting the right balance between price appeal and promotional expenditure on the product. There are other possibilities, but the main economic variables in any pricing decision are likely to be the elasticity of consumer demand,* the

*This concept is defined below, Chapter 8.

trend of demand for the product, the level of costs and the expected behaviour of rival producers following a price change.

(b) Product differentiation

Product differentiation implies a degree of uniqueness in each competitor's product. The act of offering the consumer a product with the same general characteristics as those of other producers, yet distinctive in some particular features is a common and effective way of competing for a larger market share. Competitive marketing activities cover a wide range of products. Such products as toothpaste, cereal breakfast foods, razor blades and television sets, all use product differentiation as a means of attracting custom. If differentiation of the firm's product persists over a long period, clearly the business derives some slight monopoly advantage from having a unique product: the only detergent which contains 'bluinite' or the only car that 'floats on fluid'. There is nothing paradoxical in this idea. 'The chief cause of monopoly (in a broad sense) is obviously competition.'[10] Firms strive to compete and expand their markets through product differentiation and to be more successful than their rivals. Professor Chamberlin writes:

A general class of product is differentiated if any significant basis exists for distinguishing the goods (or services) of one seller from those of another. Such a basis may be real or fancied so long as it is of any importance whatever to buyers and leads to a preference for one variety of product over another. The result of such product differentiation from the viewpoint of the market is as follows:

Where such differentiation exists, even though it be slight, buyers will be paired with sellers not by chance and at random as with pure competition but according to their preferences.

Product differentiation takes various forms. It may be based upon certain characteristics of the product itself: patented features, trade marks, trade names; peculiarities of the package or container, if any; singularity in quality, design, colour or style. While many firms make cereal breakfast foods, each brand has its peculiarities of crispness, nourishment, etc. While many firms make perfumes, Lanvin Arpège is, to those initiated in such matters, a very different commodity from Chanel No. 5. Differentiation may also be based on conditions surrounding the sale of the product, such as convenience of sellers' location, reputation and goodwill and various other links which attach customer to seller.[11]

Professor Chamberlin tends to look on product differentiation as an element conferring monopoly power on the seller. Professor Lawrence Abbott, however, uses the term, 'quality competition' for what is essentially the same phenomenon; the term 'quality' being used to refer to all the qualitative properties of a product: size, shape, design, materials used, etc.[12] This approach views quality variability as essentially part of the competitive process. Such quality variability can be *vertical*, where one quality is considered 'superior' by nearly all buyers, superiority usually being indicated by a high price; or *horizontal*, where there is no clear-cut agreement regarding quality differences because people's tastes differ. Product competition between quality levels is likely to be most intense where levels are adjacent but otherwise may be small. Product competition within horizontally different quality levels is usually much more intense, depending on how far people's tastes are unchanging or easily shifted from one product to another.

Underlying product differentiation (or quality competition) are the great range of differences in consumer tastes, incomes, locations of buyers—in fact all those things which determine the satisfaction a buyer gets from purchasing one firm's product rather than that of a rival. Sellers must therefore seek to discover those qualitative aspects of a product which satisfy consumers and cause them to buy it. A business must make the most of its individuality and special character and seek to establish a differential advantage by appealing to needs or attitudes of the buyer. Whether the costs of obtaining such an advantage will be justified by future results, is, of course, subject to uncertainty like every business decision, but there are also costs of doing nothing while competitors gain advantages. Product competition is necessarily highly dynamic in today's conditions of rapid technological change. A successful business which can offer a differentiated product of better quality at a competitive price will obtain increased sales—and earn higher profits—wholly or partly at the expense of rivals. But rivals must be expected to respond and neutralize or offset the initiator's advantage by offering the buyer something more effective and obtaining a differential advantage for themselves. The process of initiation and response, however, usually takes time and the response of rivals to a product improvement will usually be slower and less certain than response to a price change. Thus a firm which competes through product differentiation can often obtain some enduring differential advantages and limited monopoly power.

But the degree of differentiation must be carefully judged. An over-specialized product may have too limited a market; while one which is too little differentiated will be indistinguishable from rival products. Competition in these circumstances will obviously require adequate market research and promotional activity before a new product can be marketed.

(c) *Innovation*

The nature of innovation and its relationship with profit were discussed earlier. Innovation describes what is probably the most important kind of industrial competition. Professor Schumpeter has stressed that the kind of competition which counts in capitalist reality, as distinct from the textbook picture, is 'the competition from the new commodity, the new technology, the new source of supply, the new type of organization—competition which demands a decisive cost or quality advantage and which strikes not at the margins of the profits and the outputs of existing firms but at their foundations and their very lives'.[13]

No hard and fast line can be drawn between product differentiation and innovation, the former often being an inevitable by-product of the latter. Every imperceptible variation in a product, such as the addition of a new ingredient to toothpaste, is in some sense an innovation. But it is better to reserve the term 'innovation' to describe those more fundamental changes in technology and organization which result in new and successful products and services. For example, the development of man-made fibres has enabled superior quality fabrics to be used for a wide variety of clothing; fundamental developments in electronics since the second world war have made possible the introduction of a wide range of new products ranging from the electronic computer to the transistor radio; similarly atomic power may ultimately supersede conventional methods of producing electricity and propelling ships, even though as yet it has no decisive cost advantages over conventional methods. This is what innovation consists of: fundamental scientific discovery resulting in new technology, new goods and services usually for the mass market and wide consumer acceptance.

It must not be thought that innovation can easily be used as a short-run competitive device in the same way as price variation or minor product differentiation. Where, however, a successful innovation is introduced and gains wide consumer acceptance, the long-term competitive advantages to the producer may be very substantial. Naturally, innovation is not easy, particularly for smaller firms. It must necessarily be based on the results of adequate industrial research and development, which, if not provided internally by the firm, must be bought from outside or obtained on a co-operative basis. There are also human and organizational problems in managing innovation as well as severe problems of finance for smaller firms. Some small firms manage successfully to overcome these difficulties and some have shown good records of innovation and growth. Professor Bruce Williams has warned against easy generalization about the impact of industrial research on the size of firm. While in the United States half the industrial scientists and engineers are employed in eighty of the biggest firms and in Britain more than one half of those employed on research and development were in sixty-one establishments, it does not follow that innovation is confined to large organizations. Radical changes in processes and products often come from small firms and from people outside the recognized trade. Further, innovation is not always directly dependent on research and development in the industry concerned; computers and automatic controls have had an impact on a wide variety of firms in other industries. On the whole, the science-based industries have a better record of innovation and growth than the older craft-based industries, which suggests that the progressiveness of industries may be more properly attributed to the technological basis of production than to size. Certainly firms with a research and development department, work-study section, technical sales staff, etc., have created groups of people from which there will be strong internal pressures to innovate. External pressures are also important, however, since what innovations a firm can make or is pressed to make, depends on the help or stimulus it gets from its customers, suppliers and competitors. This depends on the extent to which science is applied to industry and the level of education and sophistication of consumers.[14] Consumer acceptance is essential to the success of an innovation.* The principles on which new products are selected are mainly psychological, depending on the perception of differences in the product itself and the claims made on behalf of the product regarding its function and performance. How far the expectations created by product characteristics or claims are fulfilled determines whether or not the product will be generally accepted.

*It will be discussed in Chapter 10, below.

(d) Promotional activity

Promotional activity is a wider concept than advertising, though advertising may be regarded as its most important form. Other forms which promotion may take are personal selling and devices such as trading stamps, premiums, dealer aids—all of which are devices to expand sales of the firm's product. Advertising is some-times associated only with product competition, but to view it simply as an alternative to price competition is misleading since a primary function of advertising in a modern mass society is to provide an economical means of transmitting information, whether about prices or products. In a complex modern society it would be inordinately expensive and quite impracticable to rely on personal selling to communicate information about a firm's product. Advertising can provide this information much more economically and can aid competition by offering the consumer a wider range of goods on which to spend his income.

Besides providing information, however, most advertising is persuasive. The techniques employed to persuade potential buyers to buy A's product rather than B's are growing increasingly sophisticated. Much advertising is based on the long familiar principle of association, by which an attempt is made to associate the product with the individual's basic motivations. Consumer attitudes can be changed by skilful advertising and new buying habits and brand loyalties created, though these are sometimes more perishable than is supposed.

The effects of particular types of advertising can only be deter-mined by psychological and sociological analysis though it is perhaps significant that some psychologists show a healthy scepticism about the effectiveness of some modern methods of motivational research, subliminal advertising and other recent developments.[15]

As a factor in economic competition, advertising is obviously indispensable to the modern business because no price or product variation can be communicated to the consumer without it and because some persuasion must be used to overcome consumers' resistance to new products. In markets already divided among producers of well established brands, entry by a newcomer is only possible, if at all, after extensive market research and heavy promo-tional spending. Advertising can break down barriers to competi-tion and often open up new markets to a firm's products. But the process of making consumers change their minds is often costly and should not be undertaken without careful consideration of the expected return to the business. This requires the application of economic analysis, which is discussed in Chapter 10. But it may be noted here that, in a competitive economy, a business undertaking advertising expenditure must also consider the likely response of its rivals to an advertising campaign. Rival companies' advertising campaigns can often neutralize each other.

4. UNDERSTANDING COMPETITION

Peter Drucker[16] has argued that the two most important functions of management are marketing and innovation. Whether or not one accepts this proposition, modern business management can profit from understanding the nature and process of competition in a modern industrial society. First, management should understand the rationale of the free enterprise system within which its own business decisions have to be made and the purpose, aims and limitations of that system. Secondly, management must have full knowledge of the markets and market situations in which its own business operates and of the policies that are appropriate to those market situations. Thirdly, it is necessary to have an understanding of the competitive process and how the variables in the process—price, product, innovation and promotional activity—may be manipulated in enlarging market shares. Fourthly, the sources of monopoly power should be understood since many businesses enjoy a minor degree of such power, if only from their own brands or products. A business should also be fully conversant with the nature and purpose of the law relating to monopoly and restrictive practices.[17]

Most modern businesses operate in oligopoly conditions. Changes in the pricing, output, product or promotional policy made by one firm will usually have direct effects on the sales of particular competitors who may be expected to react strongly to such changes. A business must study and understand the competitive process of initiation and response in pricing, marketing and promoting its product against the competition of such rivals. These matters will be taken up in Chapters 9 and 10.

NOTES

1. Quotation from Daniel J. Boorstin, *The Image*, p. 227.

2. See, for example, Machlup, *The Political Economy of Monopoly*, Bain, *Industrial Organization* (1959) and *Barriers to New Competition* (1956).

3. Adam Smith, *The Wealth of Nations*, book IV, part ix.

4. Full explanation of these points clearly requires detailed analysis for which there is not space here. For such a discussion and analysis of competition by economists of differing shades of opinion, the interested reader is referred to: Adam Smith, *The Wealth of Nations*; Marshall, *Principles of Economics*; Chamberlin, *The Theory of Monopolistic Competition*; Joan Robinson, *The Economics of Imperfect Competition*; Schumpeter, *Capitalism, Socialism and Democracy*; Hayek, *Individualism and Economic Order*; Rothschild, 'Price Theory and Oligopoly', *Economic Journal*, 1947; Neale, *The Anti-Trust Laws of the U.S.*; Phelps-Brown and Wiseman, *A Course in Applied Economics* (part II).

5. For a full explanation of this analysis, the interested reader should consult any one of the standard texts, for example, Stigler, *The Theory of Price*; Stonier and Hague, *A Textbook of Economic Theory*; Boulding, *Economic Analysis*.

6. J. Downie, *The Competitive Process*.

7. Joan Robinson, *Exercises in Economic Analysis*, p. 167.

8. Joan Robinson, 'Imperfect Competition Revisited', *Economic Journal*, 1953.

9. See below, Chapter 9.

10. Joan Robinson, 'Imperfect Competition Revisited', *Economic Journal*, 1953.

11. Chamberlin, *The Theory of Monopolistic Competition*, chs. IV and V.

12. Lawrence Abbott, *Quality and Competition*.

13. J. A. Schumpeter, *Capitalism, Socialism and Democracy*, p. 87.

14. B. R. Williams, 'Some Conditions of Useful Competition', *Yorkshire Bulletin*, 1959, p. 75.

15. See J. A. C. Brown, *Techniques of Persuasion*, ch. 7.

16. Drucker, *The Practice of Management*.

17. For reasons of space, this increasingly important matter is not discussed here. The principal legislation affecting the UK is to be found in the *Monopolies and Restrictive Practices (Inquiry and Control) Act*, 1948; *Restrictive Trade Practices Act*, 1956; *Re-Sale Prices Act*, 1964. Discussion of the operation of the 1956 Act and cases are included in *The Registrar of Restrictive Trade Agreements Reports* and the *Reports of the Monopolies Commission*. Discussion by economists may be found in John Heath, *Still Not Enough Competition*; Stevens and Yamey, *The Restrictive Practices Court*; and Guenault and Jackson, *The Control of Monopoly in the U.K.* For an American comparison, see Neale, *The Anti-Trust Laws of the U.S.*

6

COST

> If accounts are bound to be untruths anyhow . . . there is much to be said for the simple untruth as against the complicated untruth, for if the untruth is simple, it seems that we have a fair chance of knowing what kind of untruth it is.
>
> K. BOULDING

1. LONG-RUN INFLUENCES ON COST: LOCATION, SCOPE, SIZE

In establishing a business, certain fundamental questions have to be settled at the outset. These are questions of *location* of firms and plants, their *scope* in terms of processes carried on and products and services marketed, and their *size*. These are in some sense basic and irrevocable decisions. At least they do not have to be made as frequently as short-run output decisions. Such decisions about where to locate a new plant, how far to diversify production, and on what scale production should be carried on—whether in large, medium or small sized plants—are obviously important because they exert a long-run influence on costs of production.*

Location

For the business, location is a question of choosing the place where production can be carried on at lowest cost. This could no doubt be done if all relevant costs were known and measurable. Usually and unfortunately, however, they are not. Professor Florence has pointed out that:

. . . factories are durable and we must realize that decisions to locate factories somewhere taken in the past by the profit motive would not always be the decisions taken now under present circumstances, and even at the time were not always in each individual case taken on a strict calculation of profit.

*The term 'production' in economics refers to the creation of utilities, whether of form, place or time. It is therefore defined more broadly than in conventional usage.

Professor Florence suggests the following analysis of possible situations.

(1) The firm makes the decision irrationally, with no calculation of profits, e.g. factories have been built without thought in the habitual location of the industry.

(2) The firm calculates the profit, but incorrectly for the time itself, e.g. firms, because the initial costs are smaller, take over existing premises that happen to be for sale. They fail to weigh in the balance the long-term costs of a possible unsuitable location. Since decisions on new locations are only taken rarely in the course of a single-plant firm's history, its staff may not be experienced or trained to evaluate the factors involved. A large multi-plant firm might do better.

(3) The firm calculated the profit correctly for the first time itself, but:

(a) incorrectly for present-day circumstances;

(b) correctly for present-day circumstances.

(i) profit no measure of *social* benefit over cost;
(ii) profit a fair measure of the balance of social benefit over cost.

This analysis sets out the logic of location decisions and shows that 3(b), which looks at costs and revenues in the future, is the only logical policy for the firm. If wider national and social considerations are brought into the reckoning 3b(ii) is the logical policy.[1]

Nowadays all location decisions are influenced by their possible national and social consequences. Besides State expenditure on health, housing, education, roads and so forth, questions of regional development, local employment policy, the preservation of amenities and the avoidance of congestion, are sufficiently important to the welfare of society to justify intervention by the Government in location decisions. No business is entirely free to determine the location of its plants independently of Government location policy.

What considerations should a profit-making business take into account in deciding the location of its plants? Emphasis is often placed on proximity to markets and, where this is not feasible, on proximity to raw materials and availability of transport. It is argued that, *in the absence of good reasons to the contrary*, a commodity should be produced as near to the market as possible. Service industries clearly must be located at or near to the point of ultimate consumption. On the other hand, extractive processes such as the mining of iron ore and coal must be carried out where the raw material is found. Most industries are subject to conflicting pulls: the pull of the market and the pull of the raw materials. If these were the only considerations in industrial location, a plant might be optimally located where transport costs were lowest. If the raw material was bulky and heavy and expensive to transport, relative to the cost of transporting finished goods, optimal location would be near to the raw material, and vice versa. Indeed, 'there would be no location problems for manufacturing establishments if transport and communications were costless' (and time-less).[2] In today's complex industrial economy, however, there are many other influences on location than materials and markets. The determination of optimal location usually requires consideration and reconciliation of many conflicting factors or 'pulls', all of which can, in principle, be evaluated in terms of cost. In calculating such a cost, however, it is *future* costs that are relevant to business decisions and it must be understood that today's costs may not be relevant to the future. Raw materials are exhaustible or may be rendered superfluous by technological change. Means of transport and communications change and so do their costs. Similarly, population is growing and becoming increasingly mobile, while consumer spending habits are subject to change, which can influence the size and importance of a firm's main markets. Thus a location decision made today in terms of knowledge of today's circumstances may be out-of-date five or ten years hence. Some attempt to forecast future costs, demand and technological and sociological changes is necessary if a rational location decision is to be made.

Edwards and Townsend[3] have identified some of the most important factors that businesses consider in choosing a location for efficient industrial operations. These are:

(1) Manpower, in all its complex aspects.

(2) Supplies of components, subcontracting facilities and professional services.

(3) Power, particularly the availability of modern sources such as oil and electricity.

(4) Water.

(5) Raw materials, a declining influence in recent decades because of improved transport, growth of 'science-based' industries of high brain but low material content, development of heavy and bulky consumer durables and growth of assembly industries drawing materials from many sources.

(6) The main markets, such factors as maintenance of adequate

stocks, reducing risk of damage and the need for efficient after-sales service probably being more important than actual costs of 'distribution'.

(7) Personal communication, important because many businesses prefer to avoid 'fragmentation' of management resulting from dispersal.

(8) Waste disposal, important, for example, in chemicals and chemical-based industries.

(9) The ethos of the locality.

(10) Site facilities, particularly important for very large plants.

This list underlines the importance, in modern conditions, of transport, manpower and sources of power. Each firm will attach differing importance to the several locational criteria. Some factors —e.g. costs of materials or the wage bill—are fairly easy to quantify in terms of costs and benefits in alternative locations. Others are subject to considerable uncertainty. The important thing is that the objectives of any particular business should be decided upon and locational criteria clearly specified. Appropriate techniques of operational research may help in location decisions. Linear programming techniques of the 'transportation model' type could, for example, be applied to this problem.

Scope

The *scope* of the firm's activities must certainly be considered at the beginning of a business's operations and frequently re-considered as the firm grows in the light of costs and profitability. Questions of scope are usually discussed as problems of *integration* and *diversification* of the firm's activities. What processes or transactions should be carried on within the firm? Should the firm integrate and carry on a variety of processes within its own organization? Or should it specialize narrowly on a few things, using the market and relying on other specialists to supply its materials and to assemble and market its products—i.e. practice dis-integration? Should it produce and sell a wide range of finished products—i.e. diversify its product range?

A fundamental economic principle states that specialization results in production at lower unit cost. Adam Smith first expounded the advantages of the division of labour. The principle was inherent in Henry Ford's application of standardization and interchangeability to his mass-produced model-T car, while the principles of task-specialization and functionalism have been reiterated in management literature since F. W. Taylor's *Scientific Management*. Applied to the firm, the principle states that, *for a given size*

)

of plant or firm, greater specialization on a few processes, transactions and products results in larger-scale production at lower costs. Modern mass and process production requiring intensive capital investment, highly trained personnel carrying out highly specialized tasks, long runs of production, standardization of parts and components and simplification of the finished product can and do unquestionably lower cost of production per unit of output. The advantages of specialization coupled with large-scale production are therefore formidable. Why then do many firms apparently go against this principle by integrating and diversifying their activities?

Mrs Penrose states that 'there are very few, if any, completely undiversified firms if "product" . . . is defined narrowly'.[4] Certainly there is plenty of evidence of diversification among the larger British firms. Dunning and Thomas[5] mention some examples:

Unilever Ltd. (supplies) . . . a wide variety of manufactures including soap products, vegetable oils and fats, ice-cream, sausages, frozen foods, fish, soups, perfumes and so on. The Distillers Co. Ltd. is a whisky-and-gin combine . . . active in the bio-chemicals, plastics, alloys and industrial alcohol fields. The products (of Imperial Chemical Industries Ltd.) range from explosives, dyestuffs, sulphuric acid and caustic soda to terylene, plastics materials, pharmaceutical products and paints. Tube Investments Ltd. . . . is linked with virtually all of Britain's principal industries through supplying such products as steel tubes, electrical equipment, paint, bicycles, aluminium alloy products and so on.

Such companies have frequently diversified by acquiring, or combining with, existing firms and plants of a more specialized nature. The process has been stimulated by scientific developments in which more than one branch of industry has been concerned. 'Most of the large firms', writes Mrs Penrose, 'lay great emphasis on the possibilities of diversification, and we know that the speeches and writings of management experts, business executives and "informed commentators" extol its virtues.'[6]

There are some difficulties in defining reliably the terms 'integration' and 'diversification', though these should not be regarded as synonymous. Both are concerned with adding new processes and products to the firm's existing range of activities. *Integration* usually means enlarging the scope of the business by adding a new process or intermediate product, as an alternative to a market transaction. *Diversification* usually means enlarging the firm's ultimate product line, though to complicate matters, the term is often used in a broader sense.[7] Economists differ in their opinions regarding the efficiency of integration and diversification by the firm. Thus:

. . . the operation of a market costs something and by forming an organization and allowing some authority (an 'entrepreneur') to direct the resources, certain marketing costs are saved. The entrepreneur has to carry out his function at less cost . . . than the market transactions. . . . (Coase)[8]

The more a plant of a given size is integrated the smaller must be its scale of operation. Integration thus means smaller-scale operation and, on our hypothesis, a lower efficiency. . . .
. . Integration within a plant or a firm must be suspected therefore of small scale inefficient production till it is proved innocent. (Florence)[9]

In the long-run the profitability, survival and growth of the firm does not depend so much on . . . a widely diversified range of products as . . on the ability of the firm to establish one or more wide and relatively impregnable 'bases' from which it can adapt and extend its operations in an uncertain, changing and competitive world. (Penrose)[10]

Such differences of opinion turn out to depend on whether one regards the firm as of given size in a static environment or whether one takes account of change and growth, as a comparison of the traditional and modern analyses of integration and diversification shows.

The traditional analysis of integration[11] tends to take the size of the firm as given and largely ignores problems of growth. It identifies four types of integration:

(1) *Horizontal integration* is an addition to the scale of production of the same article, through extension or combination.

(2) *Vertical integration* is the combination in the same organization of consecutive operations such that the finished product of one is the raw material of another. Such integration may be *backwards* towards the raw material or *forwards* towards the market. Motives for *backward* integration may include the need for regular and reliable supplies of raw materials, the existence of monopoly elements in the supply of materials, the belief that uniform quality standards are better maintained within the organization than by buying out. Justification for these motives must ultimately depend on how they affect costs and profits. *Forward* integration may occur when the firm wants to push sales, where existing distributive organization is costly and inefficient, or where retail outlets possess strong monopoly power. Complete forward integration is,

however, rare because of the technicalities and complexity of the marketing process.*

(3) *Lateral integration* is the production of many different sorts of products within a firm of given size. Such products usually *diverge* from common raw materials or processes (e.g. engineering or chemical products) or *converge* on the same market (e.g. agricultural machinery and supplies).

(4) *Diagonal or service integration* consists of the provision within an organization of auxiliary goods or services (e.g. a firm may design and produce its own tools and machines).[12]

If we regard the conditions under which the firm operates a static, it is unlikely that integration—the opposite of specialization —will be to its advantage. Given the known advantages of special ization and given the size of the firm, integration can only result in lower costs if there are special over-riding advantages, such a common overhead costs or continuous processes. However, it i naive to regard the firm as being of given size. Most firms toda exist in an environment of growth and innovation. Specialization implies loss of flexibility. Research and the development of new products and services 'is the logical response of the individual firr to the challenge inherent in the Schumpeterian process of creativ destruction. After all the specialized firm is vulnerable. . . .'[1] Mrs Penrose, in her penetrating analysis of diversification, argue that the modern competitive process, described by Schumpeter a a process of creative destruction, instead of destroying the larg firm, forces it to be more creative. This creativity manifests itse in greater diversification which takes the form of a greater variet of final products, increases in vertical integration, and increases i the number of 'basic areas' of production in which a firm operates. Primary importance is attached to the firm's technological bas Diversification and expansion based on a high degree of compe tence and technological knowledge in specialized areas of manufa ture is the best way of ensuring for the firm a strong and endurin position. A strong market position without fundamental techn logical competence could clearly leave the firm in a precario situation. Moreover, while technical economies of scale withi the plant may already be exhausted *as far as any specific product*

*Often, of course, firms arrange with one another for part, at least, of th activities to be linked on a co-operative basis (e.g. export marketing, developme or large-scale construction projects). Such integration by co-operation may undertaken through *ad hoc* groups or trade associations. For reasons of space it not discussed here. See, however, Edwards and Townsend, op. cit., ch. XI.

concerned, considerable *overhead* economies may still be available to the firm through diversification; i.e. by expanding production into new ranges of products for which markets are readily available.

Firms often diversify to safeguard against uncertainty. It is commonly believed that the production of many products is the most effective 'hedge' against all kinds of adverse changes.[15] Some firms have successfully diversified and reduced their vulnerability in this way, but there are dangers in such a policy. To be successful, a diversified firm must have access to and devote sufficient resources to development and innovation in *each* of its main product areas. Failure to do so may mean loss of markets to competitors. In some industries, consumer acceptance of a product depends on whether the producer can reasonably claim to be one of the 'leading producers' or whether a firm carries a 'full line' of related products.[16] This tends to widen the basic areas of production in which a firm must be competent and create barriers to the entry of new firms, with insufficient capital or managerial skills.

Decisions on the *scope* of the firm's activities (diversification and integration) influence costs in a complex way. The problem is larger than the simple economics of specialization, since the modern firm must innovate in order to survive. The criteria to apply in such decisions are those of *cost* and *profitability*. Long-term profitability, rather than short-run profitability or stability of earnings, is the correct criterion to apply for major decisions against a background of change and growth. Incremental or short-term profits may, however, be relevant for short-run product line decisions where motives for diversification spring from the existence of surplus capacity or common costs.

Size

In an environment of growth and innovation, the idea of an optimum size of firm may appear remote from the everyday problems of management. Size cannot however be ignored. The size of plant and firm, and the extent to which existing capacity is used, are important determinants of cost per unit of output. The formal relationships between cost and output will be discussed in the second part of this chapter. Here we summarize the broad economic principles underlying those relationships.

The superior efficiency of large-scale production—increasing returns to scale—has been extensively discussed by economists, management specialists and technologists.[17] It needs little elaboration here. Most economists assert that the size of the firm is influenced by four considerations: (1) technical factors; (2) managerial factors; (3) marketing factors; (4) financial factors.

Technical economies favour the large plant or firm. Economies arise through (a) specialization; (b) superior techniques—since only large firms can afford to install large machinery and employ 'best practice' technology; (c) increased dimensions—large units being generally proportionately more efficient than small ones, and only large plants fully utilizing 'indivisible' units to capacity; and (d) economies of linked processes—which can be carried on more economically together than separately, and only larger firms, attaining a scale of output equal to the least common multiple of different capacity outputs of each stage of production.

Managerial factors are less certain in their effects. Specialization of the management function—e.g. use of functional specialists, production planning techniques, computers, etc.—available only to larger firms—increases managerial efficiency. Economists used to argue, however, that problems of top co-ordination ultimately become so great in large organizations that managerial diseconomies set in. The hypothesis that large firms encounter increasing costs through managerial diseconomies is not proven. Such a proposition is logically valid on very restricted assumptions, but has little relevance where modern management techniques and executive development programmes are widely applied. Modern writings on this subject speak rather of the 'receding managerial limit' than of managerial diseconomies.[18]

Marketing arrangements are complex and varied and sweeping generalization is best avoided. Large firms usually have cost advantages over small ones in the market. On the *buying* side, there are economies where a large order is supplied to specification, economies of buying in bulk, economies of transport from handling on a large scale, and from the skill of a specialized buying staff (provided they do not make mistakes). On the *selling* side there are economies from using a specialized selling organization to the full, and from the ability to hold larger stocks. There may be limits to the attainment of these economies, especially if heavy selling costs are needed to expand the market or if production is on too small a scale to enable marketing economies to be reached. Generally, however, the large firm has access to economies of marketing which are not available to the small firm.

Financial factors also favour the large firm. It is easier and cheaper for the large business to obtain capital than for the small (especially the new) business. The large firm can borrow more easily and cheaply and needs proportionately smaller reserves for contingencies. New businesses, in particular, find finance more difficult to obtain than the large going-concern with a proven trading record.

The foregoing discussion indicates that, in modern conditions of production, large firms have considerable economic advantages and that large-scale production can be carried on at lower unit cost than production on a small scale. The propositions just discussed are fundamental to the explanation of the economist's long-run average cost curve and relevant to the subsequent analysis of costs.[19]

2. PRODUCTION AND COSTS

The production process is a system of asset transformation; production cost is the evaluation of this transformation.

The most fundamental concept of cost . . . is that it represents the transformation ratio in production, i.e. that ratio in which the input assets are transferred into the output assets.[20]

In order to make a profit, a business must be able to sell its output assets at a greater price than the total transformation cost. Transformation cost itself, particularly in manufacturing industry, consists of the initial cost of purchasing the raw materials which are to be processed and the conversion cost—e.g. wages and other expenses required to convert this basic material into a marketable commodity. A knowledge of this cost is essential for managerial planning.

The economic classification of cost

Economic theory has distinguished between the short-run and the long-run and, within these time periods, has concentrated on the relationship between cost and output. Here we are concerned with the short-run, since it is obviously most relevant to day-to-day managerial decisions.

The short-run is defined as a period in which at least one element of factor input is in fixed supply, so that it is not possible to alter the amount of this factor available to the firm. Under these conditions, as additional units of a variable factor are added to the fixed factor, then the additional output (marginal product) brought about by the addition of the variable factor will first increase, then remain constant and finally decrease. This decrease in the marginal product is not caused by any diminution of quality of the input factors but is due entirely to the fixity of supply of the one factor. The usual illustration of this 'natural' law is to take land as the fixed factor and add labour to it, but the law is equally valid if plant and machinery are taken as 'fixed'. Even if, to begin with, additional output results, eventually the situation would be reached when there were so many units of labour to the fixed amount of land or plant that the addition of one more would have no positive effect, and ultimately cause total output to diminish. Intuitively this law seems true because marginal product cannot increase indefinitely; if this were so it would always be beneficial to reduce the amount of fixed factor and add more and more non-fixed factor to it, i.e. an infinitely small amount of fixed factor would be the best situation for a firm. Nor can it remain constant indefinitely: if this were so any quantity of output could be obtained by simply adding more and more units of the variable factor, which experience seems to contradict. Therefore, if marginal product cannot increase or remain constant indefinitely, it must decrease. If this is so, the firm's cost schedule will appear as in the table on facing page.*

This can be represented diagrammatically and the resultant cost will be:

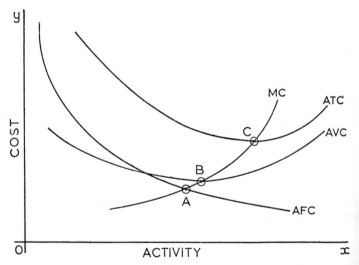

*Note we are only concerned here with the relationship between cost and output in the short-run and have ignored the fact that the level of output itself will have an effect on the unit prices which have to be paid for the factors of production.

SHORT-RUN COST SCHEDULE (ECONOMICS)

UNIT COSTS

Units of variable factor	Total output	Marginal product	Total fixed cost £	Total variable cost £	Total cost £	Average fixed cost £	Average variable cost £	Average total cost £	Unit marginal cost £
1	1	1	10	5	15	10·00	5·00	15	5·00
2	3	2	10	10	20	3·33	3·33	6·66	2·50
3	6	3	10	15	25	1·67	2·50	4·17	1·67
4	10	4	10	20	30	1·000	2·00	3·00	1·25
5	14	4	10	25	35	0·71	1·79	2·50	1·25
6	17	3	10	30	40	0·59	1·76	2·35	1·67
7	19	2	10	35	45	0·52	1·84	2·36	2·50
8	21	2	10	40	50	0·48	1·90	2·38	2·50
9	22	1	10	45	55	0·45	2·05	2·50	5·00
10	21	−1	10	50	60	0·48	2·38	2·86	

From this diagram certain observations about business decisions and the level of production can be deduced. Under normal circumstances the production range will be to the right of point C because it is only there that two conditions essential for profit maximization can be satisfied: (1) that the marginal costs of producing one unit of output exactly equals the marginal revenue which the sale of that unit produces—the necessary condition of profit maximization;* (2) price must be greater than average total cost if a profit is to be made. Under exceptional circumstances it may, in the short-run, be worthwhile for the business to accept a level of output greater than position B even though total costs are not covered, because to the right of this point, it will still be covering its average variable costs and so providing a 'contribution' towards fixed costs from which in the short-run it cannot escape.

The accounting classification of costs

The classification of costs into fixed and variable and the effect of variations in the level of activity on these is useful, too, for the analysis of certain business decisions, but also for these a more detailed analysis of the cost components is required and traditionally it is the accounting classification which has provided this.

The prime function of all accounting systems is to record costs as they arise and to relate them to a specific unit so that appropriate decisions can be made. Because of the extent, variability, and alternative uses which can be made of a firm's resources it is impossible for an individual to contain in his own mind all of the various combinations and permutations that can arise. A form of classification is required. The traditional accounting approach is to classify by function, such as factory, selling, administration and by nature, e.g. material, labour and expenses. Within these categories further subdivision can take place according to the requirements of the particular organization, for example, factory could be further analysed by department and material by its constituent components, but in any event these costs when classified are identified with the cost unit as the following statement illustrates.

*These concepts were mentioned above, p. 15. They are formally defined in Chapter 9, section 2, below.

TRADITIONAL ACCOUNTANCY COST CLASSIFICATION

PRODUCT X—DEPARTMENT A—COST BY PROCESS

	Process 1	Process 2	Process 3	Total
	s. d.	s. d.	s. d.	s. d.
Direct material	7 6	—	—	7 6
Direct labour	1 6	6	6	2 6
Direct expenses	3	—	—	3
Indirect material	—	—	—	—
Indirect labour	0·5	0·5	—	1
Indirect expenses	3 0	1 0	1 0	5 0
TOTAL	12 3·5	1 6·5	1 6	15 4

PRODUCT X—FACTORY COST BY DEPARTMENTS

	Department A	Department B	Department C	Total
	s. d.	s. d.	s. d.	s. d.
Direct material	7 6	2 0	1 0	10 6
Direct labour	2 6	6	9	3 9
Direct expenses	3	—	—	3
Indirect material	—	—	—	—
Indirect labour	1	1	1	3
Indirect expenses	5 0	1 0	1 6	7 6
TOTAL	15 4	3 7	3 4	22 3

PRODUCT X—TOTAL COST (OF PRODUCT)

	Factory/ works	Selling distribution	Administra- tion	Total
	s. d.	s. d.	s. d.	s. d.
Direct material	10 6	1 3	—	11 9
Direct labour	3 9	1 0	—	4 9
Direct expenses	3	—	—	3
Indirect material	—	—	—	—
Indirect labour	3	6	3 0	3 9
Indirect expenses	7 6	5 0	3 6	16 0
TOTAL	22 3	7 9	6 6	36 6

However, even within these main classifications further rearrangement is often required so that the costs can be assembled in a
manner most convenient for the particular problem under consideration. For reporting purposes a distinction must often be
drawn between period costs and activity costs. Period costs are
those which are a function of time and *not* of the activity of the
business, for example, rent, part of depreciation cost, etc. Even a
cursory glance at accounting literature discloses a prolific display
of cost description—responsibility cost, controllable cost, opportunity cost, imputed cost, policy cost, etc., and the important
point that emerges is that, while an accounting system can
classify costs for certain purposes, it cannot classify them for
every purpose. All that an efficient accounting system can do is
to record information in sufficient detail and provide a convenient store from which basic data can be retrieved and
rearranged as and when required. It also clearly indicates the
futility of using cost figures without reference to their particular
use or purpose. Differences of opinion which arise over cost
problems—e.g. whether or not one method of valuation and
recording a cost is superior to another—are more often a conflict of purpose rather than of conception. However, there are
differences between economic theory and accounting theory as to
how costs move in relation to activity.

Cost movement and activity

Accounting theory tends to segregate the relationship of different items of cost with activity as the following diagrams illustrate.

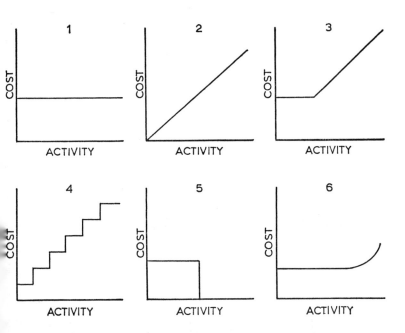

(1) Rent of premises with an annual lease.

(2) Fixed royalty per unit produced.

(3) Rental of reproduction equipment where there is a minimum charge which allows a stated quantity of reproductions thereafter at fixed cost per additional reproduction.

(4) This is a step cost, for example, supervisory expenses where one supervisor is required for every fifty work people and each workman has a constant output per hour.

(5) The rent of premises which do not have to be paid once a definite number of man hours have been worked.

(6) Material costs where the first x lbs are at a flat charge, the next x lbs are at a lower unit cost than the first x and so on.

Although there is this variety of cost behaviour patterns for many purposes accounting theory adopts the simple economic distinction between fixed and variable and allocates all costs to either of these categories. Unlike economic theory, however, a different assumption is made as to the shape of these curves, particularly the average variable and marginal cost curves which are assumed to be linear in that each additional unit of output results in an identical addition to cost as the previous. As follows:

SHORT-RUN COST SCHEDULE—ACCOUNTING

UNIT COSTS

Total output	Marginal product	Total fixed cost £	Total variable cost £	Total cost £	Average fixed cost £	Average variable cost £	Average total cost £	Unit marginal cost £
1	1	10	5	15	10	5	15·00	5
2	1	10	10	20	5	5	10·00	5
3	1	10	15	25	3·33	5	8·33	5
4	1	10	20	30	2·50	5	7·50	5
5	1	10	25	35	2·00	5	7·00	5
6	1	10	30	40	1·67	5	6·67	5
7	1	10	35	45	1·43	5	6·43	5
8	1	10	40	50	1·25	5	6·25	5
9	1	10	45	55	1·11	5	6·22	5
10	1	10	50	60	1·00	5	6·00	5

The assumed accounting relationship between cost and activity can be expressed graphically as follows:

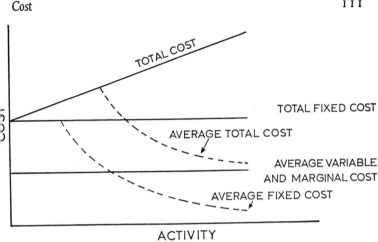

A comparison, therefore, between the accountant's cost and the economist's cost will indicate the following:*

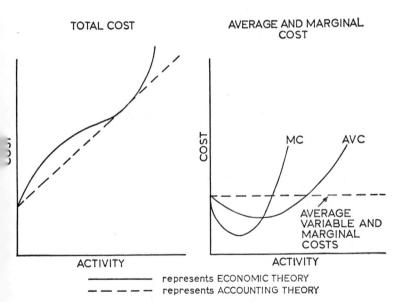

——————— represents ECONOMIC THEORY
— — — — — represents ACCOUNTING THEORY

*Note that we are concerned here with the response of cost to changes in the level of activity and not how the physical factors involved—material, labour, etc.—should be priced.

Is the assumption of the economist or the accountant the more realistic for decision making based on short-run curves, such as those of average and marginal cost? Economic theory does not attempt to describe what happens in specific instances. Rather, by a process of abstraction, it deduces what must happen—e.g. to costs—if certain assumptions hold and certain economic 'laws'— e.g. variable proportions—are assumed to operate.[21] For decision making in the firm, it is also necessary to know what *does* take place, which requires a knowledge of the assumptions made by the business about cost relationships and whether these assumptions can, in fact, be justified. The economist's theory of cost behaviour is perfectly rational, given its limited assumptions. However, many empirical studies tend to support the views of accounting theory. For example:

. . . the total cost function is linear over substantial ranges of output and this linearity holds not only where a single process is being used at various levels but also where two processes are being used simultaneously at various levels.

Two major impressions, however, stand out clearly. The first is that the various short-run studies more often than not indicate constant marginal cost and declining average cost as the pattern that best seems to describe the data that have been analysed. The second is the preponderance of the L shaped pattern of long run average costs that emerges so frequently from the various long run analysis.[22]

. . . there are those who will argue that expense with relation to volume does not take the form of a straight line when charted but rather rises and falls in steps. This may be true with a single expense classification but, where a number are involved, the steps in each classification will invariably occur at different times, thus tending to offset each other. As a result in practice, the line of expense with relation to volume takes on a surprisingly smooth and uniform appearance.[23]

Average cost (total adaptation) descends like the left hand branch of a capital U swiftly at first and then more gently. Decreasing costs with size are almost universal but the U seldom turns up again. *Sharply increasing costs with size are practically unknown and even slight increases are rare.*[24]

An interesting attempt to overcome this conflict between formal economic theory which postulates a short-run U-shaped cost curve and empirical evidence which denies increasing costs has been made by Hirshleifer:[25] His thesis is based on the proposition that the term output or activity is not one-dimensional in that it is determined by both volume and rate and that when this is recognized and long and short run are redefined in terms of long and short production runs then it can be shown that 'marginal costs are a rising function of the rate of production, a declining function of the volume of production'. As output is therefore a combination of these two factors the relative importance of each will determine the final relationship between cost and activity. Thus both the accounting and the economic view may be correct according to which dimension is assumed to be the more important. It may well be that empirical studies based on Hirshleifer's analysis will validate his hypothesis. In the remainder of this chapter we shall assume that the linear relationship between cost and output is the one most likely to be relevant to business decisions in the short run. The main justification for this is that most business decisions are based not on actual costs but on a projection of these costs into the future through standards and budgets. These projected costs are based on an anticipated level of activity or capacity and, unless there are significant deviations from this, it is assumed that the linear relationship holds good. When activity does deviate significantly, the original set of cost curves will no longer be valid and a new set will have to be constructed to represent the results of decisions taken in light of these abnormal circumstances. With economic theory, in the short run, this is not possible because of the fixity of certain factors. However, in accounting theory, fixed costs are only defined as being fixed in one direction, i.e. they must be incurred and cannot be escaped though, if management desires, they can be increased. It is interesting that Hirshleifer in his analysis moves towards the accounting concept of fixity:

What 'fixes' a fixed factor is not that you cannot vary it immediately, if you desire but that you do not want to vary it in response to only a temporary fluctuation of demand (short production run).[26]

In addition, the added benefit from obtaining true marginal costs as opposed to assumed linear marginal costs must be weighed against the cost of obtaining this information. If the difference between the true marginal cost and the assumed cost is not likely to be significant enough to lead to different decisions, or at least to better decisions, then it will not be an economic proposition to obtain this and, for many purposes, linear relationships do provide a sufficient approximation to actual. A further advantage of linearity is that it is more convenient analytically. Not only is it particularly suitable for mathematical manipulation, but also it is easier to analyse and interpret results in a non-mathematical language—an important consideration for business decisions.*

The following diagram assumes a linear relationship and shows the relationship between output, total revenue, total cost and profit.

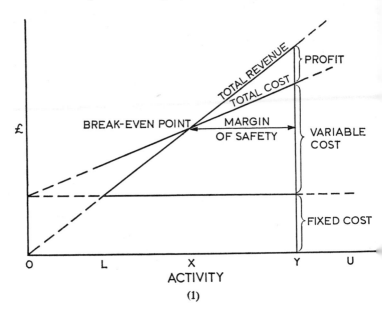

(1)

Diagram (1) is the conventional break-even chart, which indicates the level of output required to break-even when neither a profit or a loss is earned—OX. The budgeted profit which it is estimated will be made (or has been made if dealing with actual results) at the forecast output level OY; and the margin of safety OY—OX, i.e. the amount by which output can fall below the estimate before a loss will be incurred. At an output level below L and above U on the X-axis, the lines of cost and revenue have been broken. This is to denote that it is unlikely that at output levels outside these two points the cost structure depicted by the graph will be valid, rather, even in the short run, management would take decisions which would alter this structure. Perhaps the main advantage of break-even analysis as such is as a medium for presenting total information in a clear concise fashion so that the

*Even where the actual situation is non linear often the only way to tackle the problem is to assume linearity.

many details do not obscure the overall picture of what planned action entails. There are many different forms of such graphs.

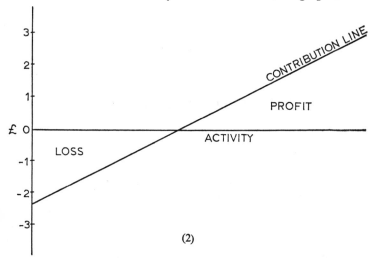

(2)

In diagram (2) rather than plot the cost and revenue curves, the contribution line, i.e. the difference between revenue and variable cost, is shown starting on the Y-axis (negative) at the total of fixed costs.

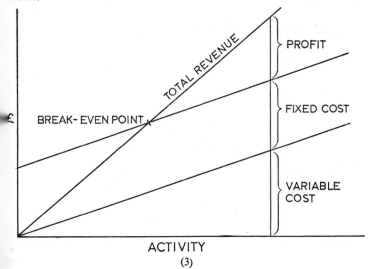

(3)

In (3) the fixed costs have been shown above the variable costs so that the contribution to fixed costs and profit is more clearly shown.

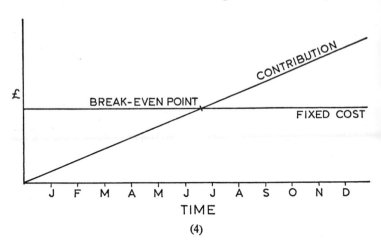

(4)

In (4) the contribution over the time period under review is shown. This indicates the level of fixed expenditure to which management has committed the organization and how soon in the decision period (not necessarily a calendar year although this is what has been shown) this will be covered and a profit begun to be made. It is on the relationships shown in these graphs that the accountant's contribution formula is based.

$$\text{Sales} - \text{Variable costs} = \text{Contribution}$$
$$\text{Contribution} - \text{Fixed costs} = \text{Profit}$$

From this it can be seen that the break-even point in terms of activity equals

$$\frac{\text{Fixed costs}}{\text{Contribution per unit}}$$

and in terms of money

$$\frac{\text{Fixed costs}}{1 - \dfrac{\text{Variable cost per unit}}{\text{Selling price per unit}}}$$

There are four main profit factors, viz. the quantity produced and sold, total fixed costs incurred for this purpose, selling price per unit, and variable cost per unit. If profit has varied or is to be altered then this has been or can only be achieved by varying one or other of these factors. (It is accepted, of course, that within each of these categories there will be a mass of other subsidiary factors.) One of the main advantages claimed for the linear relationship is that, in dealing with an uncertain future, elementary model building enables us to measure the effect of a change in one or other of the profit factors.

Management is often faced with complementary profit factor decisions, e.g. will a reduction in selling prices stimulate such an increase in the quantity demanded as to result in increased profit? In order to calculate this the company will need to know the shape and elasticity of its demand curve[27]—and such information may not be available. However, from the profit factor equation one can easily compute, assuming a continuance of the present circumstances, what level of sales will be required to maintain the same profit, given a reduction in price. While this need not necessarily indicate the true position it does give management a first idea of the magnitudes involved. For example, suppose that a firm is faced with a position which shows a profit of £1,000 in that

$$Q \quad = \quad 2,000 \text{ units}$$
$$SP \quad = \quad £5 \text{ per unit}$$
$$VC \quad = \quad £4 \text{ per unit}$$
$$FC \quad = \quad £1,000$$

and it is suggested that selling prices should be reduced by 10 per cent to stimulate demand, then if

$$Qn \quad = \quad \text{New quantity sold}$$
$$SPn \quad = \quad \text{New selling price per unit}$$
$$VCn \quad = \quad \text{New variable cost per unit}$$
$$FCn \quad = \quad \text{New fixed cost in total}$$
$$Pn \quad = \quad \text{New profit}$$

For a proposed position to be at least as good as the current position then we require that $Pn \geqslant P$ and the effect of a reduction in selling prices will require a minimum new quantity sold of

$$Qn \quad = \quad \frac{Q(SP-VC)}{SPn-VC}$$

or the old contribution in total divided by the new contribution per unit.[28]

Therefore, if selling prices are to be reduced by 10 per cent the new quantity which will have to be sold to maintain the present profit position will be

$$\frac{2,000\ (5-4)}{(4\cdot5-4)}$$

=4,000 units, i.e. a 100 per cent increase in sales.

This will give management an initial idea of whether or not a proposed line of action is worthwhile. Thus in the above example, while the company may not know its demand curve, it may be able to indicate with confidence that, even if selling prices are reduced by 10 per cent, quantity sold will certainly not double. Some of the simple formulae which can quickly provide this initial appraisal of a suggested variation in a profit factor are as follows:

(1) Given a change in selling price

    1.1 the new quantity must be $Qn = \dfrac{Q(SP-VC)}{SPn-VC}$

    1.2. the new marginal cost must be $VCn = (SPn-SP) + VC$

(2) Given a change in quantity

    2.1. the new selling price must be $SPn = \dfrac{Q(SP-VC)}{Qn} + VC$

    2.2. the new variable cost must be $VCn = SP - \dfrac{Q(SP-VC)}{Qn}$

(3) Given a change in variable cost

    3.1. the new selling price must be $SPn = (SP-VC) + VCn$

    3.2. the new quantity must be $Qn = \dfrac{Q(SP-VC)}{SP-VCn}$

(4) Given a change in the level of fixed costs

    4.1. the new selling price must be $SPn = SP + \dfrac{FCn-FC}{Q}$

    4.2. the new variable cost must be $VCn = VC - \dfrac{FCn-FC}{Q}$

    4.3. the new quantity must be $Qn = Q + \dfrac{FCn-FC}{SP-VC}$

The above models are convenient devices for indicating both the apparent feasibility of a course of action and which profit factor seems most likely to respond in the manner desired.*

We have seen that there are many different cost relationships. This makes it difficult to decide which expenses should be allocated to which category because, in many cases, they do not entirely fit into either a fixed or variable type. Expense types can be regarded as a spectrum, at one end of which items are clearly fixed and at the other clearly variable; in between there will be those of a semi-fixed and semi-variable nature. For many decisions, however, a twofold classification has to be made.

Locating the items on a spectrum is itself not easy and the techniques adopted for doing so range from observation of what has happened in the past to statistical methods of correlation and regression analysis. Certain other considerations complicate the analysis of fixed and variable expenses. Such a classification relates to a specific time period in the sense that in the immediate short run all costs are fixed but eventually all must be variable. Consequently, when the time period is altered the fixed and variable classification will alter accordingly. As it is not really possible to fit business decisions into discrete short and long run categories each decision must be looked at in isolation. The segregation of fixed and variable is also dependent on the type of decision which is being taken. For example, if a company rents premises, then in controlling the production costs of the products manufactured there, rent is a fixed expense. However, if the decision is whether or not to close these premises and transfer the production elsewhere, then rent is a variable expense. Most cost accounting systems are designed for cost control, one of the basic assumptions of which is continuity, i.e. the intention that the production process or unit will continue in operation. The classification of costs for this purpose therefore takes this assumption into account and if decisions are made, based on this cost classification, with different underlying assumptions then confusion must clearly result.

The common cost problem

Unless one article only is produced it will be difficult to identify directly certain costs with specific products and yet this must be

*Another use of the above is the accounting technique in profit planning of 'contribution per limiting factor'. This, however, has been superseded by the much more sophisticated operational research technique of linear programming, see below, pp. 124–32.

done if the full cost of a product is to be determined. To economists this is known as the joint cost problem. However, we can distinguish two types of joint cost. There will be certain facilities, such as equipment, building, personnel, etc., which will be involved in the production of many different products, for example, the costs of the accounting function of a large industrial combine jointly, although not necessarily equally, incurred in supervising all of the products which the various units within the combine produce. These costs would not be described by the accountant as joint costs but rather as indirect costs; the description 'joint' being reserved for the situation where the processing of material automatically results in two or more distinct products being produced, for example, when gas is produced from coal, coke and other products also result and these will have as joint cost the purchase price of the coal.

There has been, and still is, much controversy over the methods and techniques for allocating indirect cost to products. The 'full versus direct' cost controversy is too extensive, however, to discuss at length here. The rightness or wrongness of allocating indirect costs, by necessity on an arbitrary basis, to products can only be judged in relation to the decision making process. To state that the only costs which should be taken into account are those relevant to the particular decision, the usual conclusion of the direct cost proponents, is only a pious restatement of the basic problem, not a solution to it. In an uncertain world where the information required for a decision must be inadequate, the basic belief of 'full costers' is that these are the most relevant costs whereas 'direct costers' believe the opposite in that

. . . it (direct costing) frees management from the uncertainties of calculating what constitutes 'normal' performance and from the belief that 'normal' full costs should somehow control, that it encourages management to follow pricing practices which produce greater profit, and that it avoids the illusion of wealth that comes from producing for inventory when inventory is made to absorb period costs.[29]

A more detailed examination of the joint product situation will help clarify the nature of the common cost problem.

This arises when the processing of material results in more than one end product. This may occur even if it is possible to produce these products separately if the combined cost of so doing will be greater than when they are produced jointly. Up to the point of separation of these products there will be common costs and the task is to apportion these so that unit product costs can be ascertained. This task usually falls to the accounting function and the methods adopted for doing this have been severely criticized by many writers.[30] The various methods used can be grouped into two main types: those based on *market values* and those based on a *quantitative unit*.

With the market value method the belief is that common costs should be apportioned to products according to their ability to pay, e.g. if by purchasing £15,000 of material and spending £5,000 of labour processing this three products are produced—20,000 units of A, 10,000 units of B, 10,000 units of C—then the apportionment of the £20,000 of common costs could be as follows:

JOINT COST ALLOCATION STATEMENT

Joint products	*Number of units produced*	*Selling price per unit*	*Total sales value*	*Joint cost allocation*	*Joint* costs per unit*
		s. d.	£	£	s. d.
A	20,000	20 0	20,000	12,500	12 6
B	10,000	14 0	7,000	4,375	8 9
C	10,000	10 0	5,000	3,125	6 3
—	40,000	—	32,000	20,000	—

Such a method is exceedingly arbitrary and means that a change in the price of one product not only affects its cost but also the cost of the others, viz.:

JOINT COST ALLOCATION STATEMENT

Joint products	*Number of units produced*	*Selling price per unit*	*Total sales value*	*Joint cost allocation*	*Joint costs per unit*
		s. d.	£	£	s. d.
A	20,000	18 0	18,000	12,000	12 0
B	10,000	14 0	7,000	4,667	9 4
C	10,000	10 0	5,000	3,333	6 8
—	40,000	—	30,000	20,000	—

*Any additional expenditure required to put the products in a marketable state would be added to these figures to arrive at the product unit cost.

Users of the quantitative unit method believe that there is more logical relationship between the physical properties of the final products and costs than with market values and costs. Using the preceding illustration, if A, B and C were of the same size, weight, consistency, etc., then the apportionment could be:

JOINT COST ALLOCATION STATEMENT

Joint products	Number of units produced	Joint cost allocation	Joint cost per unit
		£	s. d.
A	20,000	10,000	10 0
B	10,000	5,000	10 0
C	10,000	5,000	10 0
—	40,000	20,000	—

In many instances the unit of output will not provide a fair physical comparison and some method of conversion will have to be applied, for example, if the weights of A, B and C were 2 lbs, $1\frac{1}{2}$ lbs and 1 lb respectively, then using this as a basis of allocation would give

JOINT COST ALLOCATION STATEMENT

Joint products	Number of units produced	Equivalent weight in lbs	Joint cost allocation	Joint costs per unit
			£	s. d.
A	20,000	40,000	12,308	12 4
B	10,000	15,000	4,615	9 3
C	10,000	10,000	3,077	6 2
—	40,000	65,000	20,000	—

These methods are also very arbitrary, but there cannot be a 'correct' method of apportioning joint costs and for decision purposes the main criticism levelled against them is that, by appearing to give a degree of precision to these costs which they do not possess, product decisions are made in isolation without realizing the complementary affects which they will have, since the production and sale of one necessarily affects the position of the other joint product. The question must be asked, therefore, why these common costs are so arbitrarily separated and apportioned. There are many reasons and, as in so many other economic problems, the best method for satisfying one reason will not necessarily coincide with the best for another. One is to determine the income of a period. It is unlikely that all joint products will be sold in the same accounting period and, therefore, to determine income and also the financial position, a cost valuation will have to be given to the joint products which have been sold and to those which are still in stock. An allocation is also required for taxation purposes.

More important, perhaps, is the justification of the allocation of common costs on organizational grounds. From the management viewpoint, the allocation of common costs is an organizational problem not an accounting one. Just as 'full costers' believe that their method is more likely in the long run to lead to better decision making, so too is the allocation of common costs to joint products justified on this ground. The methods adopted are never held out to be valid but only reasonable. Reasonableness can be justified only in relation to the organizational structure and, where joint products are involved, such a structure may operate better if joint unit costs are prepared. This is especially so when the joint products require different methods of finishing, packaging, marketing, etc., and where autonomous selling companies are established for each product line. In these circumstances an attempt must be made to develop unit costs for establishing intra-company prices, and even if a market valuation or market price method is adopted, this is usually allied to some internal cost concept. Although there are problems in doing this and the results obtained are obviously open to misinterpretation, it is believed that an arbitrary measurement is better than none at all and that the problems which arise if this is not done are more serious than if it is. Even where these techniques are criticized at a conceptual level, as a decision making tool they are usually regarded as acceptable:

In making our decisions, we are reduced, as with joint costs, to the total consideration of the situation. We must list all the alternatives and simply choose the best.[31]

Thus, although the allocation of common costs may perhaps be justified, be they indirect or joint, it should not be done in a fashion which covers the degree of arbitrariness in their construction otherwise such figures will be a source of error. Hence the Boulding quotation at the beginning of this chapter:

There is something to be said for a certain naivete and simplicity in accounting practice. If accounts are bound to be untruths anyhow, as I have argued, there is much to be said for the simple untruth as against the complicated untruth, for if the untruth is simple, it seems to me that we have a fair chance of knowing what kind of untruth it is. A known untruth is much better than a lie.[32]

3. OPERATIONAL RESEARCH

One of the most important developments in the field of management science has been the emergence of the specialist function known as operational research. Although its roots are to be found in military studies it is now an accepted service in all areas of administration which require planning and control. Operational research—OR—is usually defined as the application of mathematical techniques to the solving of business problems. Such techniques are not the exclusive province of the OR worker and he cannot claim uniqueness on this ground as, to a varying extent, the industrial economist, accountant, and methods engineer also use mathematical techniques. However, the OR worker does, it is maintained, distinguish himself and his specialism by the scientific method which he adopts. Unfortunately, there is no universally accepted definition of the scientific method other than perhaps that which a scientist uses! However, the approach of the scientist is to construct on the basis of actual observations of phenomena hypotheses which can readily be falsified, hoping eventually to explain firstly why the phenomena occur and secondly to formulate a law which describes this. For the applied scientist the observation of actual events is not always possible. The engineer who wishes to construct a tunnel cannot, because of costs if nothing else, build a series of actual tunnels. He must revert to model building, that is describing the event and evolving the hypothesis on a model constructed in the laboratory. It is this latter approach which OR has brought to bear on management problems which themselves are a consequence of having to make decisions in complex situations. The construction of business models presupposes that measurements of the factors which enter into these are available and the first requirement for an OR approach is to set the boundaries of the particular system which is to be examined so that these variables can be identified and then measured.

OR and measurement

The application of mathematical techniques to business problems requires quantifiable data so that models can be constructed and the effect of variations in them tested. However, often the required information is not available or perhaps the real cost of collecting it is prohibitive. To overcome this use is made of mathematical statistics and simulation. Decisions based on quantified data require an appreciation of the significance which can be attached to such data as, for example, whether observations indicate that a real change in circumstances has taken place or whether it is merely a chance effect. The statistical techniques most commonly used for this are sampling, probability, and factorial analysis. All business decisions have an underlying statistical foundation. The impact of OR has forced an explicit recognition of this, in particular because in the complex situation with which OR is concerned intuition is not always a reliable indicator of probability and of chance.

The scientific approach based on observation has at least three distinct stages: the collection of data; the construction of hypotheses based on the data; and the testing of these hypotheses on a sufficiently large number of occasions to determine the significance of the apparent results. All of these stages present difficulties in the context of business problems. The cost of information retrieval has already been considered. In addition, there is usually a time limit for decisions. Simulation, a model building process based on probability, is one means of overcoming these difficulties. Suppose a company must decide on the size of telephone switchboard it wants installed in a new building. Little information about the number and timing of calls in and out may be available except that there is a belief that the probabilities are one in three the line will be in use at any minute of the day. (This belief in this particular case may be based on an activity sample of present switchboard operations.) By putting three markers numbered 1, 2 and 3 respectively in a hat and by drawing one out at a time, always replacing, it is assumed that if a 1 or 2 is drawn a line would not be required but if a 3 is then it would. Sixty drawings will indicate the pattern for one hour, one hundred and twenty for two, and so on. Different probabilities could have been stipulated for different times of the day, if required. Similar procedures could also be adopted to determine the length of time calls would take when the line was in use. Given then this data a picture of what would happen if one,

two, three or more lines were installed and the probability significance given to the chances of a line being available under the
various circumstances can be constructed. This is a simple illustration and an electronic computer may be required as the problem
becomes more complex. It is possible to produce from a computer
in a short time the equivalent of months of actual experience.

The field of inventory control provides another interesting
example of mathematical model building. There are various costs
associated with holding stock, for example, interest on capital,
insurance, obsolescence, and there are also costs associated with
not holding stock, such as ordering, lost sales, reduction in customer
goodwill. These costs will tend to move in opposite directions when
the size of inventory is altered and this movement can be expressed
graphically in relation to the quantity ordered at one time as
follows:

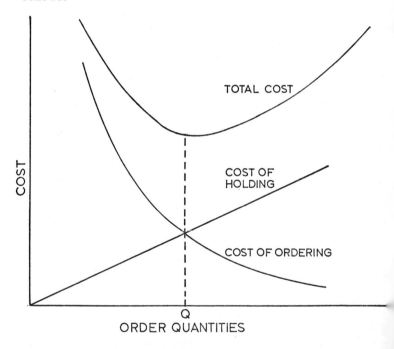

If it is possible to express the total cost curve in equation form
then the order quantity, and thus the average stock, which gives the
minimum total cost can be found. Such an equation can be found

if certain severe assumptions are made about the behaviour of stock usage and receipts and it can be shown that if

Co = Cost of placing an order

D = Demand during time period t

Q = Order quantity

Ch = Cost of holding per unit for time period t

Then Cost of ordering = number of orders × cost of placing an order

$$= \frac{D}{Q} \times Co$$

Cost of holding = average stock × cost of holding during t

$$= \frac{Q}{2} \times Ch$$

$$\therefore \text{ Total cost} = \frac{D.Co}{Q} + \frac{Q \, Ch}{2}$$

Under these circumstances total cost is at a minimum in respect of order quantities when

$$Q = \sqrt{\frac{2 \, D.Co^*}{Ch}}$$

To construct this model what appear to be fairly unrealistic assumptions have to be made. These assumptions are:

(1) The only objective is to minimize cost;

(2) The quantity demanded is known with complete certainty;

(3) Stock usage is even throughout the period;

(4) There is an insignificant (no) time lag between placing an order and receiving the goods.

* $Tc = \dfrac{D.Co}{Q} + \dfrac{Q.Ch}{2}$

Differentiation in respect of Q

$\dfrac{dTc}{dQ} = -\dfrac{D.Co}{Q^2} + \dfrac{Ch}{2}$

Tc will be at minimum when

$\dfrac{Ch}{2} - \dfrac{D.Co}{Q^2} = 0$

By rearrangement $Q = \sqrt{\dfrac{2 \, D \, Co}{Ch}}$

Despite this, it illustrates the value of model building because by expressing the decision in this fashion an understanding of the basic problem is made much simpler through the highlighting of the relationship which exists between the variables. It can be deduced that, if there is a functional relationship between the amount of stock held and the level of sales, then it is the square root of sales which should determine this and stock levels which are determined, for example, on a 'number of weeks sales' are based on a wrong principle. It is often also found that total cost in the neighbourhood of the optimum order quantity is relatively insensitive to small variations in the quantity ordered. This is only a generalization but it has particular significance where the amount invested in stock is a large proportion of total investment. All that the model does, of course, is to provide a starting point for investigation by giving a 'paper' figure which is compared with current practice and if the order quantity so computed differs radically from actual then this may be because an important variable has been omitted from the calculation. This may be a variable which is either difficult or perhaps impossible to quantify such as the loss of customer goodwill or the risk of obsolescence. The model helps get these in perspective and may indicate that apparently management are placing a much greater/less value on these than they apparently intend or believe. Or the value of a variable may be incorrectly estimated, or perhaps management is not pursuing a policy of optimization.

Mathematical programming

The most popular type of programming is linear programming, the main purpose of which is to identify the optimum contribution of limited resources. The linear assumptions which underlie this such as that product costs increase by an identical amount per unit or that selling prices per unit stay constant irrespective of the quantity sold have already been justified in certain circumstances. The application of linear programming presupposes that there is some objective which has to be achieved—with most linear programming examples this is usually either the maximization of profit or the minimization of cost—the objective function. This objective function is a dependent variable in that it is a function of several other factors, the availability of at least one of which is limited. Given these conditions linear programming requires formulation of the relationship between the dependent variable and the independent variables and then computes the optimum solution out of all of the available feasible solutions. This can be applied in determining product mix, storage utilization, machine allocation, etc. A simple illustration will help clarify the approach.

The objective is to maximize profits and this is to be done by producing product A and/or product B, both of which require processing on two machines, 1 and 2. A requires two hours on both machines 1 and 2, while B requires three hours on machine 1 but only one hour on machine 2. There are only twelve and eight hours available on machines 1 and 2 respectively. A has an estimated contribution to profit of £6 per unit and B £7 per unit. Here we have a dependent variable profit which is to be maximized and which is a function of two independent variables A and B, the production and sale of which are limited by the machine time available. This can be expressed in linear programming terms as

$$\text{Maximize P (Profit)} = 6A+7B \text{ subject to constraints}$$
$$2A+3B \leqslant 12$$
$$2A+B \leqslant 8$$
$$A \geqslant 0$$
$$B \geqslant 0$$

The answer to the above can be obtained graphically (see p. 130).

When dealing with many variables, however, the graphical method is impracticable and recourse must be had to algebraic techniques. Most of these follow an iterative—i.e. trial and error—procedure by starting with a feasible solution and then testing by substitution to see if the result shows an improvement. This is continued until no further improvement can be made. In the above illustration, by taking the feasibility area and systematically computing the profit at each of the corners of this, comparison of the resultant profit will give the optimum position, viz.:

Step	Feasibility area corner	Output A	B	Contribution A	B	Total
				£	£	£
1	0·0	0	0	0	0	0
2	4·0	4	0	24	0	24
3	3·2	3	2	18	14	32
4	0·4	0	4	0	28	28

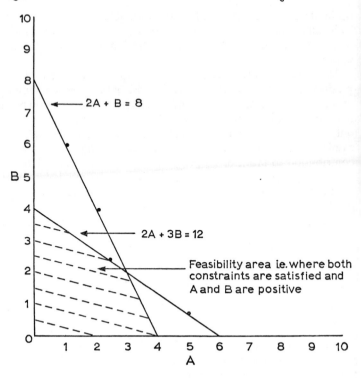

The above graph shows that the position of maximum profit will be
achieved when 3 of A and 2 of B are produced, i.e. the extreme point
on the feasibility area which lines on a line parallel to the line $A=6$,
$B=7$.

Therefore, the optimum step is number 3. Methods of solving the
problems amenable to graphical treatment have been developed
which may or may not require a computer according to the number
of steps involved—an example of this is the Simplex method.

A special application of the linear programming technique is the
Transportation Model. This is applied when there are supplies of
'product' in more than one location and these have to be distributed
to more than one point. If there are three warehouses, A, B and C
at which 40, 50 and 60 units are in stores and these must be sent to
three outlets, 1, 2 and 3, in quantities of 50, 40 and 60 respectively
and if the transport costs are as follows:

A to 1	30/- per unit
A to 2	70/- ,, ,,
A to 3	40/- ,, ,,
B to 1	80/- ,, ,,
B to 2	50/- ,, ,,
B to 3	60/- ,, ,,
C to 1	40/- ,, ,,
C to 2	50/- ,, ,,
C to 3	70/- ,, ,,

then it would be a long and difficult operation to determine by rule of thumb an optimum delivery schedule. However, an application of linear programming techniques reduces this to quite a simple operation which indicates that the optimum/minimum cost position is

$$
\left.
\begin{array}{l}
\text{40 from A to 3} = 1600/\text{-} \\
\text{30 from B to 2} = 1500/\text{-} \\
\text{20 from B to 3} = 1200/\text{-} \\
\text{50 from C to 1} = 2000/\text{-} \\
\text{10 from C to 2} = \ \ 500/\text{-}
\end{array}
\right\} \quad £340
$$

With linear programming the answer may often be in fractions which must be rounded up to whole numbers in order to give a realistic position. However, if required, allowance for this can be built into the programme when the term *integer programming* is applied. The final type of programming—*dynamic programming*—discards the linear assumptions and while it has a great potential for business purposes in those situations where linearity can be shown to be false, at present its impact, for obvious reasons, has been much less than that of linear programming.

In conclusion, how does the approach of OR differ from that of conventional economic theory? Probably the main distinction may be found in the emphasis which OR—in common with modern thinking about cybernetics and organization theory—places on the information system and on the communication of information to the decision maker. Traditionally, as was indicated in Chapter 2, economics has tended to neglect problems of obtaining, processing and communicating information to and within the firm. It has usually analysed business behaviour, assuming knowledge and objectives to be given. In the future, however, there seems likely to be a much closer integration of the work of the OR man whose skill lies in clarifying the logic of a business decision through

quantitative analysis, the organizational theorist whose special
concern is with communications and the nature of organizational
decision-making, and the normative micro-economist whose
strength lies in his ability to recognize and systematically analyse
relevant objectives, criteria and concepts—e.g. profit, cost,
economies of scale. Thus, economics will continue to contribute
much to our understanding of business efficiency. But it will itself
benefit from the growth of new disciplines which make the business
firm their object of study.

What we are witnessing, therefore, is not so much a revolution in the
theory of the firm as a deepening and broadening . . . which we hope
will lead to better understanding of the complex systems of human
behaviour in the framework of both small organizations and of large.[33]

NOTES

1. Florence, *Logic of British and American Industry* (1953), pp. 89–90.

2. Edwards and Townsend, *Business Enterprise*, p. 143.

3. op. cit., p. 143.

4. Edith T. Penrose, *The Theory of the Growth of the Firm*, 1959. The 'product' concept is of course highly elusive. How do we define 'product' meaningfully to decide whether or not diversification exists?

5. Dunning and Thomas, *British Industry: Change and Development in the Twentieth Century*, p. 53.

6. Penrose, op. cit., p. 151.

7. Unfortunately, economists have not adopted consistent definitions. Dr Penrose, for example, seems to regard *integration* as a special case of diversification (op. cit., p. 145), though it is difficult to see why the older terminology should be employed in this restricted sense.

8. Coase, '*The Nature of the Firm*', reprinted in *Readings in Price Theory*, published by American Economic Association, 1953.

9. Florence, *The Logic of British and American Industry* (1953), p. 74.

10. Penrose, op. cit., p. 137.

11. See, for example, Florence, op. cit., p. 44 et seq. and pp. 74 et seq.

12. Edwards and Townsend, pp. 205 et seq., for a discussion of the reasons why firms do this.

13. Penrose, p. 112.

14. Penrose, pp. 104 et seq.

15. Penrose, p. 132.

16. Penrose, pp. 134–5.

17. For economists' views on this subject, see Florence, op. cit.; Edwards and Townsend, op. cit.; Stigler, *The Theory of Price*, etc.

18. Penrose, ch. 4.

19. The formal analysis in terms of cost curves is discussed in most elementary and intermediate economic textbooks, e.g. Stigler, Stonier and Hague, op. cit. See also, however, Chamberlin, *Towards a More General Theory of Value*, part III, for a discussion of some conceptual matters. Also Wiles, *Price, Cost and Output*.

20. Boulding—'Economics and Accounting, the Uncongenial Twins', in Baxter and Davidson in *Studies in Accounting*.

21. It is instructive to compare this with the way the physicist proceeds. See Toulmin, *The Philosophy of Science, passim*.

22. J. Johnson, *Statistical Cost Analysis*.

23. H. C. Doofe, NAA Bulletin, 1959.

24. P. D. Wiles, *Price, Cost and Output*, 1963 ed., p. 213. For other evidence supporting these views, see:

(1) P. W. S. Andrews, *Manufacturing Business*.

(2) Dean, *The Statistical Determination of Costs*, University of Chicago Press.

(3) P. H. Douglas, 'Are there Laws of Production?', *American Economic Review*, XXXVIII, March 1948.

(4) R. H. Solow, 'Technical Change and the Aggregate Production Function', *Review of Economics and Statistics*, vol. XXIX, August 1957.

25. Hirshleifer, 'The Firm's Cost Function: A successful reconstruction', *The Journal of Business*, July 1962.

26. Hirshleifer, op. cit. For practical illustrations of this attitude see the discussion on uncertainty in Chapter 4 above.

27. See Chapter 8 below for a definition of this term.

28. Proof: $Qn(SPn-VC)-FC = Q(SP-VC)-FC$
$$Qn(SPn-VC) = Q(SP-VC)$$
$$Qn = \frac{Q(SP-VC)}{SPn-VC}$$

29. Chamberlain, *The Firm. Micro-economic Planning and Action*.

30. For example, see Wiles, op. cit.

31. Wiles, op. cit.

32. Boulding, op. cit.

33. K. E. Boulding and W. A. Spivey, *Linear Programming and the Theory of the Firm*.

COST CONTROL

*Any fool can learn to stay within his budget, but I have seen only
a handful of managers in my life who can draw up a budget that
is worth staying within.* NICHOLAS DREYSTADT

1. AIMS AND PURPOSES OF COST CONTROL

A common factor for all organizations is that their objective, or
objectives, should be achieved at minimum cost and this has led to
the development of cost accounting systems. An information
system designed for cost control must both produce information
which is sufficiently detailed and accurate to allow decisions to be
made and also ensure that it is available soon enough for these
decisions to be effective. Accounting systems designed for the
production of financial statements do not satisfy these requirements. This is not surprising when one considers that the original
role of financial accounts was one of stewardship, the prim

LEGEND TO FACING ILLUSTRATION

Ratio

1. Earnings/Total net assets
2. Earnings/Sales
3. Sales/Total net assets
4. Sales/Cost of sales
5. Sales/Fixed assets
6. Sales/Net current assets
7. Production cost/Cost of sales
8. Selling cost/Cost of sales
9. Administration cost/Cost of sales
10. Sales/Plant
11. Sales/Land/Buildings
12. Sales/Goodwill

Ratio

13. Sales/Stocks
14. Sales/Cash and debtors
15. Sales/Current liabilities
16. Material cost/Production cost
17. Labour cost/Production cost
18. Overhead cost/Production cost
19. Equipment/Plant cost
20. Motor vehicles/Plant cost
21. Loose tools/Plant cost
22. Raw Materials/Stocks
23. Work in progress/Stocks
24. Finished goods/Stocks

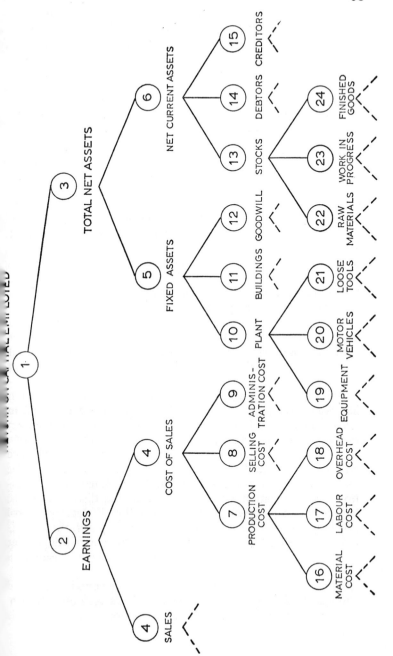

purpose was the preservation of resources—the utilization of resources was of only minor importance—and the rules and regulations which were formulated and developed for the recording of financial transactions had, as a general yardstick, this major purpose. However, cost ascertainment is only the first step in achieving the objective of cost minimization. Cost in an absolute sense is a meaningless concept and a reference point for comparison purposes must also be established. A knowledge of cost will only result in motivation if it is high or low, acceptable or non-acceptable. To make this qualification, however, some standard must be available and unless this standard or limit of acceptability is formalized then action based on it will not be consistent. The establishment of these limits has been developed both externally and internally.

External standards are applied by comparing performance with other organizations as represented by a set of ratios. Management control is facilitated through attention being drawn to those areas which show a significant deviation. Most schemes of inter-unit comparison are based on a pyramid structure which starts with the key ratio earnings/total net assets from which other important constituents can be prepared.

These do not exhaust all the possibilities. There are many other permutations of the variables listed above which produce a relevant measurement, e.g. the relationship of current assets to current liabilities.

Despite the advantages of this type of comparison its adoption has been relatively slight and the more striking development in management control systems in recent years has been the adoption of systems of budgeting to provide internal achievement standards. Although initially the prime objective was to create reference points for the control of costs these techniques have been used for many other managerial functions such as planning, communication, decentralization, co-ordination, etc., and this multiple use has created many problems in their operation. Budgetary control is closely associated with standard costing. However, the latter is only a more detailed type of budgetary control and in this chapter the word standard can be taken to be a specific sub-division of a budget.

A standard cost is only relevant to a definite period of time and can be incorporated into the organization's recording system. Standards are applied to actual production to see what this should have represented in financial terms in light of predetermined achievement levels. By highlighting the difference, or variance* between standard costs and actual costs, management is able to concentrate attention on those items where achievement deviates significantly from what was expected.

If an actual cost differs from standard there can only be two reasons for this. Either more or less input factors have been needed to achieve the given output and/or a higher or lower price has had to be paid for them. The application of this reasoning requires that actual and standard cost should be expressed in terms of quantities and prices of input relative to output. In most situations output will be units of production or sales and input will be the material, labour and expenses which are required to achieve these. This can be represented as follows:

Actual cost	= Actual quantity times Actual price
A C	$= A Q \times A P$
Standard cost	= Standard quantity times Standard price
S C	$= S Q \times S P$
Total cost variance	= Actual cost less Standard cost
	$= A C - S C$
	$= (AQ.AP)-(SQ.SP)$

In allocating the total cost difference between input quantity and input price the convention adopted in the United Kingdom is that the variations in input quantity are priced at standard. This is justified by the assumption that in most situations those responsible for controlling input usage are not responsible for the prices paid for it and reports which measure their performance against standard should not be affected by variations over which they have no direct control.

Standard cost control is based on responsibility accounting in that cost variations are identified with the individual responsible for incurring these. The exercise of control can only be through motivation and motivation presupposes the authority necessary to take action. It is, therefore, unreasonable and irrelevant to identify an individual with items of expenditure which do not come under his control and authority.

If cost variations due to the usage of input factors are to be priced at standard then this quantity variance will be got by evaluating at standard price the difference between the actual

*Not to be confused with the statistical concept of that name.

quantity of input factor for actual performance and the standard quantity of input factor for actual performance.

$$S P (AQ-SQ)$$

By difference it can then be deduced that the remaining portion of the total variation due to fluctuation in input prices will be given by the difference between the actual price of input factor and the standard price of input factor multiplied by the actual quantity of input factor, or

$$A Q (AP-SP)*$$

These conventions only present a realistic assessment of the situation when both quantity and price variances move in opposite directions but when both are either above or below standard then part of the total variance is a combination of both price and quantity factors which is arbitrarily allocated to one or other of the major categories as follows:

Example 1

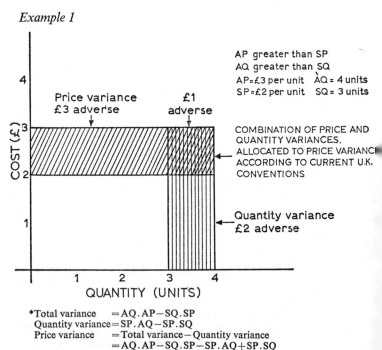

*Total variance $= AQ.AP-SQ.SP$
Quantity variance $= SP.AQ-SP.SQ$
Price variance $=$ Total variance $-$ Quantity variance
                   $= AQ.AP-SQ.SP-SP.AQ+SP.SQ$
                   $= AQ.AP-SP.AQ$
                   $= AQ (AP-SP)$

Example 2

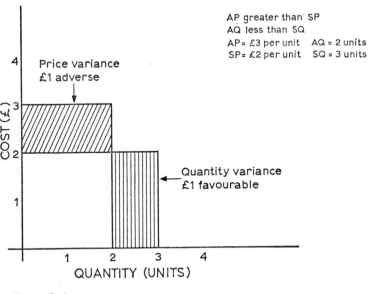

AP greater than SP
AQ less than SQ
AP= £3 per unit   AQ = 2 units
SP= £2 per unit   SQ = 3 units

Price variance
£1 adverse

Quantity variance
£1 favourable

COST (£)

QUANTITY (UNITS)

Example 3

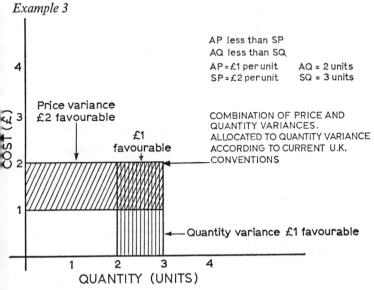

AP less than SP
AQ less than SQ
AP = £1 per unit   AQ = 2 units
SP = £2 per unit   SQ = 3 units

COMBINATION OF PRICE AND
QUANTITY VARIANCES.
ALLOCATED TO QUANTITY VARIANCE
ACCORDING TO CURRENT U.K.
CONVENTIONS

Price variance
£2 favourable

£1
favourable

Quantity variance £1 favourable

COST (£)

QUANTITY (UNITS)

The total cost difference is therefore divided between price and quantity and any further analysis is directed towards evaluating the reasons for this. Because of the difficulties of quantifying the reasons for price variations, e.g. negligent ordering, further analysis has tended to be concentrated on input quantities by taking the specific reasons for the excess or reduced input usage and pricing these at standard, e.g. alterations in capacity, lost time through a power cut, change in the mix of materials, etc.

The initial procedure therefore is to take the actual level of activity and then to ask the simple question 'what should this have cost?' With direct costs the answer is relatively easy because of their assumed linear relationship with activity. However, within a specific range of activity there are certain expenses which are fixed and consequently do not have this relationship. For accounting purposes if a full costing system is in operation a fixed standard cost per unit must be calculated. Full costing exists when any costs, other than direct, are identified with cost units, and this must be done on the basis of an anticipated level of activity. This two-fold analysis can be illustrated as follows:

(1) *Activity and expenditure similar to standard*

Estimated output	= 100 units
Standard fixed cost	= £100
Standard fixed cost per unit	= £1
Actual output	= 100 units
Actual fixed cost	= £100
Standard fixed cost for actual output	= £100 (100 × £1)
Total variance	= Nil

(2) *Expenditure similar to standard but a variation in activity*

Actual output	= 80 units
Standard fixed cost for actual output	= £80 (80 × £1)
Actual fixed cost	= £100
Total variance	= £20 Excess

(3) *Activity similar to standard but a variation in expenditure*

Standard fixed cost for actual output	= £100 (100 × £1)
Actual fixed cost	= £130
Total variance	= £30 Excess

(4) *Variations in both activity and expenditure*

(Actual output as 2)

(Actual expenditure as 3)

Standard fixed cost for actual output	=	£80 (80 × £1)
Actual fixed cost	=	£130
Total variance	=	£50 Excess
	=	£30 due to increased expenditure and
		£20 due to decreased activity

For many items, particularly fixed expenses, it will not be possible or worth while to express the amount which should have been spent in a relevant price times quantity relationship and all that will be available is the total amount budgeted to be spent. There are many difficulties to be overcome before such a system can be implemented. There are the technical accounting problems of identifying factor inputs with a relevant output unit, relating cost movement to activity and/or time, the allocation and treatment of joint costs, the construction of technical specifications for standards, and in general the establishment of information systems which achieve a balance between the requirements of accuracy and speed. Even when these technical accounting problems have been apparently overcome there are still the managerial problems of a cost control system and it is with these we are primarily concerned.

2. THE MANAGEMENT PROBLEMS OF A COST CONTROL SYSTEM

The development of cost control systems is a product of the complexity of operation and communication within a large organization where there are many variables associated with each decision. As Churchman has postulated[1] measurement becomes necessary when precision is required, i.e. when fine distinctions have to be drawn and or when the results obtained in one connection may be used in another where the circumstances are different from those prevailing when the original results were obtained. By linking cost ascertainment records with budgets and standards a measurement system can be developed which integrates planning and control. This integral relationship and the dependence of each sub-unit in the system on another also provides a means for co-ordinating the activities of the organization. At the same time it provides the framework within which delegation of authority can take place. By clearly defining responsibilities an individual has freedom to act within the constraint of his overall budgeted objectives.

A formalized statement of policies and objectives which such a system presupposes should also help to eliminate many of the problems which arise out of uncertainty of purpose.

The prime purpose of standard cost statements is to control costs by directing attention to specific areas where rectification is required.

When a red variance on a monthly operating statement leads a departmental head to ask—'Why am I running over on my operating supplies?' —it is performing an attention-directing function.[2]

The interpretation of such statements is in effect a situation appraisal done at different levels in the organization.

This operates through three channels. Not only does it lead to self-appraisal where those immediately concerned must decide whether or not the size of the variances indicates that corrective action is required but also higher management will have to decide whether or not they should intervene and direct their subordinates as to how the standard will be achieved. This will only be done when it appears that lower management are unable to rectify the position themselves.

Appraisal does not imply immediate intervention by the appraising body. Instead, intervention presumably is deferred until a series of successive appraisals indicates a lack of effectiveness at the lower level.[3]

Thirdly the variances may be so significant that a complete reappraisal of the objectives and policies of the organization will be required. In order that such appraisal can be carried out effectively the measurements involved should have certain characteristics. Measurements should be valid, and in this context, validity means that the information system actually measures what it sets out to measure. Secondly, they should be objective in that the results obtained should not be equivocal and finally, they should be reliable if they are to satisfy the Churchman criterion of transferability from one set of circumstances to another and from one individual to another. However, doubts have been cast as to whether or not cost control systems as they presently operate satisfy these three basic criteria. The source of the conflict is in the level of achievement which is incorporated into the budget.

3. THE LEVEL OF ACHIEVEMENT INCORPORATED INTO BUDGETS

It is the level of achievement set in the budget which determines the variance and it is the quality of the variance which is the motivating force for managerial action. However, interpretation of these cannot be done properly unless there is complete knowledge about the standard measures. To produce 100 tons of finished output a greater weight of input may be required because of process wastage or loss. This could be a function of the machinery, material or labour used. An allowance must be made for this, but how much should be allowed? The information available may show that in the past actual process loss has been of the order of 25 per cent of input. However, the technical specification may indicate that at most the process loss should only be 5 per cent of input. In setting the standard for process loss, therefore, should it be 5 per cent, 25 per cent or something in between, say, 15 per cent?

If the standard price of factor input is £20 per ton and during a control period 2,000 tons of finished output is produced for which input is 2,353 tons then at each standard process loss level the position will be:

	Process loss Actual cost	Process loss Standard cost	Variance	
(1) Standard set at 5 per cent	£7,060	£2,100	£4,960	above standard
(2) Standard set at 15 per cent	7,060	7,060	NIL	
(3) Standard set at 25 per cent	7,060	13,340	6,280	below standard

From the above it is evident that how the standard is set will determine whether the variance will be either negative, nil or positive. An actual performance in line with budget may only indicate that management's estimate of its own inefficiency is accurate. It was this that led the late Nicholas Dreystadt, Chief Executive of the Cadillac Corporation, to say

Any fool can learn to stay within his budget, but I have seen only a handful of managers in my life who can draw up a budget that is worth staying within.[4]

The problem may be aggravated because of the conflicting notions which different managerial functions may have on the level to be incorporated. The production manager may, for example, incline towards a level which he knows can be achieved, whereas the technical manager may favour that which should be achieved. The accountant and purchasing manager in any event will require an estimate of not what should be, nor what is, but what will be in order to integrate these figures with the material and financial requirement budgets. If one level is to satisfy the notions and demands of all functions then conflict is bound to arise and unless these notions are revised then interpretation will be affected and the reliability of the measurements questioned. Further complications arise through the integration of the planning and control activities which means that in practice one set of measurements will usually serve both functions. There is, therefore, the problem of a technique which tries simultaneously to provide a measure of restraint by keeping costs at a target level and also an estimate of what is likely to be achieved in the future. Budgets can be regarded as pressure devices or as measures of appraising expected performance or a mixture of both.

In one sense, this problem (arriving at an acceptable standard) arises due to an improper conception of the purpose of the budget . . . the budget is a standard, not a target, and for some items it is the average deviation that is to be minimized rather than the average costs. This is consistent with the concept of the budget as presented in this paper as an evaluation standard rather than a pressure device.[5]

If, as is likely, the measure used is biased in one direction, then interpretation will only be valid if the extent of the bias is known and it is doubtful if in most cost control systems this is ever made explicit.

An obvious solution to this is to develop the system and to distinguish between evaluation standards and pressure standards. Various factors however operate against this as a complete solution. Every variation or sophistication which is introduced into the measurement system is an additional expense. Also one of the supposed advantages of a budget system is that it acts as a co-ordinating device and if there are different levels of achievement with varying qualifications on each then this will tend to detract from this co-ordinating aspect. Even if there is a budget level set below another target level the budget may still become synonymous with acceptability and although the target is what should be aimed for, as long as the budget is achieved the results will be seen to be satisfactory,[6] in that the budget tends to be identified with aspiration and becomes the level of achievement above which is perceived a success and below which failure.

Thus it is certainly important to know to what extent the numerical size of the measurement scale influences, favourably or unfavourably, the attitude of the decision maker.[7]

The association of budgets with aspiration levels and acceptability is further strengthened by the accounting terminology which is used to describe variances. If an actual cost is higher than standard then the variance is qualified as adverse or unfavourable, whereas if the opposite is the case then it is described as favourable. Although the words adverse and favourable have a precise technical meaning—above or below standard—it is not surprising if they are often given a literal interpretation. Success will, therefore, be materially affected by the level of achievement incorporated in the budget and the setting of this will not only affect the interpretation of actual results but also the amount of effort which is put in to achieving them. Despite this the most guidance that is usually given is a very general statement that standards should not be too high as this will discourage, but on the other hand they should not be too low, otherwise this will not provide an incentive.

. . . although all budgets must be attainable they must make no concession to the obvious weaknesses of the administration or operations; they must be an absolute and realistic assessment of what ought to be achieved.[8]

However, no guidance is given as to the counterpoise which must be established between 'attainable' and 'ought to be achieved'. If there are administrative weaknesses should these be ignored entirely in the budget or should some allowance be made for them and if so how much? Is consideration only to be given to weaknesses in existing structure or should some attempt be made to construct, for the particular decision, an alternative—probably quite different —optimum structure?

It can be shown that for decision making purposes the true minimum cost of an activity cannot be determined strictly until operations have first been optimally organized, e.g. logically, one can in the final analysis only treat a particular cost as fixed and, therefore, irrelevant as far as a particular decision is concerned if one knows that the activity to which it relates is organized in the least cost way.[9]

However, although it may be possible to construct a least-cost model on the basis of an existing structure, the current state of organizational theory is such that to build a model of an optimal organization is not feasible.

In most instances with which I am familiar, there is a serious doubt that the persons who set up the standard costs were fully aware of the proper way to relate organizational structure to costs standards. Since we have as yet only tentative ways of proving what organizational structures are optimal, the cost accountants cannot be blamed.[10]

Nevertheless, unless the degree to which the optimal organizational structure is incorporated into the budget is known then an effective appraisal of the results which incorporate a comparison with this cannot be made.

Most measurement systems are subdivided for administrative purposes into a series of sub-units or decision centres. When interpreting the results of each sub-unit not only must its decision rules be known but the result must be appraised alongside those achieved in other closely related sub-units. If, for example, an increased labour rate variance is disclosed this may be related to the labour employed variance in that increased wage rates may have been granted to achieve faster work. A comparison of these interrelated variances will, therefore, require a knowledge of the level of achievement incorporated in each. This has been recognized for those activities which are obviously interrelated. However, recent simulation studies by Bonini have indicated the possibility that the results achieved in one sub-unit can affect the amount of effort put into another not so obviously related sub-unit.[11]

A basic problem with budgets is to give what they measure some significance and this can only be done if the error in the budget itself can be measured.

One of the most significant aspects of modern times is the realization that one does not measure unless one can also measure the error of the measurement.[12]

In budgetary control and standard costing the variance is the measurement based on the budget but what is the degree of error incorporated into the budget? One method[13] which has been suggested for tackling this problem draws on probability statistics. The budget is identified with expectation and is assumed to be the means of the probability distribution. In estimating the level of cost a range is given, each with the probability of occurrence and the weighted average is taken and used as the budgeted cost. By equating budgeted cost with expected value the budget then becomes the level expected to occur. Once this budget cost has been determined, by definition there must be an equal chance that random deviations from it are equally likely to fall on either side of it and that variances are equally likely to be favourable or adverse. In addition, an attempt must be made to measure the standard deviation associated with the particular budget level. This can be done by either analysing records of actual past achievements, provided the causes of deviation from past expected levels have also been recorded, or by answering such questions as 'what is the budgeted level of expenditure at which there is an even chance that actual expenditure will be greater because of non-controllable factors?' If the budget is the mean of the probability distribution and if a normal distribution is assumed (the assumption of normal distribution is not essential but it simplifies the explanation and in many cases it will approximate sufficiently well to be acceptable) then by using statistical tables a probability significance can be given to the chances of any variance being due to random non-controllable factors. For example, if the budget level of staff salaries is £20,000, and there is an even chance that actual costs will fall in the range of £18,000 to £22,000, and if the actual cost is £23,000, the variance report will indicate that:

	Actual	*Budget*	*Variance**
Staff salaries	£23,000	£20,000	£3,000 excess

However, from the information given the standard deviation can be calculated from the equation:

Budget cost $+2/3$ Standard deviation $=$ Upper limit of range
Budget cost $-2/3$ Standard deviation $=$ Lower limit of range

4/3 Standard deviation $=$ Upper limit of range
                                  $-$ Lower limit of range

$\therefore$ Standard deviation $= \frac{3}{4}$ (Upper limit $-$ Lower limit)
                                  $= \frac{3}{4}$ (£22,000 $-$ £18,000)
                                  $=$ £3,000

*The reader is reminded that this variance bears no relationship to the statistical concept of that name.

By then expressing the variance in terms of the number of deviations from the budget as follows:

$$\frac{\text{Actual cost} - \text{Budget cost}}{\text{Standard deviation}}$$

the probability of this variance being due to random non-controllable factors can be calculated.

$$\frac{\text{Actual cost} - \text{Budget cost}}{\text{Standard deviation}} = \frac{23,000 - 20,000}{3,000} = 1$$

From statistical tables the probability of a positive variance one standard deviation from the mean being due to non-controllable factors is only 0·16 (the maximum is, of course, only 0·5).

If budgeted cleaning costs are also £20,000 with a range £19,500 to £20,500 the standard deviation is £750. With actual expenditure £22,000 the number of standard deviations is

$$\frac{22,000 - 20,000}{750} = 2·7$$

and a chance that this was due to a random factor is less than 0·04 and relative to the staff salary variance more attention is required by management, although this variance is only 10 per cent of budgeted level compared to 15 per cent with the staff salaries. The limits which will determine the degree of investigation of the variance will be set by management after weighing the value of information received in terms of accuracy and detail against the cost of obtaining it. These limits should be set for both favourable and unfavourable variances as the analysis of extra-favourable results can lead to a reappraisal in the level of achievement incorporated in the budget and/or to knowledge which will be useful in improving performance in other areas. In addition to the probability significance management will also take account of the size of the variance if this is an important factor relative to the company's overall financial position. A graphical presentation of cost control figures can take account of both of these factors as follows:

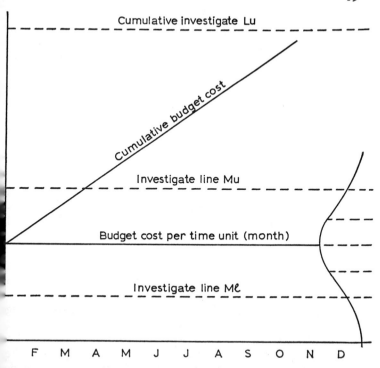

The above diagram indicates how investigation of variances can be determined by both the degree of significance and the absolute amount of the variance. For each month the upper or lower limits, Mu and Ml, for investigation have been determined by the probability significance of the deviation. However, in addition, because of financial considerations, if the cumulative total goes beyond the cumulative investigate line Lu the investigation will also take place.* Apart from providing a measure of the significance of the variances disclosed in cost control systems the use of probability statistics would appear to offer other advantages in that it would give more precision to the definitions used in budgetary systems and remove to some extent, the emotive connotations of present terminology. The substitution of expectation for budget or standard requires an explicit statement that the budget is neither a target nor a pressure device but simply what is expected under current

*The above analysis is mainly relevant to accountancy fixed costs although with slight modifications it can be applied to accountancy variable costs.

circumstances to take place. Variances are neither favourable nor adverse but simply greater or less than expectation. The level of expectation is, of course, a subjective probability estimate which to a large extent is dependent on judgement. However, it is the level which management feels is most likely to be achieved given present circumstances, not a target level to be used as an incentive nor a perfect level representative of the optimum organizational structure. While subjective probability as a decision rule criterion is open to criticism,[14] nevertheless, if future decision theory is to be based on probabilities it provides an opportunity for management decision to be expressed in this form. Finally, by emphasizing the importance of estimating the likely extent of deviations from budget as well as the absolute level attention is directed towards those activities where it is difficult to correlate activity of performance with the level of expenditure and consequently, the control exercisable by management is weakest, or where uncertainty is greatest.

Whether or not the actual procedure for establishing budgeted levels of achievement affects the efficiency of the system is still an open question. While some authorities[15] argue that lack of participation in the setting of such levels tends to defeat its co-ordinating aspect, creates tension, and has other undesirable side effects, others[16] believe that it is the existence (or absence) and size of a clearly defined goal which affects worker motivation, not the degree of participation. The present state of opinion is both inconclusive and contradictory and it is only possible to deduce certain control hypotheses which should be taken into account when such systems are constructed.

Although initially, the control system will be assessed from the viewpoint of the organization it should also be looked at from the viewpoint of the individual, to see how it affects his freedom of choice and the structure of his reward system. In particular, it should be considered whether it is possible for the individual's results to satisfy the budget constraints but still produce a position which conflicts with the overall goal or goals of the organization. This implies that there should be complete knowledge of the level of achievement which is incorporated into the budget and also a clear understanding of the policies and objectives of the organization which this is meant to reflect. A budget is a means not an end and only achieves its purpose if its achievement results in organizational policy being achieved. This will only happen if the budgeting system works with the organizational structure and does no conflict with it. How this can be achieved is an open question and there is obviously more than one answer. However, it would appear that while dissection of the budget into small units is required for administrative purposes the sub-units should still be grouped together for reporting and appraisal purposes into larger identifiable sectors. The concept of the responsibility centre has already been discussed but it would appear that unless these responsibility centres can be identified with an overall yardstick of company performance then they are not suitable as they will not provide an incentive for sub-unit performance to be geared to that of the main unit. Suggestions have been made that these should be identified with profit centres which themselves are identified with the reward and penalty* system of the organization. Finally, a control system will only operate if it is seen to be regarded by management as important and this requires management sponsorship. Although many checks and controls to detect budget 'monkey business' can be instituted either internally or by extending the recourse to external comparisons, in the last resort a control system must depend on management integrity.†

NOTES

1. Churchman, *Prediction and Optimal Decisions*.

2. H. Simon, *The Controller*, January 1965.

3. Shillinglaw, 'Divisional Performance Review: an extension of budgetary control', in Bonini, ed., *Management Controls*.

4. Quoted in Drucker, *The Practice of Management*, p. 74.

5. Shillinglaw, op. cit.

6. Stedry, A., Aspiration Levels, Attitudes and Performance in a Goal Orientated Situation, *Industrial Management Review*, 1962.

*Not necessarily exclusively financial.

†*Budget 'monkey business'*. The term 'monkey business' refers to the practices which are adopted by individuals in order that their personal goal rather than organizational goal will be achieved. An example of this would be a salesman not submitting documentation which indicated an achieved sale in a period when the budget has already been achieved so that it will be awarded to him during the next period. Another example would be a production supervisor ordering excess supplies in a period when he knows that he cannot achieve his position so that he can start off next period in a position of advantage compared to his colleagues. Perhaps the most common example is when towards the end of the budget period an all out attempt is made to spend up to the budget irrespective of its worthwhileness and 'just a little bit over' in order to prove the budgeting ability of the supervisor and prevent an underspending in this period being used as a justification for reducing the budget next period. While this latter reason may not strictly be termed 'monkey business' it is indicative of a lack of trust in the budgeting process resulting in a lack of managerial integrity.

7. Churchman, op. cit.

8. Fleck Committee, *N.C.B. Report of the Advisory Committee on Organization.*

9. Amey, 'Accounting as a Tool of Management', *District Bank Review,* December 1964, No. 152.

10. Church, op. cit.

11. Bonini, op. cit., 'Simulation of Organizational Behaviour'.

12. Churchman, op. cit.

13. Bierman, Fouraker and Jaedicke, *Quantitative Analysis for Business Decisions.*

14. See Churchman, op. cit.

15. Argyris, *The Impact of Budgets on People.*

16. Stedry, op. cit. French, Kay and Meyer, *A Study of Threat and Participation in an Industrial Appraisal Situation.*

8

DEMAND ANALYSIS AND FORECASTING

> But scientists, who ought to know
> Assure us that they must be so. . . .
> Oh ! let us never, never doubt
> What nobody is sure about.
>   HILAIRE BELLOC

1. THE ELEMENTARY ECONOMICS OF DEMAND

The total revenue, or gross receipts, of a business over any period of time, past, present or future, depends on the price at which it sells its output and the quantity it sells in its several markets. It is from this figure of total revenue that total costs, defined for management purposes in terms of opportunity costs, must be deducted to arrive at a figure for business income or profit.*

If future costs were known and given for each possible volume of sales, the future income or profit of the business would depend entirely on expected total revenue, which would depend in turn on future demand for output. But in any event, demand analysis and the related problem of demand forecasting must have a central place in the business planning process. First, they enable the variables influencing the demand for the firm's products to be identified and understood and used as the basis for the whole planning and budgeting process. Secondly, by showing the forces that determine demand, they indicate how these may be manipulated in planning for profit. This implies an *active* approach to controlling demand and not the mere passive acceptance of forecasts.

The economist's demand curve shows the quantity of a good consumers will buy at every possible price over a relevant range. In all cases, however, the demand curve depicts demand (quantity

*See above, Chapter 3.

demanded) as a function of price. There are at least three types of demand curve: (1) industry demand curve showing the quantity purchased by all consumers of that industry's product at each price; (2) the demand curve for the individual consumer, showing how much he or she buys at each price; (3) the demand curve for the product of the firm, showing how much it can sell at each price —otherwise known as the sales or average revenue curve.

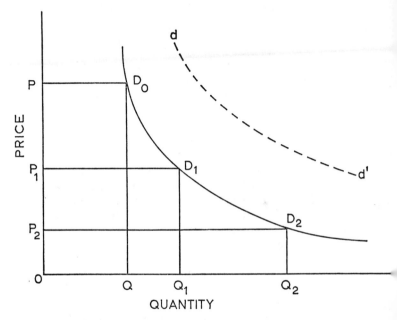

Thus, in the diagram, D_0, D_1, D_2 are points on the demand curve for a hypothetical commodity X. At price OP, a quantity OQ of X will be bought; at OP, quantity OQ, etc. It is logically possible to draw such a demand curve on the assumption that price is continuously variable and that demand varies continuously with price. In practice, however, serious problems arise in 'fitting' a demand curve to limited statistical data. We may note certain fundamental characteristics of the economist's demand curve:

(1) Demand is treated as a function of price, price being the independent variable. Contrary to usual mathematical practice, economists represent price on the vertical axis and quantity demanded on the horizontal axis.

(2) The graph refers to a single point of time, so that all but one of the prices and quantities must be hypothetical. This 'static' assumption implies reversibility of the price-quantity relationship, an assumption unlikely to be borne out in practice. Because a consumer bought a certain quantity at a certain price six months ago, it does not follow that he will buy the same quantity at the same price six months hence.

(3) The demand curve normally has a negative slope indicating that, as price rises, less is bought. Except for a few goods and services of 'snob' appeal, or where the consumer argues that 'it must be good because the price is high', this type of demand curve most readily accords with observed experience. The shape of the demand curve may be explained theoretically in terms of the *substitution effect* and the *income effect*. The former shows that when the price of a commodity falls, other prices remaining the same, the consumer must substitute that commodity for other commodities he had previously bought and which have now become relatively dearer. The latter shows how a fall in the price of a commodity, other things being equal, causes the consumer's real income to rise so that he can now buy a little more of all things—including the good whose price has fallen. The income and substitution effects will normally reinforce each other, causing the consumer to buy more of the good whose price has fallen.

(4) Most important, the price-quantity relationship represented by the demand curve assumes that other things remain unchanged. Clearly price is not the only influence on demand, though it may be the most important. In order to obtain a simple representation of how quantity demanded varies with price, 'other influences' must be ruled out, in particular:

(a) The influence of expected further price changes in the same direction as any given change in price,

(b) Changes in consumer tastes, needs or preferences,

(c) Changes in the prices of related goods,

(d) Changes in consumer income,

(e) Changes in the amount of advertising,

(f) Changes in consumer credit facilities, e.g. mortgage or hire purchase terms.

A change in any one of these things—the parameters—would be represented by a *shift* in the whole demand curve. A rise in income might, for example, produce a new demand curve d d', indicating that, at any price, the consumer would buy more than before. Such a shift in demand is clearly a very different thing from the price-determined change in demand as one moves along a given demand curve. For this reason, vague expressions such as 'rise in demand' are best avoided since they do not make it clear which sort of change we are talking about. What is clear is that demand is a function of many variables (tastes, prices of other goods, income, advertising, etc., and probably many others according to the nature of the goods and services sold) and that such elaborate relationships can only adequately be dealt with by introducing mathematically more complex demand *functions*. The demand curve concentrates exclusively on the price-quantity relationship.

Elasticity of demand

For many purposes we are less interested in the actual quantity bought at any price than in *how much* a price change influences the quantity demanded. This degree of *responsiveness* of quantity to a change in price is termed *elasticity of demand*, which will not be the same for all goods or for different ranges of price on the demand curve for a particular product. One of the most important forces underlying elasticity is the presence or absence of competing substitutes for a commodity. There are no good substitutes for salt or bread and doubling their price might not greatly affect the quantity bought, indicating a relatively inelastic demand. If, however, the price of air travel were doubled the users could turn to railways, buses, private cars and sea travel instead for their holidays and recreation and demand for seats on airlines would probably drop very sharply, indicating a fairly elastic demand.

How do we measure elasticity? One possibility might be to measure the marginal effect of a price change $\frac{\Delta P}{\Delta Q}$, or to use the derivative $\frac{dP}{dQ}$. This measure would give a larger value of 'elasticity', the flatter the demand curve. Actually this formula is concerned with *absolute* changes in price and quantity and it is not very helpful to divide tons or bushels by dollars or shillings and expect to come up with a meaningful result. We therefore employ a measure of elasticity which deals with *proportionate* or *percentage* changes in price and quality. The economist's formula for price elasticity of demand for commodity X is therefore:

percentage change in quantity of commodity X demanded*

percentage change in price of commodity X

This can be expressed mathematically as

$$e = \frac{\dfrac{\Delta Q}{Q}}{\dfrac{\Delta P}{P}} \text{ or } \frac{\Delta Q}{Q} \times \frac{P}{\Delta P}$$

Five categories of elasticity are customarily distinguished:

(1) perfectly elastic demand ($e = \infty$), where no reduction in price is needed to cause an increase in quantity demanded;

(2) absolutely inelastic demand ($e = 0$), where a change in price, however large, causes no change in quantity demanded;

(3) unit elasticity of demand ($e = 1$), where a given proportionate change in price causes an equal proportionate change in quantity demand (and the demand curve takes the form of a rectangular hyperbola).

(4) relatively elastic demand ($e > 1$), where a change in price causes a more than proportionate change in quantity demanded;

(5) relatively inelastic demand ($e < 1$), where a change in price causes a less than proportionate change in quantity demanded.

The formal relationships between elasticity of demand and the firm's total revenue can also be summarized:

	Elasticity less than unity ($e < 1$)	*Unit elasticity* ($e = 1$)	*Elasticity greater than unity* ($e > 1$)
Price RISE	Total revenue RISES	Total revenue UNCHANGED	Total revenue FALLS
Price FALL	Total revenue FALLS	Total revenue UNCHANGED	Total revenue RISES

It should be pointed out that our formula $\dfrac{\Delta Q}{Q} \times \dfrac{P}{\Delta P}$ gives a measure of *arc elasticity*, values of Q and P being the average of the two end values, and measuring average responsiveness over some

*Strictly, since the demand curve has negative slope, a minus sign should be inserted before this formula.

finite stretch of the demand curve. An alternative possibility is to measure *point elasticity* of demand. To do this it is necessary to apply the derivative concept and make change in price and quantity infinitesimally small. Thus, point (price) elasticity of demand=

$$\frac{dQ}{Q} \times \frac{P}{dP} = \frac{dQ}{dP} \times \frac{P}{Q} \text{ (substituting the derivative } \frac{dQ}{dP} \text{ for } \frac{\varDelta Q}{\varDelta P})[1].$$

For management purposes, it may be possible to apply the concept of elasticity to other variables than price. Thus, while

(1) *price elasticity* of demand = $\dfrac{\text{percentage change in quantity demanded}}{\text{percentage change in price,}}$

(2) *income elasticity* of demand=$\dfrac{\text{percentage change in quantity demanded}}{\text{percentage change in income,}}$

(3) *promotional elasticity* = $\dfrac{\text{percentage change in sales}}{\text{percentage change in advertising expenditure,}}$

(4) *cross-elasticity* of demand = $\dfrac{\text{percentage change in quantity of commodity A demanded}}{\text{percentage change in price of commodity B}}$

(Where products A and B are substitutes, then cross elasticity is positive; where products are complements, cross elasticity is negative.)

Other concepts of elasticity could be defined and applied to business decisions and it should also be remembered that markets can be divided up into areas, product groups, etc., and demand concepts applied to each of them.

Economic indicators

For some business purposes, especially forecasting, aggregate demand concepts and appropriate economic indicators may be relevant.[2] The actual and forecast size of gross national product and the magnitude of its components, consumer spending, public spending on current account, together with public and private fixed investment, will influence the demand for products and services of particular industries. These and other macro-economic quantities are important economic indicators. Such indicators are rather like the dials and gauges an aircraft pilot relies on, except that economic indicators show the broad trends of economic activity in the whole economy and in various sectors. Useful statistical relationships between these values and the demand for the output of a particular industry, firm or major product, can often be discovered and used as a basis for business forecasting.

The use of economic indicators has been pioneered in the United States by such bodies as the National Bureau of Economic Research, which first employed them in business cycle analysis. In the past two decades, many useful, reliable and up-to-date statistical indicators have been available in the United Kingdom. Among the most useful are those published quarterly by the National Institute of Economic and Social Research, which also provides quarterly forecasts of the economic situation and occasional forecasts of demand in various sectors of the domestic and world economy, and the reader is referred to recent numbers of *National Institute Economic Review* for an up to date list of them together with explanation.

These data are largely derived from such official publications as the Blue Book on *National Income and Expenditure*, published annually. Other data are obtained from the *London and Cambridge Economic Service Quarterly Bulletin* (published quarterly in the *Times Review of Industry*). The official *Index of Industrial Production* is published monthly in the *Board of Trade Journal* and the *Monthly Digest of Statistics*, which also provide much additional statistical information. In addition, the *Ministry of Labour Gazette* contains statistics on income, prices, employment and production. Data on foreign trade are available in the monthly *Overseas Trade Accounts* and *O.E.C.D. Foreign Trade Statistical Bulletin*. Useful short-term forecasts of demand are also conducted by the Confederation of British Industries in its four-monthly surveys of industrial trends.[3] Since for forecasting purposes it is often necessary to establish some relationship between aggregate economic series and individual company or product demand, such statistical data provide essential information for the business economist.

2. A DIGRESSION ON THE SOCIO-ECONOMIC
ANALYSIS OF DEMAND

Recently, several economists have criticized orthodox micro-economic demand theory because of its apparent neglect of important psycho-sociological factors. Their ideas, when more fully developed, may possibly contribute more to managerial economics than the 'arid formalism' of conventional theory and are therefore briefly mentioned here.[4]

Robin Marris of Cambridge relates his analysis to a dynamic theory of the firm. One way in which the firm can grow is by diversifying its product range. Diversification can be either (a) imitative or (b) differentiated. Marris, following Duesenberry,[5] shows that conventional demand theory is inadequate for the analysis of differentiated diversification, largely because it is a static theory and consumers' demand curves are not independent. The consumer may well be concerned with 'the maximization of the rate of refinement of preferences', rather than the achievement of a stable state within a given system. Thus Marris's theory of demand, instead of considering adjustment to price changes among established commodities, emphasizes the process of inter-personal stimulation and want creation.

People buy a product they have not previously purchased as a result of 'socio-economic' contact and stimulation by another consumer or family, who have already bought one, rather than because of reading or hearing advertisements. Once a person has been stimulated to buy a new commodity in this way, he possesses a 'want' or 'need' where he had none before. Thus, it is argued, demand is largely the result of inter-personal stimulation and want creation, though there must be some *pioneers* as well as *sheep* or things would never get started. Marris describes the characteristic early history of a new commodity in an affluent society roughly as follows: When it is introduced, the number of immediate consumers is small because pioneering is a minority activity. As time passes, pioneering purchasers increase but in the absence of other influences would probably ultimately cease to grow. If pioneers give their contacts a good account of the product, they may, however, stimulate them into purchasing it and these sheep may, in turn, stimulate others. Thus a chain reaction may spread consumption far beyond the pioneering frontier.

Stimulation requires socio-economic contact. One is stimulated by one's friends and sometimes by one's neighbours. But not everyone with whom one is in social contact is a 'socio-economic' contact. 'A socio-economic contact is a person with whom one has a relationship such that his consumption behaviour is capable of influencing one's own.' These tend to be limited to persons with whom one is in general contact, i.e. whom one sees and speaks to fairly regularly and, among them, to those with whom one shares enough relevant values for the contact to be economic as well as social.

Marris's interesting thesis is clearly related to John Kenneth Galbraith's 'Dependence Effect'. According to Galbraith, 'one man's consumption becomes his neighbour's wish . . . the process by which wants are satisfied is also the process by which wants are created. The more wants that are satisfied, the more new ones are born'. Galbraith's theory is less formalized than that of Marris and is part of his larger thesis on the Affluent Society. The following is the nearest he comes to a formal statement of the Dependence Effect:

As a society becomes increasingly affluent, wants are increasingly created by the process by which they are satisfied. This may operate passively; increases in consumption the counterpart of increases in production act by suggestion or emulation to create wants. Or producers may proceed actively to create wants through advertising and salesmanship. Wants thus come to depend on output. In technical terms it can no longer be assumed that welfare is greater at an all round higher level of production than at a lower one. It may be the same. The higher level of production has merely a higher level of want satisfaction. There will be frequent occasion to refer to the way wants depend on the process by which they are satisfied. It will be convenient to call it the Dependence Effect.

Finally, we mention Mr Ronald Brech, formerly head economist at Unilever, who takes the view in a book 'designed to stimulate imagination' that 'long-term economic analysis must include a study of the socio-psychological and sociological aspects, and in particular an analysis of the inter-relationship of economic, psychological and sociological factors determining consumer behaviour'. While it is relatively straightforward to project statistically economic data, Mr Brech points out that it has not as yet been possible to project over time psychological and sociological factors. This is of minor importance for relatively short-term forecasts of, say, five years, as current psycho-socio-economic factors can be assumed to be constant. Equally for the long-term forecast of say twenty-five years, it can be assumed that these factors will have already been fully reflected in monetary demand and personal expenditure. But for the period of ten years, which Mr Brech takes as the half generation, a vital one for business purposes, prediction with any degree of confidence is most difficult, since this involves timing the development of the psychological and sociological trends. Society does not develop at a constant pace and projection of economic trends for periods of around ten years may give misleading results unless socio-psychological factors are taken into account.

Mr Brech also emphasizes the highly complex nature of the demand for products:

> For income to become a status symbol, its size must be demonstrable . . . income must be reflected in the purchase of goods and services, though not necessarily any goods and services, because goods and services demonstrate a particular standard only when society has accepted them as such. This at once raises a complication, since the purchased goods and services that help to form our social-psychological environment are in turn conditioned by that environment, although occupation, education and culture have their part to play.

Recognizing that an adequate psycho-socio-economic analysis of demand has not yet been fully developed, Mr Brech considers the significance, for an adequate theory, of such psychological factors as the new attitude to obsolescence, attitudes to leisure, the significance for social status of products that offer freedom from drudgery and the significance of goods and services that offer freedom from the tension of modern life. Aspects of social changes which affect long-term demand are also considered, such as education, emancipation of the housewife, younger marriages, later retirement and the size of the household. He also discusses the relevance for the analysis of consumer demand of the phenomenon of the 'onion-shaped' society. In today's mass democratic society technological change and re-distribution of income through taxation and subsidy tend to push most people into the middle-income group.

One purpose of this short digression into the socio-economic analysis of demand is to suggest a cautious approach to employing highly formalized techniques of economic forecasting, some of which will be briefly introduced in the next section, without a full and imaginative recognition of the broad psychological and social influences on demand.

26-7-70

3. DEMAND FORECASTING

The importance of demand or sales forecasting to business planning can hardly be over-emphasized. Sales constitute the primary source of revenue for the business, while production for sale gives rise to most of the costs incurred by the firm. The sales forecast is the key to the sales budget which is crucial to the whole comprehensive budgeting process.[6]

A distinction should be made between a *forecast* and a *budget*. A *forecast* is a prediction or estimate of a future situation, which tries to indicate the level of activity which might be realized under given conditions. A *budget* is an objective to be attained as part of a general plan, usually expressed in financial terms and used as a technique of management control. The forecast therefore precedes the plan or budget; the latter being usually intended to change the result from that forecast by changing the conditions on which the forecast was based—for example, by improving the product or by additional spending on sales promotion.

The sales forecast and sales budget are thus crucial since so many other things depend on them. A business normally makes a number of related forecasts, plans and budgets. The sales budget determines the production plans, inventory plans and the level of employment the business expects to offer. It is also used to establish a profit objective, a capital budget and, as the basis of financial planning, to compute future cash flows and sources of funds. Standard costs and variances at some assumed level of output will similarly be computed on the basis of the sales budget.

The sales forecast itself is a concept capable of differing interpretations and applications. There are at least six factors involved in the sales forecast.

First, how far ahead? A business may forecast for any convenient period of time ahead. There is nothing sacred about calendar dates and time periods should be selected which are relevant for the particular business. *Short-run forecasting*, usually defined as any period up to one year, can be distinguished from *long-run forecasting*. The effect of present policies, whether internal, such as sales promotion campaigns, or external, such as tax changes, cannot usually be predicted for more than about a year ahead. Experienced and informed judgement may be more important in the short run than statistical forecasting, though useful numerical methods have recently been developed for short-run forecasting. For long-run forecasts, reliance is usually placed on statistical techniques, though judgement is still required in identifying the variables—more especially those over which management has some control—likely to affect future sales. In the still longer run, any realistic forecast must include a study of socio-psychological aspects discussed above.

Secondly, sales forecasting may be undertaken at different levels. (a) *Macro-economic* forecasting is concerned with business conditions over the whole economy, usually measured by some appropriate index or estimate of industrial production, national income or expenditure. Such external data, nowadays fairly readily available, constitute the basic assumptions on which the business must base its forecasts. (b) Forecasts are made at *industry* level, often by trade associations, which supply the results to their members. These are based on surveys of consumers' intentions and analysis of statistical trends, or the use of simple or multiple correlation based on some general series for the economy, such as disposable income. The business may use such forecasts to compare trends of industry sales with its own current and expected sales and so determine its market share. (c) Forecasts at the level of the *firm* are those with which we are mainly concerned in this chapter.

Thirdly, should the forecast be general or specific? The firm may find a general forecast useful, but it usually needs to be broken down into commodity forecasts and forecasts by area of sales. Many firms require separate forecasts for home and export markets. Selection of products or product groups for sales forecasts must be made with care. Too much detail may obscure the over-all picture; too little may provide an insufficient basis for budgeting purposes. Some businesses make a detailed forecast of the mix of models, styles and accessories.*[7]

Fourthly, problems and methods of forecasting are usually different for *new* products from those for products already well *established* in the market, for which sales trends are known and the competitive characteristics of the product well understood.

Fifthly, it is important to classify products as producers' or capital goods, consumer durables, or consumer goods and services. Economic analysis indicates distinctive patterns of demand for each of these different categories. The demand for capital goods, being a derived demand, usually fluctuates differently from and more violently than final consumer demand. The *acceleration*

*It has been stated that 'the permutations and combinations are so enormous that it would be possible to turn out an entire year's production of over 1.5 million Ford cars and never duplicate any car previously built'.

principle shows how a small change in final consumer demand can cause greatly magnified changes in the demand for capital goods.*[8] Total demand for consumer durables is made up of two parts: part being additions to the existing stock and part the replacement of old products that have worn out. Both are usually, to some extent, postponable in a business recession. According to modern Keynesian economic thinking, final consumer demand is a function of income. As income increases, consumption also increases but at a slower rate. This relationship is not reversible in the sense that once a high level of consumption has been attained it is not quickly abandoned if income should fall.

Finally, in every forecast, special factors peculiar to the product and the market must be taken into account. The nature of competition in the market, how far the situation is complicated by uncertainty or non-measureable risk and the possibility of error or inaccuracy in the forecast must be seriously considered. Sociological factors influencing changes in taste are of dominant importance in some markets, e.g. ladies' hats or hula hoops.

Before considering methods and techniques of business forecasting, we would particularly emphasize that there is no easy method or simple formula which enables an individual or a business to predict the future with certainty or to escape the hard process of thinking:

When all is said and done, none of us can predict major political and military upheavals, to say nothing of natural disasters, and no amount of wishing such problems at the bottom of the sea or pretending that they are already there will be of much help in policy formation and judgement.[9]

This is not to imply that forecasting cannot and should not be made more scientific. Better forecasting can only come from a fuller understanding of the principles governing economic activity and of the inter-relationships between economic variables. A trained economist or statistician, who understands the nature of demand and its determinants, is likely to make a more competent business forecaster than the naive amateur who indulges in irrational guesswork.

There are really two dangers to be guarded against in forecasting. One is that we may be blinded by a mathematical formula. The discovery that consumer sales have, in the past, been influenced by say half a dozen variables which can be formalized into an

*The validity of this principle depends on the assumptions made.

equation, may lead us to believe that this precise formulation represents an eternal truth and, moreover, is the whole truth. In business, however, it is unsafe to rely too heavily on the continuity of history.* Mathematical and statistical techniques are essential in clarifying relationships and providing techniques of analysis but ultimately they are not substitutes for judgement.

But the other danger is that we may go to the opposite extreme and regard forecasting as something to be left to the 'judgement' of so-called 'experts'. The role of judgement in business forecasting should, however, be properly understood. We may agree with Bassie that judgement is one of the prime requisites for good forecasting; the other two being information and analysis, all three being regarded as interacting.[10] Judgement, in this sense, means correctly interpreting information, carefully selecting an appropriate forecasting technique, evaluating forecasts made by others, deciding how much weight to attach to different forecasts and how much confidence to place in what is predicted. Learning from experience is an important part of good judgement, which consequently leans heavily on the use of historical analogy. Analogy however can at best establish only probable inference. It can provide a basis for further analysis, but cannot of itself establish certainty. Because a seasonal cut of 10 per cent in the price of television sets last year was successful in clearing surplus inventory, it does not follow that the same policy will be successful this year. Moreover, judgement is likely to be all the more reliable when expressed quantitatively. In short, what is needed is 'some common sense mean between pure guessing and too much mathematics'.

Fundamentally, there are two approaches to the problem of business forecasting. One is to obtain information about the intentions of spenders by such means as market research, surveys, economic intelligence, etc. The other is to use past experience as a guide and, by extrapolating past trends, to suggest the level of future demand. The first method tends to be used for short-term forecasting, the second tends to be suitable for long-term forecasting. This is by no means invariably the case. Both rely to some extent on judgement. We shall now consider both methods in turn.

*For example, one of the variables known to have affected the demand for bus services in the 1950s was rising ownership of television sets. In the mid-1940s it would have been absurd to have included such a variable in a demand equation and if by the 1970s television ownership is universal such a variable could probably be completely ignored.

The interview and survey approach

The most direct approach to demand forecasting is to ask those who know consumers' future spending plans—principally the consumers themselves. *Field surveys or interviews* may take many forms: they may be made by a company's sales organization, by its headquarters market research staff, by specialized market research and consumer opinion research organizations, etc. The method adopted will depend on the nature of the product and the market.

The simplest case is where a headquarters market research staff regularly obtains market information from a select list of regular customers. Newbury[11] describes a company manufacturing slide fasteners, which, following initial personal contacts, every six months sent out letters to a select list of customers for about twenty different slide fastener applications, each customer being asked to estimate requirements for the next six months.

Many businesses make use of their own *field selling organization* to determine the customers' buying plans. Such sales force surveys might be used to supplement independent estimates made by headquarters' economics and market research staffs and are normally only suitable for short-term forecasting. Where the company has its own sales force, organized on a product and/or district basis, each salesman is asked to estimate sales for say the coming year or six months. A similar procedure may be followed where sales are organized through a main distributor and dealer network. Regular checking and supervision of sales force surveys at a higher level is essential if the results are to be of any use.

Use of the sales force has the apparent advantage of enabling companies to obtain detailed forecasts of sales by product and district without setting up an elaborate new organization for the purpose. There are, however, inherent disadvantages in relying on salesmen's forecasts. Salesmen are probably temperamentally unsuited to forecasting and their estimates are unlikely to be based on objective analysis of economic forces affecting their particular market. A business which, as an afterthought, turns over the unfamiliar job of forecasting to a salesman trained and motivated for the primary task of selling the product, is not likely to get the job well done. Better results are likely to result from interviews based on good contacts at management level between sellers and prospective customers.

Surveying the buying intentions of customers is not a large

problem in industrial markets where the manufacturer is in direct contact with his customer and where buyers are usually large and few in number. If twenty major customers take 85 per cent of total sales, and 500 customers take the remaining 15 per cent, detailed surveys can be concentrated on the intentions of the twenty large buyers, the remainder can be aggregated and a sales forecast made on the basis of past experience.

It may, however, be unwise to rely on the buying intentions of principal customers where there is a substantial time lapse between stated intention and customers' final approved buying plans. This difficulty can be overcome by close and continuous contact between management and forecasting staffs of both seller and customer.

Consumer field surveys—Sample surveys are used in mass markets for standardized products where there are formidable difficulties in discovering the buying intentions of household consumers. It is clearly impracticable to ask millions of potential consumers what they intend to buy. Use is therefore made of sample surveys. Nowadays, with advances in sampling and interviewing techniques and the development of improved statistical methods based on probability theory, consumer surveys can be designed to yield information in considerable detail about consumer intentions in different markets and sub-markets. Much survey work is now carried on by specialized research agencies, such as A. C. Nielsen, the Attwood Consumer Panel, the Government food and expenditure survey, etc. The use of public opinion polls to forecast election results—or more strictly to assess voters' intentions—is perhaps a more familiar application of sample survey techniques. The TAM (television audience measurement) ratings provide information about television viewing. Some agencies regularly supply clients with *current* information about such things as sales performance or consumer acceptance of products. This, of course, is distinct from forecasting *future* sales, though current information may be useful to businesses as a basis for their own forecasts. Agencies can generally provide a service to manufacturers at much lower costs than if each firm had to carry out its own survey.

The design and use of sample surveys requires knowledge of theoretical principles and practical experience. Modern statistical techniques employed in sample surveys can become quite complex and are fully treated in advanced statistical texts. A few general comments may be made here.

A sample survey differs from a census or full count since in the former every unit in which we are interested is included, while the latter takes in only a representative fraction of the whole 'population', but from which we can infer characteristics of the whole. From a carefully selected sample of say, 3,000 consumers we may thus deduce the buying intentions of several million consumers. The reasons for taking a sample are fairly obvious—the sheer impracticability of taking a full count; the speed of collecting information, which is essential if the forecast is to be of any use as a basis of business policy; the greater accuracy of such a survey conducted by specialists; and lower cost.

Fundamental problems in sampling concern inaccuracies in collecting information and sampling errors. These are quite distinct. Inaccuracies in collecting information can only be rectified through improved interviewing techniques and questionnaire design, thus limiting response errors. Even so, infallible forecasts cannot be guaranteed because people do not act as they say they will. Sampling errors are concerned with two things. (a) Bias occurring in the selection of a sample. The sample may not be random in the sense that each unit has not the same chance of being selected. Selecting and interviewing a sample from every tenth name in the telephone directory need not give a valid sample of consumers' spending habits, since ownership of a telephone may be confined to particular social and income groups. (b) Chance errors arise because no sample exactly reproduces the characteristics of the whole population. Provided, however, the sample is a random one, the chance element can be specified in terms of confidence limits. The determination of the size of sample depends on the size of sampling error that can be tolerated. The increased accuracy of a larger sample can usually be obtained only for an additional money outlay. This must be weighed against the costs to the business resulting from failure to minimize sampling error.* The 'best' designed survey can only mean one which minimizes cost for a given error, or minimizes error for a given cost. The selection of a random sample is most reliably carried out with the aid of a table of random numbers. This overcomes the possibility of bias, which very easily creeps into the sample where the investigator relies on subjective or other unscientific procedures. Wherever the personal judgement of the investigator is permitted to influence the selection of the units, the sample will not be properly random. A careful check for these and other sources of bias should be made in assessing the results of a sample survey for forecasting purposes.

*It is an elementary statistical principle that sample error is inversely related to square root of sample size.

F*

Sometimes, it is convenient to divide the population into distinct groups or strata, from each of which a random sample may be taken. Thus, a sample might be selected from a population on the basis of area, income range, etc. Where such supplementary information is used to select the sample, we speak of *stratified random sampling*. In both simple and stratified random sampling, expense of carrying out the sample is a prime consideration. Sometimes there is no ready frame, or list of units of population to be sampled, or population may be constantly changing. Geographical or other factors may make contact with the sample by interview or mail very costly. Cost of carrying out the sample must again be balanced against the money value to the business of having accurate information and the cost of a sample survey should be carefully compared with the cost of other methods of forecasting of comparable accuracy.

While better techniques have made surveys much more reliable in recent years, sample improvement cannot eliminate response errors. Though these can be much reduced by improved questionnaire design and improved interviewing techniques, a basic difficulty remains: the danger of creating information where it does not exist. Respondents may be quite undecided and indefinite about their own intentions. An interviewer, however, can usually get people to 'co-operate' in giving some kind of answer.* When pressed for an opinion the uninformed respondent may make unguarded statements about his intention to buy a new, untested, product which he has never seen, or an old one of which he has no experience. Or a businessman may record 'no change' as an indication of his uncertainty. Both pieces of false information are useless as a basis for forecasting. It is no part of an interviewer's task to create information that does not exist.

Forecast based on composite management opinion. Some businesses determine their sales forecast by asking individuals in a selected group of top management for an estimate of future sales. Independent forecasts may then be reviewed by a committee of top management or by the chief executive. The advantages are said to be that only a minimum of statistical work is required, thus saving costs of surveys, etc., and that a number of different viewpoints are

---

*Or, to quote Mr John Betjeman:

> The mass-observer with the Hillman Minx
> (Unwitting he of all the knowing winks)
> The more he circulates the bitter ales
> The longer and the taller grow the tales.

brought to bear on the forecasting problem. Its weakness is that it tends to substitute opinion for analysis of the situation. Insofar as the opinions of top management are based on experience and carefully considered judgement this may be useful. But judgement, if it is to be of value, should be based on reliable and well ordered information, not on guesswork or the vague reconciliation of conflicting opinions.

A panel of experts may also be used for business forecasting. This method can be carried out on a survey basis or simply rest on the collective judgement of the experts in question. Clearly the selection and composition of the panel—whether from those recognized as good forecasters, or from specialists in some functional field—is important. Much also depends on how the so-called 'experts' carry out their forecasting, whether by systematic analysis or on the basis of their own judgement. A survey of expert opinion is no more or less than the *average opinion* of the 'experts'. While some may have reached their answers by systematic analysis, their opinions are likely to be swamped in the averaging out process by those who have based their opinion on cruder forms of judgement. Frequently, the opinion of a group of experts does no more than reflect the dominant bias which is no better than sounding the general state of business opinion. Indeed, whenever the opinions either of 'experts', the sales force, or a group of top management are used as the basis of the sales forecast, it is pertinent to examine the facts, assumptions and the logic of the arguments by which their results are reached.[12]

Projecting past experience as a method of forecasting
Numerous techniques of forecasting by projecting past experience have been devised in recent years, though the science of forecasting by mathematical methods is still probably only at an early stage of what appears to be a promising development. Most of these techniques are fairly complex and some require considerable mathematical competence. Here we shall consider only a few possible approaches to the problem. For a full discussion the reader is referred to the specialist literature on the subject.

Regression and correlation analysis. This uses statistical and econometric techniques to investigate the nature and extent of relationships between variables. One of the variables may be time. The use of trends and time-series analysis will be discussed later. A time series is a series of values of a dependent variable—e.g. sales—as it changes from one point in time to another. Regression and correlation analysis explores the relation between a dependent variable—e.g. sales—and independent variables—e.g. income, price, advertising expenditure, etc.* Such relationships, established from past data, may be used as a basis for predicting the future. Analysis can be undertaken at varying degrees of complexity. In *simple correlation* the function has only one independent variable— e.g. sales may be shown inversely correlated with price. *Multiple correlation* uses a function in which there are several independent variables. A regression equation may be drawn up to show the relationship between sales and several independent variables. This terminology is briefly explained below.

The use of such analysis in sales forcasting can never be entirely a substitute for sound judgement. Confining attention to the most frequently used linear forms, a past correlation pattern can only be a reliable guide to the future if it can be safely assumed that the same forces will continue to operate in the future as operated in the past, or if an appropriate modification of past patterns can be made on the basis of good judgement. In particular, evidence of a high degree of correlation between two variables does not imply causation. The fact that sales were high in a year when disposable incomes were known to be high resulting in a strong positive correlation between disposable income and sales, does not entitle us to infer that high incomes caused the high sales: strictly all we can infer is that the data are not inconsistent with such a relationship. Reliance on correlation must therefore be based on our knowledge that the two variables are in fact related. Furthermore, even if a valid causal relationship can be established from past data, it cannot necessarily be relied on as a basis for projection into the future for forecasting purposes.† Its use must again be tempered with knowledge of the specific series and careful judgement. Thus qualified, regression and correlation analysis may be regarded as one of the forecaster's most useful tools. The subject can become fairly technical,[13] but the main elements of the analysis are:

(1) determining a curve (in the simplest case a straight line) relation to describe the average relationship between two or more variables. This is often called the regression equation.

(2) determining how well the regression equation describes the relationship between the two or more variables. This can be done by measuring the dispersion around the regression line by

*Or any appropriate macro-economic indicator, as discussed above, pp. 158–9.

†Problems arising from several variables and their possible inter-relationships are briefly mentioned below, p. 178.

computing the *standard error of the estimate* and calculating the actual degree of association between the variables by the *coefficient of correlation*.

The procedure in the first case is simplest in the case of linear regression and it is usually easier to work in graphical terms. A scatter diagram showing the relationship between sales and the association value of a second variable is drawn. The trend of the relationship may be established either by visual inspection or by more exact statistical methods such as fitting a curve or function by the method of 'least squares' or 'maximum likelihood'. The curve can then be expressed as an equation. Where the relationship existing between disposable income X, and sales Y, is linear, b in the equation $Y = a + bX$, where b is the change in Y per unit change in X, is the regression coefficient.

Suppose we draw a graph measuring the X variable on the horizontal and the Y variable on the vertical axis. The X variable might for example be the amount of *advertising* expenditure undertaken by the firm in particular years and the Y variable the money value of *sales* in those years. For each year we thus have a pair of values of the variables X and Y, which can be plotted on a *scatter diagram*.

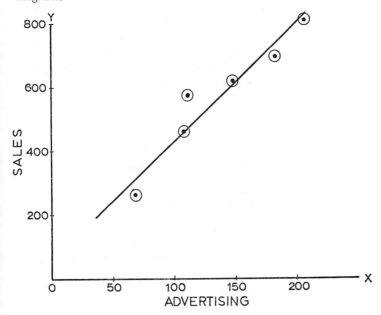

If sufficient data were available, a large number of points would appear on the diagram, and provided some relationship existed between X and Y, an appropriate curve could be fitted to the data.

Confining attention to linear relationships, such a curve could either be drawn freehand, or preferably a statistical technique of curve fitting employed, such that $Y_c = a + bX$, where Y_c is the *computed* value of Y for a given X and a and b are constants which fix the position of the line. The equation expresses the *average* relationship between Y and X (Y_c being different from particular observed values of Y) and is called the *linear regression* of Y on X.

The problem of fitting such a curve to the data involves minimizing the total deviations between plot points (observed values) and the line. This cannot be done simply by drawing the line such that the sum of all such variations is minimized since large negative deviations would largely cancel out large positive deviations. If, however, we square the deviations to get rid of minus signs, we can be certain that our line will fit the data closely, since any large deviations either positive or negative would at once be thrown up. The procedure, therefore, is to draw the line such that $(Y - Y_c)^2$ (the sum of the squares of the vertical deviations of the observed points from the line $Y_c = a + bX$) is minimized. This procedure is known as fitting a curve by the method of least squares.* Other more sophisticated survey fitting techniques exist, such as maximum likelihood, which requires some information about the probability distribution of random influences which influence the values of Xs. This can be a complex and consequently expensive procedure, though standard programmes for computers are now available for use with this technique.

*Mathematically, we require

$$W = \Sigma(Y - Y_c)^2$$
$$= \Sigma(Y - a - bX)^2 \text{ to be a minimum.}$$

By partial differentiation of W with respect to a and b and by equating the partial derivatives to zero, we have

$$\Sigma(Y - a - bX) = 0$$
$$\text{and } \Sigma(XY - aX - bX^2) = 0$$
$$\text{i.e. } \Sigma Y = Na + b\Sigma X$$
$$\Sigma YY = a\Sigma X + b\Sigma X^2 \quad \Big\}$$

These two equations are known as the normal equations for determining a and b and can be solved for a and b. By determining the numerical values for a and b such that these equations hold, then the line $Y_c = a + bX$ will have the property that $\Sigma(Y - Y_c)^2$ is at a minimum. This procedure can be extended to deal with more complex cases of equations containing many variables and various types of curved functions.

The second problem concerns how good is the relationship between the variables—advertising expenditure and sales—as a basis of forecasting the business's sales? This depends on two things: (a) how good is the relationship as an explanation of past behaviour? (b) will the same relationship continue in the future as in the past? (b) is a question of judgment as much as of statistical analysis. (a) can be measured by measuring the extent of the scatter or dispersion of actual values around the regression line. *The standard error of estimate* measures dispersion around the regression line (the relationship between the standard error and the regression line being analogous to that between the standard deviation and the mean in measuring dispersion about the average in frequency distributions). *The coefficient of correlation* does not measure dispersion but rather the strength of the relationship between the variables (income and sales). Where large values of the independent variable are associated with large values of the dependent variable and small values of the independent variable with small values of the dependent variable there is a positive relation. Where large values of a variable are associated with small values of another there is negative correlation. Coefficients of correlation may be between zero and one. Perfect correlation between two variables would give a value of 1, weak correlation would approach zero.*[14]

Multiple correlation considers the dependent variable (sales) as a function of several independent (explanatory) variables (e.g. disposable income, price, age of the goods still in use by consumers, etc.). One of the simplest forms of multiple correlation might consider time and one other independent variable. But it is not always appropriate to consider time and commonly other variables are brought into the picture. In its simplest linear case such a regression equation would have the form

$$X_1 = a + B_2 X_2 + B_3 X_3 + B_4 X_4$$

where X_1 is the dependent variable (sales), X_2, X_3, X_4 are the

*The formula for co-efficient of linear correlation (r) is

$$r = \sqrt{\frac{\Sigma(Y_c - \overline{Y})^2}{\Sigma(Y - \overline{Y})^2}}$$ where $\overline{Y}$ is the mean value of Y.

The formula for the *standard error of estimate* of the regression of Y on X is

$$Sy\,(c) = \sqrt{\frac{\Sigma(Y - Y_c)^2}{N - 2}}$$ where $N-2$ is a divisor and N represents the number of observations.

explanatory variables (e.g. disposable income, price, age of goods still held by consumers), and B_2, B_3, and B_4—the partial regression coefficient—showing the change in the mean value of the dependent variable, X_1 if the explanatory variables X_2, X_3 and X_4 are changed, in turn, by one unit, the other two remaining unchanged. Thus the coefficients B_2, B_3 and B_4 each indicate what a given change in an independent variable—demand determinant—will do to sales, other things remaining constant.

Multiple regression analysis is not confined to linear forms and can involve complicated statistical techniques. Where the analysis is non-linear and is complicated by the addition of extra variables, it is desirable to try and confine the independent variables to those known to affect the dependent variable in some fairly specific way. It is also necessary to ensure that the raw data used is appropriately adjusted. Judgement must always be used in identifying causal relationships and in determining their measurability. While the need to obtain a good relationship is obviously a dominant consideration, complex non-linear regression equations which are statistically valid descriptions of past relationships should be used with extreme care in forecasting. The point is well made by Bassie:

The complexity of the analysis must, of course, be partly a matter of personal preference. But actual experience indicates what might be stated as a general rule: the more a function is complicated by additional variables or non-linear relationships, the surer it is to make a good fit with past data and the surer it is to go wrong at some time in the future.[15]

Ultimately, the concern of the forecaster must be to obtain the best set of future estimates in the light of all that is known about the variables rather than with getting a statistically perfect fit for past data.[16]

Problems of empirical determination of demand relationships. The demand curve introduced in the first section of this chapter was essentially a theoretical device. In practice, a business would like to be able to measure or estimate demand or sales volume in its various markets as a function of say price or advertising expenditure or some other appropriate variable. Or it may wish to determine its future sales from a trend based on time-series analysis of past data. Suppose, for example, that a firm has comprehensive data on its sales volume and advertising expenditure (appropriately corrected for price changes) over a period of years. It could plot advertising expenditure (independent variable) and sales (dependent variable) and proceed to fit a straight line to the data.

	t	t+1	t+2	t+3	t+4
Sales (£000)	450	530	600	680	800
Advertising (£000)	97	104	134	143	169

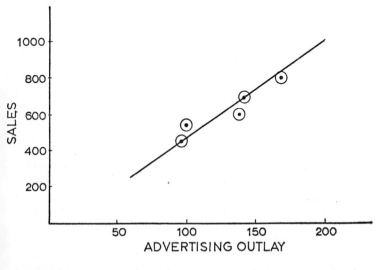

This would appear to give us the firm's advertising demand curve, so that we might be tempted to conclude that certain levels of advertising expenditure would result in a certain level of sales. In practice, however, there are many statistical pitfalls and we are not entitled to draw any such conclusion.

First, it is fairly obvious that there are other variables besides the company's own advertising which could affect the volume of sales, e.g. incomes, prices, other firms' advertising expenditure, changes in consumer tastes, etc. Clearly it would be dangerous to assume that a given change in volume of sales was caused by advertising alone and to ignore all these other possibilities. To meet this problem, it would be necessary to take into account not one but several variables—employing least squares multiple regression technique —in order adequately to analyse a demand relationship, though the usefulness of such methods is no guarantee of correct results, unless all the important variables are included. At the same time this does not mean that every possible variable has to be incorporated. Quite apart from the complexity of the analysis, complete data on all possible variables is seldom if ever available or may be far too expensive to collect.

Secondly, there is the possibility that several of the variables may themselves be highly inter-related. A good example is that of sales volume being determined by both income and years of education per inhabitant. Income and education tend themselves to be highly correlated with each other and it is difficult if not impossible to disentangle their effects on the dependent variable. Similarly price and income time series are frequently used to explain demand, but prices and incomes often rise or fall together and these two explanatory variables are often found to be highly correlated. Inability of statistical procedures to disentangle these effects can easily result in nonsense relationships being put forward. Where, in the demand relationships, there occur several variables themselves highly correlated, it is usually best to omit all but one in any statistical study.

Thirdly, some quite serious statistical problems arise where a number of variables interact mutually and are determined simultaneously. Such simultaneous relationships are quite often met in economics. The statistician's problem is to separate out the relationships from the raw statistical data at his disposal and establish valid causal relationships. This is known as the *Identification Problem*. The application of elaborate statistical regression techniques to the data without having first ascertained whether the simultaneous relationships are identifiable can be quite useless.

The Identification Problem cannot be fully described or its solution explained without the use of fairly advanced statistical and econometric techniques. The important thing in the present connection is simply to know that it exists. The easiest way of describing the dilemma it poses for the statistician is to consider any typical time series of prices and quantity sold. The data consists of a series of points which, since they represent quantity sold, must be the intersection of supply and demand curves, curves being drawn on the usual assumption that quantities supplied and demanded are governed independently by price.*

It is evident that such a series of points could be explained (a) by shifts of the demand curve along a stationary supply curve, in which case the points would trace out a supply curve, or (b) by shifts in the supply curve along a stationary demand curve, in

*These elementary economic concepts are discussed below, pp. 186–7.

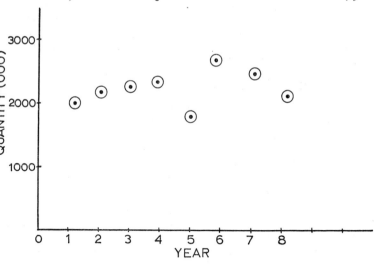

which case the points would trace out a demand curve, or (c) by shifts in both curves, in which case it would be impossible to say whether the points represented the true supply curve, demand curve or something else entirely. This, in essence, is the statistician's identification problem. How does he determine from his raw data which relationship, if any, is stationary? The solution of this problem involves the use of advanced mathematical techniques. Essentially, such tests of whether a relationship is identified rely on seeking out the causes of 'shifts' in demand or supply (or other relationship). Such disturbances or shifts can only be explained by some other influence (or variable) such as income or advertising expenditure in the case of the demand curve. If these variables appear in only one of a pair of simultaneous equations, it is possible for both equations to be identified and more generally:

In a system of n simultaneous equations, a necessary condition for identification in any one of the equations, say the ith, is that every other equation in the system contains at least one variable which is missing from equation i.[17]

This brief mention of problems of empirical determination of demand relationships is inevitably superficial. It is very necessary, however, to be aware of the serious problems that can arise in analysing demand for the firm's products from raw statistical data. Failure to recognize them can result in management decisions being based on quite meaningless statistical results. Normally, such problems are too complex for line management alone to handle and should be referred to professional statisticians or econometricians for expert advice.

Time series analysis and projection of past experience by such devices as trend curves, are being increasingly used in making forecasts for relatively long periods—i.e. periods of more than 2–3 years. The principle is to establish the growth pattern in the past and to suggest, by extrapolation, the future demand for a product, assuming the growth pattern continues unchanged. Such quantitative analysis can help in forecasting the future, though it cannot entirely dispense with the need for 'qualitative' judgements. Generally, projections based on time-series analysis are only valid (a) if non-recurring distortions have been removed from the data and (b) if the influences underlying the trend in the past can be assumed to continue into the future. While there is no 'ideal' trend or method of projection, there are usually advantages in using a straight-line trend. This is simple, easy to fit and is frequently just as logical for forecasting purposes as more complex curves.

Mention should also be made of *seasonal movements*. These may be useful for short-run forecasting. Monthly or quarterly data frequently exhibit strong seasonal movements, fixed in their periodicity, but variable in amplitude. A *seasonal index* enables us to know by how much to discount recent statistics for seasonal change.[18]

Long-term forecasting by mathematical trend curves (the ICI Study).[19] One fairly sophisticated technique of this type has been developed by ICI forecasters. Where a steady growth of demand for a commodity is apparent over a period, a mathematical trend curve may be drawn. In selecting the type of curve a moving average technique* is used to get an approximation to the underlying progress of the market over a limited period. A moving average is obtained by adding yearly demands for successive periods of a given number of years and dividing by number of years. Thus:

5. (Moving average at year t)$=Y_{t-2}+Y_{t-1}+Y+Y_{t+1}+Y_{t+2}$, where Y_t is demand in year t etc.

*In using a moving average, the selection of an appropriate number of years may be most important. This question is not pursued here but is discussed in the textbooks where the limitations of moving averages in dealing with cycles of non-constant amplitude and completely random fluctuations are also explained fully.

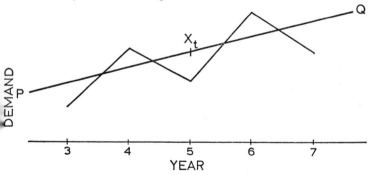

In the diagram line PQ is fitted to the demand data so that any point on such a curve represents 'average demand' at some appropriate time. The midpoint, X_t, gives an estimate of average demand at year t.

The slope of the trend—e.g. PQ is an estimate of slope at year 5— is then taken as a criterion for selecting an appropriate trend curve which is then used as the basis of the forecasting technique. By transforming the original demand data so as to produce a linear relationship with time, it is possible to decide how well a particular type of mathematical trend curve will fit the data and whether it is suitable for forecasting. This technique has been used by ICI and has been described as 'distinctly promising', though it needs to be employed with extreme care and is, like other methods, subject to limitations.

Short-term forecasting by Holt's method [20] This is a technique of forecasting by extrapolation using exponentially weighted moving averages. It was developed in the United States by Professor Holt of Carnegie Institute of Technology and has been successfully used in the United Kingdom by a number of ICI Divisions. The method is particularly suitable for production planning and inventory control for periods of six to twelve months.

Whereas a moving average of say seven months could obviously only cover the period ending with the last month for which data was available, a satisfactory moving average for the most recent months could be found by assuming demand in the next few months to be the average demand of the last few (say seven) months. This might appear to give a better forecast, but its weakness is that it would take as much account of demand six months ago as in the most recent months. Holt's Method uses a technique of exponentially weighted moving averages by which a progressively smaller weighting is given to the most distant as compared to the most recent past months. As we move further back in time the co-efficients attaching to demand in each month form a geometric progression, each co-efficient after the first being a constant fraction of the one preceding it. The formula may have to be modified to allow for changes in trend and for systematic seasonal variations. This calls for judgement. Holt's Method appears to provide a simple and inexpensive numerical routine which gives adequate short-run forecasts for many products. Similar techniques have been developed by Brown,[21] and by Box and Jenkins.[22]

Further problems of forecasting

Forecasting demand for new products. Most of the discussion so far has considered the question of forecasting demand for products already established in the market. The problem of forecasting the demand for new products is in many ways a quite distinct type of problem. Joel Dean has suggested a number of possible methods or approaches to this problem: (1) the evolutionary approach, which consists of projecting the demand for the new product as an outgrowth and evolution of an existing old product. This has obvious limitations. (2) The substitute approach, by which the new product is analysed as a substitute for some existing product. (3) The growth curve approach, which estimates the rate of growth and ultimate level of demand for the new product on the basis of some growth pattern of an already established product. (4) The opinion polling approach, estimating demand by direct enquiry of the ultimate purchasers, either by the use of samples or on a full scale. (5) The sales experience approach, offering the new product for sale in a sample market and estimating total demand for all channels and a fully developed market. (6) The vicarious approach, which consists of surveying consumers' reactions to a new product indirectly through the eyes of specialized dealers who are proposedly informed about consumers' needs. These are just some possibilities for dealing with this problem. To some extent, as in the growth curve approach or opinion polling approach, the methods already described for forecasting demand for an established product can be applied or adapted for new products.

Criteria for desirable sales forecasting procedures. What are the most desirable criteria for testing the usefulness of the sales fore-casting procedure? (1) Plausibility. Management must be able to understand and have confidence in the techniques used. Understanding is essential for a proper interpretation of the result.

(2) Simplicity and ease of comprehension. Elaborate mathematical and econometric procedures may be judged less desirable if management does not really understand what the forecaster is doing and fails to understand the procedure. (3) Economy. There is always the question of how much money and managerial effort should be employed to obtain a high level of forecasting accuracy. Costs must be weighed against the importance of the forecast to the business's operations. There is no point in pursuing very high levels of accuracy at great expense if the forecast is of no great importance to the business. (4) Availability. The technique employed should be able to produce meaningful results quickly; techniques which take a long time to work out may produce useful information too late for effective management decisions. (5) Accuracy. The problem of accuracy is an important one and some check of the accuracy of past forecasts against present performance and of present forecasts against future performance should be made. Some comparison of the model with what actually happens and of the assumptions with what is borne out in practice are most desirable.

Finally, it may be noted that the question of assessing the comparative predictive accuracy of alternative methods of forecasting is very complex. It is however one of obvious practical importance in business decisions. Whatever forecasting method is used, some attempt should be made to follow up the predictions so as to indicate the reasons for poor forecasts. Too little work has been done on this problem by economists and econometricians to offer any conclusive judgement on the matter. The study by Shupack[23] considered several possible criteria of predictive accuracy: frequency of being closest to the actual value; the overall average rank (i.e. consistently high or low over all predictions made); average deviation of prediction from actual values; size of the co-efficients of inequality; ability to predict turning point errors in statistical series. The result of applying these criteria to 387 predictions was inconclusive, as no technique was shown to be significantly better than the others. The 'best' methods on the criteria applied were better than the others only one third of the time (and worse than some alternative two thirds of the time). Perhaps the most important conclusion emerging from this study was the need for improving the specification of the model (equation) used for forecasting purposes and checking it frequently in the light of its predictive accuracy. In the practical application of forecasting techniques predictive accuracy is ultimately more important than over-concentration on finer points of statistical theory.

NOTES

1. This point and other difficulties of measurement of elasticity are fully treated in intermediate texts on economic theory, such as Stigler, *The Theory of Price*, Baumol, *Economic Theory and Operations Analysis*, and Dowsett, *Elementary Mathematics in Economics*. More advanced treatment is to be found in R. G. D. Allen, *Mathematical Analysis for Economists*.

2. Good intermediate treatments of macro-economic analysis are to be found in Ackley, *Macroeconomic Theory*, and Brooman, *Macroeconomics*.

3. See *National Institute Economic Review*, November 1963, for a description of the methods used. On statistical sources generally, see Devons, *British Economic Statistics*.

4. See Robin Marris, *The Economic Theory of Managerial Capitalism*, especially ch. 4; J. K. Galbraith, *The Affluent Society*, especially ch. 11; and Ronald Brech, *Britain 1984. Unilever's Forecast*.

5. Duesenberry, *Income, Saving and the Theory of Consumer Behaviour*.

6. See Newbury, *Business Forecasting*, ch. 15: 'The sales forecast is the keystone of the arch of the structure of planning . . . the sales forecast is the support of a corporation's budgetary programme, of its financial controls, of its planning for production and its inventory stocks'.

7. Footnote quoted from Neil Chamberlain, p. 119.

8. For a full explanation see for example Hansen, *Business Cycles and National Income*, ch. 11.

9. Prest and Turvey, 'Cost Benefit Analysis: A Survey', *Economic Journal*, December 1965.

10. J. Lewis Bassie, *Economic Forecasting*, pp. 3–4.

11. Newbury, p. 250.

12. No mention is made in the above discussion of direct approaches to fore-casting, i.e. direct market experiments. These are rarely used because they are expensive and risky, they cannot be controlled experiments and must inevitably be of short duration. See Baumol, ch. 10, sect. 3.

13. For a full analysis, see Karmel, *Applied Statistics for Economists*, ch. IX; Merrett and Bannock, *Business Economics and Statistics*, ch. 4; R. G. D. Allen, *Statistics for Economists*, ch. 7.

14. This analysis is developed in detail in Karmel, op. cit.

15. Bassie, p. 81.

16. Examples of the use of correlation analysis in forecasting may be found in *National Institute Economic Review*, November 1960, 'The Demand for Domestic Appliances', and September 1961, 'Prospects for the British Car Industry'.

17. See Baumol, p. 228.

18. See Karmel, p. 231, etc.

19. *See ICI Monograph no. 1—Mathematical Trend Curves—An aid to Fore-casting* (1964).

20. This method is fully explained in *ICI Monograph no. 2, Short-Term Fore-casting* (1964).

21. Brown, *Statistical Forecasting for Inventory Control* (1959).

22. Box and Jenkins, '*Some Statistical Aspects of Adaptive Optimization and Control*', J.R.S.S., series B, vol. 24, no. 2, 1962.

23. M. B. Shupack, 'The Predictive Accuracy of Empirical Demand Analysis', *Economic Journal*, September 1962.

9

PRICING POLICY

Trillip brought round the shirts and, to my disgust, his charge for repairing them was more than I gave for them when new. I told him so, and he impertinently replied: 'Well, they are better now than when they were new.' I paid him and said it was robbery.   DIARY OF A NOBODY

1. INTRODUCTION

Pricing is a central concern of economics. People's money incomes are determined by factor prices—e.g. wages and interest—and their real incomes by the prices of the products they buy. Here we consider pricing as a management problem: What should a business's general pricing policy be? Should prices be based rigidly on cost or should they drift with the market? How should prices of particular products be fixed? There are two ways of looking at this. One is to apply techniques of economic analysis and formulate logical pricing rules—the *prescriptive* approach. The other is to study what firms actually do about their prices—the *descriptive* approach. In this Chapter some attempt is made to discuss both.

There are no cut and dried rules for pricing, since each firm, product and market situation have some features that are unique. Three points need to be stressed at the outset. First, pricing is only one aspect of market strategy and the business must consider it together with its product and promotional policies. Secondly, pricing policy clearly depends on business objectives. Many businesses budget for a 'target' level of profit and fix their prices accordingly.[1] Sometimes, however, the forces of competition and the market are too strong to allow much managerial discretion in pricing. Thirdly, pricing policy may or may not be thought a matter of importance for the business. There is some evidence that

pricing policy is taken less seriously by businessmen than economists seem to imagine. One American study (the Brookings study)
of pricing in large corporations found 'that most of the executives
with whom the interviews were conducted did not ordinarily concern themselves with pricing details; instances appeared in which
they were not intimately aware of how their products were priced
. . .'[2] and that 'the administration of the pricing function tends to
reflect the nature of the product and the customs of the trade
appropriate to it'.[3] This is not to be taken as implying that pricing
ought to be regarded with comparative indifference. Questions
which every business must ask are: (1) how important is pricing in
the promotion of its products, in controlling sales volume and
achieving planned profit targets? (2) how adequate is present
pricing policy and organization compared to what ought to exist?

2. THE ELEMENTARY ECONOMICS OF PRICE

Two tools of elementary economic analysis must be understood
before the pricing policy of the business can properly be discussed.
These are:

(1) the principles of supply and demand in competitive markets;

(2) the application of the marginal analysis to the profit-
maximizing firm.

Supply and demand

This well-known analysis applies to the competitive industry and
to competitive markets, the best examples of which are those commodity markets where prices are determined by free competition
among buyers and sellers. In this analysis, the *demand curve* for the
industry is drawn according to the principles outlined in the
previous Chapter. The supply curve is assumed to have positive
slope,* the quantity supplied to the market being shown as a
function of price, assuming that techniques of production do not
change. The supply curve and its elasticity are ultimately explainable in terms of costs.[4] Given the supply and demand curves, there
can be only one price (and output) consistent with clearing the
market. This is the equilibrium price, at which price will settle if
there are no further disturbing forces operating in the market.[5]
Such a price is said to *clear the market*, since there are no unsatisfied

*Though some writers have argued that, for manufactured products, the supply
curve of any one industry is perfectly elastic.

buyers or sellers. Equilibrium does not imply 'a state of sodden inertia',[6] but may represent the cancellation of powerful forces.

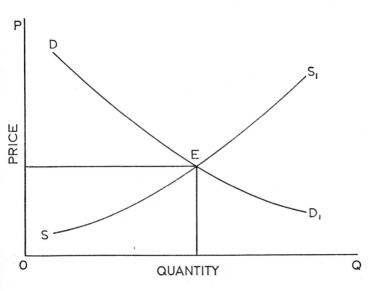

Supply and demand curves showing equilibrium price at E

Equilibrium will be disturbed and eventually re-established at some other price and output if the 'parameters' change, causing the whole curve of demand or of supply to shift upwards or downwards—e.g. if fundamental changes in technology or prices of inputs were to occur, the supply curve would shift bodily resulting in a new equilibrium price. We may also note that the equilibrium of supply and demand need not always be stable. Cases do occur where the mechanism apparently works in the wrong direction and prices instead of tending towards equilibrium may exhibit violent fluctuations without ever reaching equilibrium.[7] Fortunately such cases are comparatively rare, but they are known to occur with some agricultural products.

How is this analysis related to the pricing policy of the firm? Near perfectly-competitive markets of the type we have just been analysing exist mainly for staple commodities. *The Financial Times*, for example, lists commodity prices every day for base metals such as lead, zinc, copper, tin, for cocoa and coffee, shipping freights, grains—i.e. wheat, maize, oats, barley—rubber, sugar, jute, wool and meat. Normally, only businesses concerned with primary or non-manufacturing production would be concerned with the production and sale of such commodities and hence would be obliged to accept the going market price for them. Nevertheless, the Brookings study cites several large American corporations whose pricing policy is dominated by acceptance of going market prices. For example, in the meat packing business, Swift and Co.'s selling as well as buying operations were found to be determined largely by the market.[8]

The marginal analysis

Economic theorists employ the marginal technique to analyse output and pricing policies of the profit-maximizing firm. The use of the marginal tools could, however, be applied to other types of maximizing behaviour. Until recently, economic literature on price and output determination has assumed a firm interested in maximizing profit. The simplest models of profit-maximizing behaviour assume that the firm produces one product and has full knowledge of its costs and revenues over relevant changes of output. This is clearly an over-simplification. However, the rules of rational business behaviour can best be derived from simple analytical models.

The marginal analysis is concerned with a maximization problem. It is essentially mathematical and can be precisely stated in terms of the calculus.[9] The general rule of marginalism is however intuitively obvious once we have a clear understanding of the nature of cost and demand conditions encountered by the firm. As regards *costs*, it has already been shown* that average cost, AC, at any output

$q, = \dfrac{TC}{q}$ (where TC is total cost) and marginal cost, MC,

$= TC_q - TC_{q-1}$. Similarly, on the *revenue* side, given the demand curve for the firm's products, average revenue, AR, for any output

$q, = \dfrac{TR}{q}$ and that the marginal revenue, MR, $= TR_q - TR_{q-1}$.

Given these marginal amounts, the marginal rule then states quite simply that the firm will reach its profit maximizing output where MC and MR are equal. Any other output must be less profitable to the producer.

*Chapter 6.

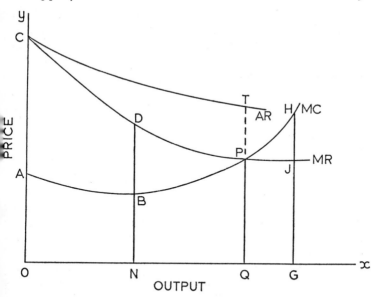

In the diagram, MC and MR are the marginal cost and marginal revenue curves of the profit maximizing firm. If we exclude fixed costs which represent commitments already entered into and are not therefore relevant to present decisions about pricing and output, the area under the MC curve measures the total (variable) costs of producing any output. Similarly the area under the MR curve measures the total revenue from the sale of any output. The area of maximum profit is APC for output OQ at which the marginal cost curve intersects the marginal revenue curve.* At outputs below OQ, for example ON, the area of profit is less. At higher outputs, for example OG, PHJ representing a loss must be deducted from the profit area APC, leaving the firm worse off than at OQ. The general rule of marginalism may therefore be re-stated:

In making a business decision, if an alternative leads to a greater increase in revenue than it costs it will increase profits and should

*This is a necessary condition of equilibrium of the firm. The sufficient conditions for equilibrium are that marginal costs should equal marginal revenue and that the marginal cost curve should cut the marginal revenue curve from below.

be decided on. If it leads to a greater increase in costs than in revenue it should be rejected. This test can be applied either to proposed increases or decreases in output or to proposed decreases or increases in price which automatically determine the quantity of output that can be sold in any market.

In mathematical terms, 'marginal' cost and 'marginal' revenue are concerned with infinitesimally small changes in cost and revenue. For practical business purposes it is more useful to speak of incremental cost and incremental revenue which refer to finite changes in costs and revenues associated with a variation of output or other business decision. It should be noted that the marginal rule tells us how to maximize profit. It does not of itself tell us what price to charge at the profit maximizing output. The price appropriate to that output must be determined from the firm's demand or average revenue curve, which, like the marginal revenue curve, is derived from the total revenue curve if this is known to the business. The elasticity of the average revenue or demand curve depends on the degree of competition in the particular market.

Economic theory employs the marginal analysis to show how the firm reaches equilibrium in differing market environments. Attention is usually given to the size of output and to the relationship between Marginal Cost and Price in order to discover the effects of particular pricing policies on the economic welfare of consumers. This particular application is little used for business purposes, but the general approach of marginal theory is highly relevant for management decisions. Some applications of this and closely-related techniques are:

(1) the analysis of oligopoly;
(2) multiple products and inputs and price discrimination;
(3) sales maximization.

(1) *The analysis of oligopoly.** Oligopoly is a complex problem and cannot be entirely interpreted by the marginal analysis. One explanation however takes note of the allegedly observed fact that prices in oligopoly tend to be rigid and proceeds on this assumption. This does not enable us to determine theoretically how price is originally set at this level but the analysis can be used to show why, once such a price is established, a firm will avoid changing it. In the diagram the firm's demand curve, APB, is really made up of two demand curves. One assumes that its price changes will not be

*i.e., competition among a few firms, see above, p. 84.

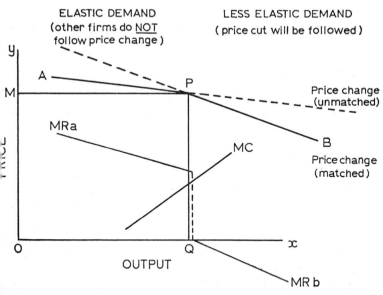

matched by competitors, the other that they will. Thus, if price is raised above P along PA, the producer is alone and loses sales heavily and because demand is elastic, gets a smaller total revenue because other firms do not raise their prices. Moving down from P to B, however, others respond swiftly to price cuts and, if demand is *in*-elastic, yield the producer a smaller total revenue. Determination of actual profitability at different prices and outputs would of course require knowledge of the appropriate cost curves.

(2) *Multiple products and inputs; price discrimination.* Marginal analysis is used to show that a multi-product firm wishing to maximize profits should allocate its scarce productive inputs in such a way that marginal revenue from any input, i, in the production of a product, X, is the same as for products Y and Z. In other words, the firm must adjust its resources so as to get equal marginal net revenues (profits) per unit of input from all products: $MNRx = MNRy = MNRz$. Any other arrangement would mean that the firm could still get higher profits by shifting some resources from products of low *marginal* return to those of high *marginal* return.

Price discrimination may be profitably practised where the firm has some 'monopoly' power, usually through product differentiation, where it sells in separate 'markets' of differing demand elasticity and where it is difficult to transfer the product from one market to another. Marginal analysis shows that profits will be maximized when: (1) output is adjusted so that marginal revenue in each separated market is the same; (2) a higher price is charged in the less elastic market; (3) total output over all markets is determined by setting marginal revenue equal to marginal cost.[10] This analysis assumes that identical 'products' are sold at different prices to different groups of customers. Where different 'products' are sold in different markets, the principle of allocating scarce inputs, previously discussed, would apply. Price differentials would be determined by differing elasticities of demand in the various markets, but need bear little or no relation to differences in cost of production. A good example is found in different classes of sea or air travel. The same reasoning underlies the principles of 'selective selling':

If sales of higher Contribution rate items can be increased, even at the cost of an equal reduction in sales of lower Contribution rate products, aggregate Gross Contributions and hence profits can be raised. For example, if the sales of high Contribution rate 'speciality' prices can be increased, profits will rise, even if dollar sales of some Contribution rate 'staple' lines fall off by an equal amount.[11]

The fundamental principle of substitution at the margin is also applied to the problem of choice of inputs to produce a given output. It can be shown in this case that the condition for the firm to maximize profit will be to hire inputs in such proportions that the marginal revenue products of all inputs used are proportional to their prices.*

$$\frac{MRPa}{Pa} = \frac{MRPb}{Pb} = \frac{MRPc}{Pc}$$

For any other arrangement of inputs it would always pay to hire less of one input and substitute more of another. In practice, neither inputs nor products can be easily switched around and knowledge of costs, prices and profits involved in the different arrangements is usually far from complete.

(3) *Sales maximization under a profit constraint.* Maximization of sales refers to maximization of the total revenue of the business, which may be a desired business goal as a measure of business effectiveness, or for reasons of stability. At the same time, however,

─────────

Marginal revenue product of an input is the increase in total revenue received by the firm by acquiring one additional unit of this input.

the business must earn an adequate profit in competition with others, so that a profit constraint must be built into the model. In the diagram, the profit maximizing output is OQp and sales maximizing output is OQs.

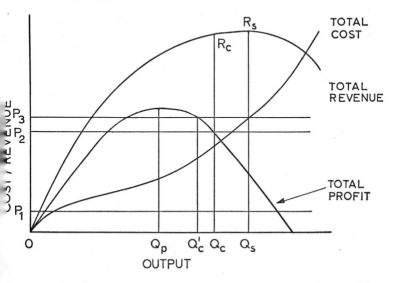

If the firm is satisfied with a profit level OP_1, sales maximizing output OQs will yield more than the minimum required profit. If, however, the firm wants OP_2, sales maximising output OQs will not yield enough. Output will then be reduced to OQc, which gives the maximum Total Revenue subject to the profit constraint. This particular model has been applied by Baumol to the oligopolistic firm.[12]

Economic theory provides a logical framework for business decisions relating to pricing problems. Its assumptions are much simpler than reality; in particular information is less readily available to a business than economic analysis assumes. Theorizing or model-building does, however, enable us to concentrate on a few relevant things and investigate their logical relationships. Theory may also be useful in pointing out areas of ignorance where further information should be sought by the firm. The marginal analysis although not always obviously applicable to the problems of a particular business is logically superior to many of the 'rules of thumb' used by many businesses in their pricing and output

G

policies and also to naive break-even charts or full-cost pricing policies which are widely used.

Marginal analysis and the use of the calculus applies to the problem of maximization where precise specifications are required to be met. In many business problems the specifications are not precise but provide for *minimum* requirements such as minimum costs or quality standards, or may require optimum production levels to be attained subject only to a certain maximum capacity being available. An acceptable solution need not meet the stated requirements precisely, but only need to fall within the minimum or maximum. Where such 'side conditions' are inequalities rather than equations, marginal analysis is generally incapable of finding a solution and resort must then be made to programming techniques, discussed above in Chapter 6.

3. INNOVATION: PRICING OVER THE LIFE CYCLE OF A PRODUCT

Robin Marris has shown that a firm whose catalogue contains none but 'saturated' products will experience growth only from secular trends.[13] Growing firms must either imitate products which others have already successfully pioneered or introduce new products themselves. How might the firm set about pricing innovations or sharply differentiated products? The monopoly pricing solution has to be rejected because very few products are so 'distinctive' that they last without imitation for more than say five or ten years. Few monopolies are permanent and it is safe to assume that most new products that are distinctive at the outset will degenerate over the years into common commodities. It is therefore better to look at the problem as one of pricing products of 'perishable distinctiveness'. The process by which the distinctiveness gradually disappears as the product merges with other competitive products has been aptly named by Joel Dean 'the cycle of competitive degeneration'.[14] It begins with the invention of a new product, and is often followed by patent protection and further development to make it saleable. This is usually followed by a rapid expansion in sales as market acceptance is gained. Then competitors enter the field with imitations and rival products and the distinctiveness of the new product begins to diminish. As its distinctiveness diminishes, the producer's pricing independence is lessened as the innovation fades into a pedestrian commodity. This is fairly typical of what happens to many manufactured products—e.g.

ball point pens, transistor radios. Throughout the cycle, changes occur in demand price-elasticity and promotional-elasticity and also in production and distribution costs. Pricing policy must therefore be adjusted over the various phases of the cycle, bearing in mind that the rate of degeneration over the cycle may be controllable.

We shall now examine briefly the pricing of a new product: (1) in the pioneer stage, and (2) in the mature stage of the product's development.

Pioneer pricing

This involves some difficult initial problems that cannot be enlarged on here. For example: (1) estimating demand for an entirely new product; (2) discovering a competitive range of price; (3) investigating probable sales from several possible prices; (4) considering the possibility of retaliation from replaced products. Assuming, however, that these problems can be solved, the important question is whether a *high* initial (skimming) price should be charged or a *low* price to penetrate the market.

(a) *A high skimming price*, together with heavy promotional spending, may be used to launch the product if conditions are appropriate. Its possible advantages are:

(i) demand is likely to be less price elastic in the early stages than later, since high prices are unlikely to deter pioneering consumers;[15]

(ii) such a policy can provide the basis for dividing the market into segments of differing elasticity.

(iii) it is the 'safe' policy where elasticity is not known and the product not yet 'accepted'.

(b) *A low penetration price* is the reverse of the skimming price, but in certain conditions can be successful in expanding the market rapidly thereby obtaining larger sales volumes and lower unit costs. It is appropriate where:

(i) there is high short-run price elasticity;

(ii) there are substantial cost savings from volume production;

(iii) the product is acceptable to the mass of consumers;

(iv) there is a threat of potential competition so that a big share of the market must be captured quickly.

Pricing in maturity

The problem here is to decide on a pricing policy for the later stages of the cycle, after imitators have invaded the market of the once unique product. The symptoms of 'competitive degeneration' should be looked for and these are likely to be:

(1) a weakening of preference for the leading brand, which will no longer stand as much price premium;

(2) reduced physical variation among products, as the best designs, etc., are discovered;

(3) market saturation, usually indicated by an increase in the ratio of replacement sales to new sales;

(4) stabilization of production methods, as cost reduction resulting from innovation is fully achieved.

It is most important to discover when the product is about to enter the mature category and to reduce price when the first symptoms appear. *Appropriate* price reductions, depending on estimated demand elasticity, should be made, *not* an open price war instituted. With the entry of competitors, the problem becomes one of oligopoly.

Oligopoly pricing

In markets of few competitors *interdependence* in decision making becomes the dominant consideration.* Each manufacturer is aware of the disastrous effects that an announced reduction of his own price would have on his competitors' prices. The appropriate pricing policy therefore becomes a problem in *strategy* and it is impossible to make sweeping generalizations about it, though if the problem can be sufficiently formalized, decision theory can work out rational solutions to particular types of problems of oligopolistic strategy. As in chess, measuring the mind of one's opponent is not an exact science, and the oligopoly problem can become exceedingly complex. We can however lay down a few general principles of oligopoly pricing:

(1) If a rival cuts his price, it is better to match the cut than to undercut his price.

(2) The fact that each seller knows that a price cut will be met promptly usually destroys the effect of overt price cuts as a means of extending market shares.

*The logic of price stability under oligopoly was briefly discussed above, p. 191.

(3) Price reductions, once made, are not easily reversible.

(4) Open price competition in oligopoly usually degenerates into an open price war.

(5) As was explained above, many businesses in this situation believe that their demand curve is *in*elastic for price cuts but elastic for price increases.

(6) Most oligopolists do not use price changes as their main competitive weapon but prefer rigid prices.

(7) Rigid prices cannot be held to uncompromisingly in a dynamic world. Therefore businesses tend to resort instead to other devices such as (a) non-price competition, (b) price leadership, (c) collusion, as an escape from the dilemma posed by the need to adjust to a changing business environment, with the need to maintain a precarious oligopoly price structure. However, price leadership and collusion may be restrained by law as 'restrictive practices'.

4. PRESCRIPTIVE: ALTERNATIVE PRICING CONVENTIONS

Probably most businesses do not consciously employ marginal techniques in their pricing policies, though there is some evidence that the best managed firms do.[16] What other pricing prescriptions do businesses use? Such prescriptions for pricing might be advocated by accountants, or trade association manuals, or are simply conventions generally adopted in the trade.

Break-even analysis

Break-even (or cost/volume/profit) analysis is not so much a pricing policy as an analysis for profit planning. As was indicated in Chapter 6,* it shows in a simplified form how costs, revenues and profits will vary with output, other things being equal.

Probably the most useful application of break-even analysis is to enable management to decide whether or not to enter on a particular branch of production. It does not tell us exactly what output to produce or indeed how to price, but simply at what level production becomes profitable. It is claimed to be an advantage of break-even charts that costs and revenue at two levels of output only need be known in order to construct the chart. This is substantially less information than is needed in marginal analysis.

*See above pp. 114–16.

However, since break-even charts are constructed on such limited information, such analysis can mislead if the highly-simplified nature of its assumptions is not sufficiently understood. In particular, all values other than those used in the construction of the chart are assumed values and linearity of revenue and cost functions may be an over-simplification. Thus as a device for profit planning, break-even analysis can give approximate results only. It may aid decision-making where information is not available, is costly to obtain or where management must make decisions quickly.

Full-cost pricing

Many businesses believe that prices should bear some fair or equitable relation to costs. The idea that 'the perfect sales price is the sum of all costs plus the profit which will yield the goal return on capital employed'[17] is typical of the approach of many businesses to pricing their products. Full-cost pricing means pricing at a level covering total costs, including overheads and selling expenses plus a pre-determined mark-up. The term 'cost-plus pricing' may be taken as broadly synonymous. The term 'gross margin pricing', as used in retailing and wholesaling operations, means a mark-up related to direct costs, whereas full-cost pricing normally refers to a mark-up related to total allocated cost.

A number of studies, beginning with the well-known pre-war study by a group of Oxford economists published in 1939,* have shown that businesses commonly set their prices by taking cost and adding a fair or conventional profit percentage. Sometimes a rigid pre-determined mark-up is applied to costs; alternatively, the mark-ups are flexible, varying with business conditions. An example of a full-cost, formula-determined price might be as follows:

Cost of materials and direct labour

+percentage addition to cover overheads (say 100 per cent)

+a percentage addition for selling expenses (say 25 per cent)

+a conventional margin for profit (say 10 per cent)

Such a formula probably over-simplifies what firms do about their pricing. More complex approaches may require a differential allocation of the overhead component and selling expenses according to the product. Nevertheless, many small businesses do apply

*Discussed in section 5 of this Chapter.

naive full-cost pricing in a mechanical way[18] largely in the belief that costs are a firm and definite basis on which to fix price. The weaknesses and limitations of such a policy must be pointed out. The definition of 'cost' itself is beset with difficulties and the cost component in the pricing formula may be quite arbitrary. 'Costs' may be (a) 'actual' cost, by which is usually meant historical cost, or (b) expected cost, which is a forecast of actual costs on the basis of existing prices, output rates, etc., or (c) standard cost, which is a conjecture as to what cost would be at some 'normal' rate of output. In none of these cases can 'cost' be regarded as definite and un-equivocal. It can, moreover, be a mistake to mark up bought-in materials and compute selling price as a fixed percentage of their cost. The correct basis for mark-up is *net output* or *value added* by the firm. Otherwise, disproportionately high prices will be charged simply because expensive materials are used, a fact which is irrelevant to the firm's own handling, conversion or selling ex-penses. In a competitive situation, such a policy could result in loss of markets.[19]

Only in the least sophisticated forms of full-cost pricing is a pre-determined mark-up rigidly applied. In more elaborate conven-tions an average mark-up on costs is computed to produce a planned rate of return on the company's investment in accordance with the firm's budgeted objectives Quite often formula prices are adjusted by the 'flexible mark-up', largely influenced by competi-tors' prices and market pressures from the demand side. Cross-sectional flexibility by customers and product lines may enable management to adapt pricing to the conditions facing a potential commodity. Variability of mark-up may be based on such factors as cost advantages or disadvantages over competitors, strength of desire to expand market share in a given product line, possibility of market segmentation, general economic situation, extent of present and potential competition, selling effort, growth plans, etc. Demand factors and adaptation to market conditions thus assume considerable importance in more sophisticated formula pricing. Some large businesses use full cost as a reference point or a useful guide to pricing, often indicating a minimum below which the business does not consider it prudent to lower prices. Actual prices may be flexible over time according to demand. Probably no full-cost formula could ever completely neglect demand, since cost per unit of output is itself a function of the level of sales.

We cannot discuss here the wide variety of full-cost formulae used by businesses. In its cruder, 'naive' forms, full-cost pricing can, however, be criticized for several obvious reasons:

(1) it ignores demand;

(2) it fails adequately to reflect the forces of competition;

(3) it exaggerates the precision of allocated costs;

(4) it may be based on a wrong conception of cost.

Incremental and future costs may be more relevant for pricing decisions than average or past costs. Full-cost pricing usually ignores this.

Why then do so many businesses adopt this pricing convention instead of the marginal approach? The answer is not straightforward because businesses vary so greatly in size, product characteristics and product range, and face varying degrees of competition in markets for their products. Some reasons why businesses do adhere to the convention of full-cost pricing are:

(1) It is said to be an ideal at which firms aim, rather than an attainable objective.

(2) Firms do not want to maximize profit. Prices based on full costs are thought to be 'fair' to consumers and competitors.

(3) Full cost is said to be the 'logical' way to maximize long-run profits. Long-run prices tend to equal cost of production in classical economic theory.

(4) Price changes are costly and inconvenient to salesmen.

(5) In practice, businesses are uncertain about the shape of their demand curve and about the probable response to any price change. This makes it too risky to move away from full cost in pricing.

(6) Businesses prefer stability and full cost is used as a guide to pricing in an uncertain market where knowledge is incomplete. This may be preferable to the high costs of getting information and the costly process of trial and error which marginalism seems to imply. Thus, full-cost pricing is not necessarily antithetical to marginalism or profit maximization. It reduces the costs of decision making.

(7) It is argued, in partial justification of full-cost pricing, that most alternative policies require that marginal (direct) cost should actually be identified and computed. This is difficult, except *ex post*, when the information may no longer be of much use for pricing. Past full costs, it is argued, may give the best possible

indication of long-run incremental costs and pricing is a long-run decision.

These reasons provide some explanation for the widespread use of full-cost pricing, but do not justify it as the logical approach to pricing. It provides no escape from the great difficulties of cost identification and allocation already discussed in Chapter 6. Direct costs still need to be calculated and a proper basis for the identification and allocation of fixed costs decided. There are, moreover, difficulties in relating the mark-up to cover overheads to the (unknown) future volume of sales. According to the full-cost formula, if one expected business activity to decline, one should logically increase this mark-up and, therefore, price. Common sense suggests that this would be highly imprudent.

Full cost is a pricing convention relying on arbitrary costs and arbitrary mark up. It is adopted because it is simpler to apply. It does not follow that it is in any sense the logical formula for optimal pricing where business objectives are known and uncertainty is taken into account. Generally, a business would do better to consider first whether better estimates of incremental cost and demand could not be obtained without great expense before applying a prescription for pricing policy which gives inadequate consideration to demand and may attribute false precision to existing cost estimates.

Going rate pricing

The opposite expedient to full-cost pricing is going rate pricing.* Whereas in naive full-cost pricing the emphasis is on cost of production, in going rate pricing it is on the market. In its simplest form, the going rate pricing prescription is simply to examine the general pricing structure in the industry and fix one's own price accordingly. Where costs are particularly difficult to measure this may seem the logical first step in a rational pricing policy. Many cases of going rate pricing are situations of price leadership. Where price leadership is well established, charging according to what competitors are charging may be the only safe policy. Going rate pricing may simply be a way in which firms contrive to escape the hazards of price rivalry in an oligopolistic market. It may be less costly and troublesome to the business than the exact calculation of costs and demand and superficially seems to have practical advantages over a highly individualistic pricing policy.[20]

*This should not be taken to imply that these are mutually exclusive. In a number of organizations, they are used together.

H

Certainly, going rate pricing is not confined to small and medium-sized businesses. The Brookings study shows how some large American companies faced what they regarded as a market-determined price and adopted a practice of 'following competition', usually implying following a price set either by the market or by a price leader. Going rate pricing is not, however, quite the same as accepting a price impersonally set by a near perfect market. Rather it would seem that the firm has some power to set its own price and could be a price maker if it chose to face all the consequences. It prefers however to take the safe course and conform to the policy of others.

Some firms follow a policy of tailoring the cost of a product to a pre-determined price. Clothing, automobiles and long-playing records are examples. These are familiar products which have reached a mature stage of their development and where both customers and rival producers have come to accept stable price relationships. Prices must be carefully set in relation to competitors' selling prices—i.e. demand and the market. Once that is done, costs must be kept within percentage limits of selling price in order to achieve profit objectives. The problem is essentially one of costing and of controlling costs at some standard output in order to provide a 'target' profit at a carefully pre-determined price. In contrast to a cost-plus theory of pricing we thus have a 'price-minus theory of cost'.[21] Such a policy must not, however, be pushed too far. Essentially some balance has to be struck between the need to price appropriately within a narrow range of competitive prices and the need to produce a product which is competitive in style and quality standards. For a business caught between such a Scylla and Charybdis it might appear that such a delicate balancing of cost and revenue is not very far removed from the economist's marginal principle.[22]

5. DESCRIPTIVE: HOW FIRMS ACTUALLY PRICE THEIR PRODUCTS

There are still many gaps in economists' knowledge of how firms actually do price their products. More research needs to be done on this subject, though business managements are not always quite certain of what principles they do follow, or resort to rationalization when closely questioned on the subject. Recent studies have used the case approach involving intensive interviews with senior company officials and follow up at lower levels. This method has elicited more reliable information regarding business pricing policies than earlier questionnaire methods. A few of the more important studies are:

(1) The Oxford study of Price Theory and Business Behaviour by Hall and Hitch, published in the United Kingdom in 1939;

(2) James S. Earley's study of Marginal Policies of 'Excellently Managed' Companies, published in the United States in 1956;

(3) The Brookings Study of Pricing in Big Business by Kaplan, Dirlam and Lanzillotti, published in the United States in 1958;

(4) The University of Kentucky study of Pricing Decisions in Small Business by W. Warren Haynes, published in the United States in 1962.[23]

The Oxford study

This pioneer study was undertaken by a group of Oxford economists in the late 1930s. Evidence from thirty-eight entrepreneurs interviewed on their pricing and output policies appeared to show that most did not aim at the maximization of profits by equating marginal costs with marginal revenue. Most of the firms were oligopolists with or without product differentiation. The explanation for their pricing policy appeared to be (1) that they were thinking in terms of long run rather than immediate profits—i.e. 'taking goodwill into account', and (2) they were thinking in altogether different terms from economists and applying a rule of thumb, namely full cost. An overwhelming majority thought that a price *based* on full average cost (including a conventional allowance for profit) was the right price, the one which ought to be charged, though most explained that they did not actually charge 'full cost' price. A few admitted that they might charge more in periods of exceptionally high demand; and a greater number admitted that they might charge less in periods of exceptionally depressed demand. Intensification of competition appeared to induce firms to modify the margin for profits which could be added to direct costs and overheads so that approximately the same price would rule for similar products within the 'group' of competing products. Both formal price leadership and unconscious price agreement was evident from the investigation.

Earley's study of 'excellently managed' companies

Earley's study was based on the replies to a questionnaire sent to 217 manufacturing companies rated as 'excellently managed' by the American Management Association, of which 110 returned usable replies. His conclusions claimed, however, to have relied on inference rather than direct questions, fortified by a search for patterns of response and tests of consistency. According to Earley, *non-marginalist* behaviour was defined as emphasizing a long-run defensive viewpoint in pricing, production and investment policy, rather than an alert attitude towards near-at-hand profit opportunities. It was also alleged to use in the main full-cost rather than incremental cost calculus in pricing, production and investment decisions.

Marginalist behaviour, on the other hand, according to Earley, implied such techniques as 'marginal accounting'. This, as practised by well-managed, multi-product companies, included such things as segmentation of costs and revenues—by market area, division, plant, etc.—and segmentation in organizational structure, each sector being a profit-making entity. It also embraced marginal techniques of planning and decision, policy making being associated with a short-dated time horizon and a lively sense of impending innovation and obsolescence.

Earley claimed to have found substantial evidence of a dynamic marginalism in these 'excellently managed' companies. There were so many exceptions to uniform full-cost pricing that it had ceased to be recognized as an objective, and he found little support for the full-cost, long-run view of business behaviour. He concluded that short views, innovational sensitiveness, marginal costing and marginal pricing were preponderant, but that marginalism was not dependent on—though it was increased by—a short-time perspective. Most of these 'excellently managed' companies did not see short-run versus long-run profitability as alternative and inconsistent goals. They tried in a dynamic setting to increase their current profits within their long-range horizons. The type of marginalism practised was not marginalism 'sitting', but a dynamic marginalism 'on the wing'.

The Brookings study—pricing in big business

The Brookings survey of giant American business corporations was made in the 1950s. It was based on a series of interviews with the top management of a representative group of large-scale enterprises engaged in primary production, manufacturing and distribution. Pricing decisions appeared to be considered by most managements as only a part of the general strategy for achieving a broadly defined corporate goal. Nevertheless, it proved possible in this study to distinguish five broad patterns of corporate pricing policy. For most of the large organizations there was clear evidence of predominance of one such policy, but 'it would be absurd to pretend that all price making by any one company was ruled by a single policy'. 'Profit maximization' was thought to be too narrow to describe corporation policies and not operationally meaningful. But profit making was a guiding principle among all the companies. The five broad classifications of corporate pricing policies were:

First, *pricing to achieve a target return on investment*, which was the most frequently stressed of company pricing goals. More than one third of the corporations studied mentioned it and it was the predominant pricing policy of General Motors Corporation, International Harvester Company, Aluminum Co. of America, E.I. du Pont de Nemours & Co., Esso Standard Oil Co., Johns-Manville Corporation and Union Carbide Corporation. There were, however, many differences in the application of this policy, depending on the product range and the emphasis or otherwise on new products. Target return pricing was essentially centred on standard cost plus target rate of profit, but this greatly over-simplified what corporations actually did. Such pricing was however found to require detailed studies of costs over a long period in order to translate the company's operating experience into realistic norms of value and unit cost and realization on investment. Some of the corporations used target return as a rigid rule; others just as a benchmark. Usually, the companies employing target-return pricing were those that enjoyed relatively protected and stable markets for their products. New products were also frequently selected for target-return pricing because they had no rivals.

Secondly, *Stabilization of Price and Margin* was a policy prob-ably favoured by a majority of companies in the study, but it usually fitted into what were regarded as more important pricing objectives. Two companies, United States Steel Corporation and Kennecott Copper Corporation, however, gave high priority to maintaining steadiness of price in their industries. United States Steel had over one-third of the basic steel capacity in the industry and was gener-ally recognized as the industry's price leader. The company there-fore carried a mantle of responsibility assumed by no other company in the industry and aimed in its pricing policy at a fair return and following a policy of selling 'at the lowest price consis-tent with cost and a reasonable profit'.

Thirdly, *Pricing to Maintain or Improve Market Position.* Some companies did not stress a target rate of return, but appeared to relate their prices to other policies which they regarded as of prior importance. One such policy was maintaining or improving market position which was followed by Great Atlantic and Pacific Tea Co., Swift and Company, Sears Roebuck and Company, Standard Oil Company (Indiana). Swift and Company regarded its meat packing activities as allowing little scope for a 'pricing policy', its buying and selling operations being much influenced by the market. Sears Roebuck and Company stated as its underlying objective 'maximum sales in every line consistent with the realization of its traditional return on investment of 10 to 15 per cent after taxes' but was at the same time anxious at least to maintain its share of the market and to perpetuate its reputation for low prices.

Fourthly, *Pricing to Meet or Follow Competition* was a policy followed by four companies studied, Goodyear Tire and Rubber Company, National Steel Corporation, Gulf Oil Corporation and Kroger Company. They were distinguished by their belief that many of their prices were fitted to conditions outside the company's control rather than to one of a number of positive pricing policies adopted by the firm itself. National Steel, for example, had a policy of 'matching the market' and it tended to disregard costs in pricing.

Fifthly, *Pricing related to Product Differentiation.* Most companies made some effort to differentiate their product qualitatively in association with a brand name rather than depending on price policy alone, product design and differentiation sometimes taking precedence over pricing. Examples included General Electric Co., American Can Co. and General Foods Corporation, though many of the other companies studied also emphasized differentiation and brand name.

The categories chosen for the various corporations were inevitably somewhat arbitrary. Many corporations can and do follow several policies simultaneously without obvious inconsistency and company goals change with circumstances. Ephemerality of goals can be regarded as a quite proper characteristic of big business behaviour in a dynamic economy. The general conclusions of this study were: (1) that large corporations generally have a fairly well defined pricing goal related to a long-range profit horizon; (2) managements usually seek a simultaneous decision with respect to price, cost and product characteristics; (3) pricing formulas are handy devices for checking the internal consistency of the separate decisions against a general company objective. No single hypothesis such as profit maximization, however, could provide an unambiguous course of action for a firm.

The Kentucky study—pricing in small business

This study covered eighty-eight individual companies with from one or two employees to more than 200. They comprised a variety of industries including manufacturing, retailing, and service industries and a few firms from wholesaling, garden or landscape nurseries and combined retail and service firms. Few of the firms were producers of a single product; the manufacturers producing a variety of goods selling in different markets, the retailers providing a variety of resaling services and the service outlets also performing a variety of tasks. Single product firms were comparatively rare. In looking at the relative importance of cost and demand factors in pricing, the main conclusions of the study were:

(1) Most of the companies did not adhere strictly to the full-cost approach to pricing, but showed more flexibility.

(2) An important minority of companies did, however, follow fairly rigid patterns in pricing, emphasizing cost rather than demand.

(3) Where full cost was used as a basis of pricing policy, it was not a rigid base but 'a reference point' which served to provide a resistance to downward price flexibility.

(4) Many of the cases, particularly those in retailing and wholesaling, used gross margin pricing. There were mark-ups on the wholesale or manufacturing price not on cost.

(5) The mark-ups used by a single firm were usually not uniform for all products.

(6) A few companies followed external guides, e.g. the lead of larger firms, thereby escaping almost completely from determining their own pricing policies.

(7) In a substantial minority of the cases the mark-up idea was not mentioned, apparently because of nebulous character of costs.

(8) In a few cases a trial and error process, in some way resembling the economist's marginal approach in search of the optimum, was followed.

The study also considered how far small businesses followed the precepts of marginalism in their pricing and whether they attempted to maximize profits. Very few firms apparently used incremental measurements in pricing, though a majority probably at least moved in the direction of marginalism by trial and error and by imitation. Marginalism was probably not pursued because:

(1) Some managers were motivated not only by the desire for profit but by other objectives, particularly of an ethical character, that called for restraint in profit seeking.

(2) The information and skills required for full application of marginalism were not easily available. Most firms could not afford much experimentation in their pricing policies, so that even the trial and error approach had limited applicability.

(3) Some managers were satisfied with less than the optimum. They were more concerned with making a reasonable living than with getting the highest possible profits and simplified life by accepting outside prices as guides.

(4) Some managers simply rejected the logic of marginalism, refusing to price any product at a level that did not return a profit above full cost.

In this Chapter, fundamental economic principles of pricing have been outlined and several alternative prescriptions and practices discussed. Because of the variety of business and market situations, no clear, unequivocal set of pricing principles suitable for all situations emerges. What we have tried to indicate are the main advantages and disadvantages of the various pricing alternatives available.

NOTES

1. Neil Chamberlain, op. cit., ch. 9, p. 191.

2. Kaplan, Dirlam and Lanzillotti, *Pricing in Big Business*, p. 5.

3. ibid., p. 245.

4. See Chapter 6.

5. This is fully explained in elementary economics texts. See, for example, Samuelson, *Economics*; Stigler, *The Theory of Price*; Stonier and Hague, *Textbook of Economic Theory*; Lipsey, *Introduction to Positive Economics*.

6. Stigler, *The Theory of Price*, p. 14.

7. See Samuelson, *Economics*, pp. 485–6 for examples. Also Lipsey, *Introduction to Positive Economics*, ch. 10.

8. Kaplan, Dirlam and Lanzillotti, pp. 184 *et seq.*

9. See Baumol, *Economic Theory and Operations Analysis*, ch. 4, and Dowsett, *Elementary Mathematics in Economics*, ch. 26.

10. For the full formal analysis, see Joan Robinson, *Economics of Imperfect Competition*, ch. 15; Boulding, *Economic Analysis*.

11. Bergfeld, Earley and Knobloch, *Pricing for Profit and Growth*, p. 53. 'Contribution rate' is the ratio of Gross Contribution—i.e. the difference between price and unit variable cost—and price.

12. W. J. Baumol, 'On a Theory of Oligopoly', *Economica*, 1958.

13. Marris, op. cit., p. 175.

14. Dean, *Managerial Economics*, ch. 7, on which much of this section is based.

15. An example quoted in the Brookings study showed that when a new dishwasher was sold at $200 instead of $250, no more than 5 per cent of additional sales was believed to result. This was because the 'service' idea of an automatic electric dishwasher was not yet so fully accepted as to make a price concession expand sales significantly. When the service idea caught on, so that sales reached about 15 per cent of market potential, demand became very responsive to price. See Kaplan, Dirlam and Lanzillotti, op. cit., p. 59.

16. Earley, 'Marginal Policies of "Excellently Managed" Companies', *American Economic Review*, 1956. See below, p. 203.

17. Quoted in Neil Chamberlain, from Keller, *Management Accounting for Profit Control*, p. 195.

18. See Haynes, *Pricing Decisions in Small Business*, p. 12.

19. See Bergfeld, Earley and Knobloch, ch. 5.

20. See Haynes, op. cit.

21. We are indebted to Mr R. L. Smyth, of The University of Keele, who first suggested this term.

22. For reasons of space, we have not discussed, as a relevant pricing method, the idea that there is a logical relationship between the price charged for similar but not identical goods supplied by the same manufacturer. Brown and Jaques have advocated 'product analysis pricing' as the best method of arriving at price quotations in a situation where there is such a large number of special orders for special products that pricing decisions must be delegated to subordinates. Their method is that the chief executive decides target prices for a sample range of articles. Other articles are then compared with the sample articles in respect of physical characteristics, bought-out components incorporated in them, etc. Target prices are calculated by a mathematical formula, actual market prices differing from these and being set by the sales department within approved limits for particular markets, customers, etc. The procedure has merit, but is administratively somewhat complicated. See Brown and Jaques, *Product Analysis Pricing*.

23. The studies referred to are:

(1) Hall and Hitch, 'Price Theory and Business Behaviour', reprinted in Wilson (ed.) *Oxford Studies in the Price Mechanism*.

(2) Earley, 'Marginal Policies of "Excellently Managed" Companies', *American Economic Review*, vol. 46, part 1, 1956.

(3) Kaplan, Dirlam and Lanzilotti, *Pricing in Big Business*, and Lanzilotti, 'Pricing Objectives in Large Companies', *American Economic Review*, 1958, p. 921.

(4) Haynes, *Pricing Decisions in Small Business*.

PRODUCT POLICY, SALES PROMOTION AND MARKET STRATEGY

> In the present age, the element of novelty which life affords is too prominent to be omitted from our calculations. A deeper knowledge of the variety of human nature is required to determine the reaction, in its character and strength, to those elements of novelty which each decade of years introduces into social life.
>
> ALFRED NORTH WHITEHEAD

1. INTRODUCTION

Pricing is only one aspect of market strategy. In a modern economy with a rising income per head consumers are problem solvers, ever seeking new and satisfying experiences in their expenditures. By introducing new products and services, by marketing superior versions of older products, by the use of advertising to suggest possible new experiences to the consumer and the particular products which enable him to achieve them, a business widens the range of choices open to consumers in the hope of expanding its own sales. Every successful business should have a product policy and keep its product line under continuous review in the light of changes in demand. Every business should also have a policy on promoting its products, deciding how much to spend on personal selling, how much to spend on advertising and which advertising media to employ. These policies must be closely integrated with pricing policy as part of a general market strategy, which in turn must be related to the objectives of the whole business.

One way of viewing the marketability of a product is to conceive all possible products as being represented in a multi-dimensional product space.[1] Each dimension represents varying degrees of some product quality, such as brand, style, colour, package, sellers' location, efficient service, etc. Any location in such a product space would thus represent some combination of product properties or quality. Actual products—those already designed and marketed—would account for only a scattered distribution of points in product space. Many would be clustered, indicating concentration of demand for a particular combination of product qualities or simply imitation by other producers of a successful product. Concentration of buyers and sellers around the same type of car, transistor radio, 'package' foreign holiday tour is a familiar enough phenomenon, sometimes referred to as the principle of minimum differentiation. Every business tries to make a product with a difference, but it must not be too different from the general run of products in that category.

In this symbolic product space, there would be vast open regions representing quality combinations and products not yet designed and marketed. Much of this space would be empty because there would be some products unlikely to be wanted by consumers. Other regions of emptiness would represent products designed but not yet technologically feasible or economically worth manufacturing.

Ideally, the development of a product should be aimed at that combination of qualities likely to gain acceptance from the largest number of consumers, consistent with a given, acceptable level of costs. This would be one among a cluster of points representing consumer wants. In practice, some decision would be necessary on whether one model should be produced in quantity in the hope of appealing to consumers whose requirements came close to this point, or whether a policy of producing several models to cater for the slight differences in quality combinations demanded should be followed.

Product research and market research can both be explained by this model. Both may be regarded as explorations of product space, searching for clusters of products representing concentration of consumer wants and determining how these wants can best be satisfied. Advertising can also be explained in terms of the amount of knowledge of where people's wants are located in product space and how these wants can best be satisfied. Advertising provides consumers with *information* (and sometimes misinformation) about the array of quality combinations of products throughout symbolic product space. More important, it *persuades* consumers that certain of these combinations can more effectively provide them with new and satisfying experiences.

2. PRODUCT POLICY

As was discussed above[2] the question of what products to produce is clearly a fundamental matter for business decision. It should not be thought that this is only a problem for the giant concern. One has only to think of the problems of the small market gardener or nurseryman or the hardware dealer to recognize that almost every business has to make decisions on product line policy. Shall the business continue to market its existing range of products exactly as before, or shall it drop some lines altogether or shall it re-design some existing lines? Decisions whether to continue or to drop or to re-design are the fundamental ones in the product-line review.

It is comparatively simple to state the criteria on which product decisions should be based, but much more difficult to apply them. Neil Chamberlain[3] has suggested two basic questions which management must answer in a product-line review: (1) by how much is each product contributing more to earnings than to costs? (2) which products are increasing and which declining in volume of sales? The answer to the second question is a matter of statistical verification of trends in sales and market share. The answer to the first raises the difficult question of 'what costs?'. For long-term planning decisions involving the introduction of a new product a firm normally expects to cover its full allocated costs. But we have seen that in most businesses there is a considerable element of jointness in costs of producing different products and, at best, problems of common-cost allocation can only be settled approximately. Opportunity cost may be the appropriate criterion for short-run decisions, whether to continue or to drop any existing product A. If there are no other products which might have been manufactured with the same fixed resources, variable cost of A is the relevant short-run opportunity cost. If, however, Product A makes use of fixed resources, its opportunity cost is the sum of its variable cost and any greater return foregone by not making product B. Products which, over a long period, fail to produce an adequate (target) return on fixed investment should clearly come under careful scrutiny for possible re-design or withdrawal. Products should not however be summarily withdrawn without consideration of possible improvements or of alternative ways in which the fixed investment might be employed to give a better return. Where a product fails even to cover variable costs and shows no likelihood of doing so it should be dropped.

Even on the earnings side the criteria we have suggested are not completely unambiguous. Many products which give apparently very poor returns may be justified on the ground that they are complementary to other highly successful products enabling the firm to offer a 'full line'. The relationship of any particular product to the company's entire product line and its importance to the firm's goodwill should never be ignored. The criterion to be used is: 'what effect would a product's withdrawal have on the sales of the company's other products or on the company's goodwill?'. Obviously a precise answer will usually be impossible, but an approximate idea is often a sufficient guide. Book profitability of a particular product may also be distorted by arbitrary common-cost allocation. Where promotional activity is concentrated on a few products, but the expenses are charged over the entire range, book profitability of each product is obviously meaningless for product line decisions. Errors of this sort can, however, be largely eliminated by establishing the profitability of broad product groups or lines as well as, where necessary, by individual products. Comparative analysis of individual product performance against average performance may also indicate appropriate product policies.

In reviewing the product line, a decision may have to be made against dropping the product, but instead of continuing it in its present form re-designing it. Product differentiation was discussed earlier.* The possibilities of differentiation even for a fairly well defined class of product are usually very great. Professor E. H. Chamberlin has pointed out:

. . . consumer goods may be of different materials, design or standards of workmanship, whether we are speaking of furniture, clothing, or household equipment. The preparation of food for sale, whether by canning, baking or other type of manufacture for consumption at home or by cooking and serving in a restaurant, affords infinite possibilities of variation with respect to the selection of ingredients, their quality, and the manner in which they are combined and prepared. The perfect and infinite variability of such 'products' as services—public utility, professional and personal is evident. In the case of barber shops, beauty parlours, laundries, cleaning establishments, etc., the quality of what is sold is a major element in the consumer's decision to buy from one seller rather than another—his choice is made as much on the basis of product as of price and probably more so.

Moving back in the productive process from consumers' goods to capital goods, it is evident without further elaboration that similar considerations apply and that all products beyond the raw material stage are highly variable for the most part on a continuous scale.[4]

*Chapter 5.

Some writers on marketing have distinguished between physical, functional and aesthetic variations of products. Thus a car may be made a few inches longer, it may be equipped with power steering and power brakes, or it may be available in a variety of colours. Certainly the product is more than the sum of its physical attributes and customers apparently attach symbolic significance to the products they buy. The importance of symbols of sex, age and social class cannot be ignored in the styling of products. Choice is made easier for the consumer when the product is symbolically more harmonious with his goals and enhances his sense of self. Thus different colours may imply either respectability or glamour, 'smoother' products may be more feminine, a particular style of suit may symbolize a social class—'You don't have to be a Director to own an X Director's suit; you just look like one'. The modern consumer does not behave like the nineteenth century *economic man*, seeking the lowest price; if he seeks at all it is for the product which gives him most psychological satisfaction. And the product, as perceived and evaluated by the consumer, is far more important than what a business thinks it is producing.

The right choice of product is thus a matter for psychological and sociological study, as well as being a question of engineering and economics. Styling and style variation usually need more emphasis as the product approaches the mature stage of its life cycle. Whilst appropriate variations must be decided within the framework of budgetary constraints, economics alone cannot determine them. Many businesses rely on their sales force to recommend style changes suggested by customers or by competition. This policy may, however, need to be reinforced by sophisticated techniques of market research.

Product differentiation, relying mainly on styling changes, has sometimes been labelled 'defensive research'—sufficient perhaps to enable a firm to hold its own in the market—by contrast with innovation, which is 'aggressive research'. Innovation is certainly a condition of above average success and a firm must have a policy on major product release. Most innovation today requires heavy expenditure on research and development. While there is scope for innovation in the small firm, the advantage is increasingly with the science-based, capital intensive industries which have attracted highly trained staff and spent substantial sums on research and development.

While the same general principles regarding consumer acceptance apply to both differentiation and innovation, the main economic problems of innovation centre on (1) how much expenditure to devote to research and development and (2) how wide ranging major new products should be. How much to spend on research and development is a major worry of most progressive managements and there is no use pretending that there is any easy answer. The normal criterion on which a business decision is made is return on investment. But how does the business measure return on research and development expenditure? Such research, especially in its early stages, can rarely be assigned to any particular product that may ultimately result from it. And frequently products have to be abandoned as obsolete even at a fairly advanced stage of their development—one has only to think of the aircraft industry's problems in recent years. Rate of return criteria may be rather easier to apply at the stage of mature development than at the research stage, but in neither case can all technical and market uncertainty be eliminated. The appropriation for research and development, as Neil Chamberlain[5] indicates, is typically in practice more an act of faith than a precise calculation. Clearly, research and development cannot just be varied proportionately to sales volume or profitability, since declining sales and profits may well be an indicator that too little expenditure has gone on developing new products. Probably the best a firm can do is to study its own and competitors' past experience closely and to try and establish relationships between relevant variables such as expenditure and return, volume of sales, goodwill and so on, but at the same time to rely to a considerable extent on intuitive judgement in this difficult area of decision.

The problem of planning major new products is that research programmes cannot usually be kept within the confines of an established 'industry'. This is not necessarily a disadvantage however. A progressive business should always be ready to shake itself free of 'industry orientation'. This has not always been successfully done. The accounting profession for example has been slow to accept operational research and systems analysis with the result that practitioners in these fields have operated independently and are challenging the autonomy of the accountant in some areas of business. This comes back to the question discussed in Chapter 6: how much product diversification should a business indulge in? It is only necessary to repeat here that the basic criteria should be those of cost and profitability, taking all relevant alternatives into account. We may, however, note that on the demand side diversification *may* be justified by the following arguments:

(1) Variation of styling of products will need to be more sophisticated as the community's cultural development advances or as a product reaches the mature stage of its life cycle;

(2) Scope for diversification and segmentation—dividing the market into groups according to demand characteristics—will depend on the type of goods, in particular whether they are frequently purchased or not. Frequently purchased products sold in a mass market may be profitably subdivided and differentiated according to geographical location, income group or other variant, whereas a commodity purchased only once in a lifetime such as a piano hardly falls into the same category.

(3) The growing demand for goods with higher labour content —e.g. cake mixes, frozen foods—may call for variation of the product in more sophisticated markets. Similarly the demand for certain types of *services*—e.g. financial and tourism—increases as living standards rise.

(4) Additional products may be justified if their demand characteristics are related to those of the existing product line, e.g. binoculars, cameras and photographic equipment, or if they benefit the sales of existing products.

Apart from general considerations of cost and profitability the argument for diversifying the product line and/or segmentation of markets must depend on the extent to which consumers can be grouped into sub-markets on the principle of 'divide and conquer'.

On the production side, differentiation, diversification and segmentation of markets *may* be justified by such arguments as:

(1) A variety of different products may stem from common raw materials and production facilities;

(2) Quite different products may emerge from a common research project or from a company pool of 'know how';

(3) Excess capacity may exist, either in plant and machinery, management research or some other productive input so that additions to the product line may be possible at little additional cost;

(4) Common distribution facilities, sales force and advertising expenditures can often be used for a wider range of products at little or no additional cost.

At the same time, it is important to recognize the economic limitations on a policy of diversification and market segmentation.*

(1) A proposed new product—however readily manufactured with existing facilities—should be rejected if it is incompatible with the present product line and the business's existing market. A prestige product may lose its prestige if it is sold with a cheaper version of the same product, however effectively the production of these two may be combined. A new product requiring unfamiliar distribution channels and marketing methods should not be embarked on without most careful study. Conversely, a proposed product which can easily be marketed alongside existing products may be incompatible with existing production methods except at prohibitive cost.

(2) The belief that a business possesses substantial unused capacity may be a myth. Apparently under-used plant and machinery may require considerable expenditure on re-tooling and re-equipment before a new product can be manufactured. Nor should it automatically be assumed that an existing sales force has the capacity to handle new products.

(3) While there may sometimes be surplus managerial skills available in the firm, diversification and widening of markets necessarily results in dispersion of managerial effort and after a certain point may call for fundamental organizational changes.

Whenever a business introduces a differentiated product or an innovation, consumer acceptance is the ultimate test of its success. The main factors determining acceptability are: (1) it must be *discernible*—sufficiently different from the old product to make it worth the consumer's while to buy and use; (2) it must be *identifiable* and distinctive—in terms of appearance and quality—from other products; (3) it must be *reproducible* at a uniform standard of quality. Inadequate attention to quality control can ruin a product's chance of acceptability.

Finally, we emphasize that the modern sophisticated consumer buys a combination of product and service. He expects to satisfy his wants by purchasing something of known and reliable quality, with appropriate styling features, ready for immediate use, attractively packaged and wrapped, with a guarantee of after-sales service, and often desires credit facilities. Imaginative marketing

*As was pointed out above, Chapter 6, pp. 100–101.

takes all these factors into account. Service offered to the consumer may relate to (1) the effective use of goods—e.g. advice on the installation of hi-fi equipment; (2) the transfer of goods—credit, packaging, delivery; (3) the selection of goods—display, advice, catalogues. A business that neglects the service aspect of marketing does so at its peril.

3. ADVERTISING AND SALES PROMOTION

Expenditure on advertising and related types of promotional activity is termed by economists, 'selling costs'. The theoretical distinction between selling costs and production costs is quite clear. The costs of producing (i.e. the costs of manufacturing, and the costs of physical distribution of the product to the consumer) a new and supposedly 'better' product are quite distinct from the costs incurred in maintaining or enlarging the market. Professor Chamberlin has recently clarified this distinction by suggesting the criterion: 'what does the buyer buy and what does the seller sell?' as defining the 'product'.[6] On this criterion, the menu on a table in the restaurant is part of (and an inescapable part of) the cost of providing the meal; the menu in the window for the benefit of those outside is a selling cost. A TV programme advertising beer is clearly a selling cost; the tail fins on a car are a production cost.

This distinction is not merely theoretical. Practically, it indicates that selling costs (advertising) can be employed to complement either price or product competition, but that selling costs are themselves quite separate and distinct from either. Alternatively selling costs may be regarded as all costs incurred to shift the demand curve for a particular product to the right. They include advertising, which may make use of a variety of media such as television, radio, national and local newspapers, magazines and hoardings. They may also include costs of door-to-door salesmen, circulars sent through the mail, gifts and samples, displays, dealer incentives and discounts, promotional campaigns. All these expenditures have one fundamental purpose: to cause consumers to buy more of a product than they otherwise would have purchased. Of all these types of selling costs, advertising through mass media may be regarded as basic; usually requiring to be supplemented by specific promotional activities aimed at building up sales of particular products in particular places.

A distinction is sometimes made between *informative* and *persuasive* advertising. In a modern economy, advertising is easily the cheapest way of transmitting *information* to consumers. Consumers want to know what the prices of products are; they want to know about special features of each of a wide variety of products. They cannot be expected to incur the expense and time to go out and find this information for themselves from factories and shops. Nor would it be possible to employ a travelling salesman to visit each customer or write to each potential customer personally. Advertising through mass media therefore is the most economical method of making necessary information available to millions of consumers. The business must scientifically seek the cheapest method of disseminating sufficient information to its consumers.

However, in the opinion of at least one product advertising agent, 'Advertising isn't a science, it's persuasion. And persuasion is an art.'[7] Certainly most advertising must be regarded as *persuasive*. In an economy where innovation is continually taking place, new and improved products being introduced and prices reduced through technological improvement and where consumers have larger incomes to spend, persuading people to buy and try new products is obviously a very important function. Through advertising, consumers may widen the range of possible satisfying experiences. Consumers need to be persuaded in choosing between alternative new and untried products and the firm must spend money on persuasive advertising in today's competitive markets in order to 'get business'. Whether or not advertising is 'scientific', the problem has its economic aspect: the business wants to achieve a desired level of sales of its products in the most economic way. Further, methods of persuading people to change their minds can be costly, and if certain methods and media proposed turn out to be too costly, sales objectives have to be modified. And in certain types of oligopolistic market advertising can and does assume very substantial and quite probably 'wasteful' proportions.

Advertising and marketing policy generally must start from the presumption that in any society, fundamental needs exist and that as society becomes more complex, these needs are becoming more numerous and varied. Consumer wants spring from such fundamental needs and the problem of marketing and advertising is to create wants 'by making consumers aware of needs by identifying specific products as a means of meeting these needs'.[8] Furthermore, turning a generalized want into wanting a specific product means convincing the consumer that the product is an acceptable way of satisfying his fundamental need. This can only be explained in terms of consumer psychology and sociological factors. Many of the technical aspects of advertising, such as choice of media, establishing brand loyalty, the relative importance attached to consumer habit formation (association principle) or impulse (emotional drives) or rational as against irrational patterns of consumer behaviour are largely outside the province of economics. The psychologist and sociologist may advise on appropriate advertising techniques: on how a specific product can be modified to meet a generalized need and on such matters as choice of appropriate media. The economist takes such technical information as his data. Recognizing that the business has not unlimited resources to spend on advertising and promoting its product, he considers such things as the cheapest way of achieving a given market share, the most effective ways a firm can use advertising to maximize or 'satisfice' its profits and the relative importance to be attached to pricing, product variation and advertising in market strategy.

Marginal analysis of selling costs

It would be possible to analyse, with economic models of varying degrees of complexity, the effects of advertising expenditure on the firm's profits and sales in alternative market situations. It is questionable how useful such an exercise would be to the firm in a decision-making situation, since much would depend on whether objectives could be clearly stated and whether the relevant variables could be identified in practice and were measurable.

The basic purpose of selling costs is to shift the firm's demand curve to the right, so that more of the product is bought at any given price. Selling costs may therefore be viewed as an alternative to price reduction as a means of expanding sales. The concepts of price elasticity of demand and promotional elasticity, discussed earlier,* are therefore relevant and if the firm has any reliable information about these ratios, it should make use of it in its choice of policy. Clearly, if promotional elasticity is high and price elasticity low, selling costs will be preferred to price cuts as a means of expanding sales and vice versa. It should also be borne in mind that promotional elasticity will vary over the life cycle of a product, declining as the product reaches the stage of maturity.

Marginal analysis treats the decision whether or not to incur selling costs as a profit maximization decision in the same way as a

*Chapter 8, p. 158.

pricing or product decision. The producer who decides whether or not to advertise is thus asking himself: 'which course of action is likely to yield maximum profits?' Reducing the problem to its simplest terms, we may say that expenditure on advertising will (1) increase the costs of the firm, (2) if successful increase the revenue of the firm. Determining the right amount of advertising expenditure thus becomes a matter of formally equating marginal cost of advertising with marginal revenue.[9] An alternative formulation which enables sales maximization to be brought within the scope of analysis has been developed by Baumol and employs the type of analysis used above in Chapter 9, section 2.

The marginal analysis of profit maximization and sales maximization is logically correct but its assumptions are so highly simplified as to make it of limited usefulness in management decisions. In particular, it is difficult to apply to the fairly typical oligopolistic market where rivals' reactions are important. It also tends to concentrate attention on the short-run consequences of advertising, ignoring the fact that advertising can have a cumulative and delayed effect and that it may be more appropriate to treat the problem as an investment decision. In practice, too, measurement of the effects of advertising expenditure on demand are likely to be very difficult to isolate and measure, and all the usual statistical and econometric problems of empirical demand estimation, such as the identification problem,* are likely to be encountered. It may therefore be true that 'economic theory . . . has never been able to handle advertising with any great conviction'.[10] Formal economic analysis is, however, useful in isolating and thereby clarifying relevant concepts and variables in the advertising decision.

What businesses actually do

Joel Dean has identified five possible ways in which advertising budgets are determined:[11]

(1) The percentage of sales approach bases the advertising budget on a fixed percentage of sales, either past or expected future sales. This provides a convenient working formula, but in terms of economic theory it has little or no foundation mainly because past or present sales volumes have nothing to do with the cost or worth of expanding sales further. It confuses cause and

*See above, Chapter 8, p. 178.

effect since promotional activities cause sales and are not the result of them.

(2) The 'all-you-can-afford' approach apparently implies that the more profitable and more liquid the financial position of the business, the more advertising should be undertaken. It can be criticized: (i) because present profitability and a high degree of liquidity are not necessarily related to potential benefits likely to be achieved through advertising; (ii) liquid resources have many possible uses both within and outside the business and other things being equal they should be employed where they yield the highest return and not be blindly and arbitrarily earmarked for advertising or any other purpose without regard to the expected return.

(3) The return on investment approach acknowledges that advertising increases immediate sales and, at the same time, contributes to the goodwill of the business by increasing future earning power. The expected stream of future cash flows resulting from today's advertising expenditure, discounted at an appropriate rate of interest, enables a present value to be determined and the usual capital budgeting techniques described above to be applied.* This does not, however, get over the difficulty of identifying which of a business's cash flows are attributable to advertising, and the dilemma posed by the quotation: 'I know half the money I spend on advertising is wasted, but I can never find out which half' is not easily resolved. Another difficulty is to separate the short-term effects of advertising from the long-term. A week-end newspaper or TV advertisement designed to increase sales of a detergent in the shops at the beginning of the following week could hardly be treated as an investment decision. Long-term institutional advertising of the 'Guinness is Good for You' and 'Persil washes whiter' variety are principally designed to create a favourable brand image and to build up consumer loyalty and are clearly in the nature of investment decisions.

(4) The 'objective and task' approach operates on the principle of first defining advertising objectives, second outlining specific tasks necessary to attain the objective and third determining the cost of attainment. This method has some basis in logic and could, with appropriate adaptation, provide the basis for treating the decision as a problem of operational research. As in all such problems, however, the question of defining the objective is fundamental.

*Chapter 4, p. 42 et. seq.

since a specific objective is presumably not worth attaining *at any cost.*

(5) The competitive parity approach bases the firm's advertising outlay on what other firms in the industry are spending—e.g. the proportion of total industry advertising expenditure incurred by a particular firm would depend on its share of the total market. In oligopolistic markets where rivalry is intense, such methods, it is argued, may help to stabilize market shares and prevent dangerous competitive retaliation. Such an approach however provides no criterion by which the costs and benefits of additional advertising may be evaluated. What rivals spend need not be relevant to the size of advertising outlays a particular firm should make.

4. MARKET STRATEGY—THE DECISION THEORY APPROACH

Clearly, marketing decisions, involving as they do pricing, product and advertising variables, are exceedingly complex. Is it possible to formulate any model that could isolate relevant variables and provide a rational basis for marketing decisions? Or must such problems be left to 'hunches' or guesswork? One approach towards a solution of the problem is through decision theory and the theory of games, briefly mentioned in Chapter 4.*

In principle, it is possible to formulate a marketing problem in terms of objectives, available strategies, states of nature and behaviour of competitors (the last two of which may range from certainty, through risk, to uncertainty) and to use the device of the pay-off matrix to determine the correct choice of strategy. This is a useful exercise in that it clarifies the logic of the situation. In practice, however, difficulties arise from the tremendous number and dimensions of available marketing strategies (e.g. design, brand name, packaging, pricing, choice of outlets, and advertising); and also from formulating the wide variety of possible activities of numerous rational competitors and possible states of nature.

To illustrate this imagine that the decision-maker's strategy includes 5 possible product designs, 5 patterns of distribution and 5 methods of communicating with the consumer. This is a total of 625 strategies. If there are 4 competitors it is not unreasonable to assume that each of the competitors has 625 strategies available. Presuming that there are 5 states of nature then the number of different conditions that can prevail is 476,837,158,203,125.[12]

*See above, Chapter 4, section 6.

It has been suggested that such problems might be handled (1) by considering only a few factors at a time (which encounters difficulties of sub-optimization), or (2) by considering outcomes and sub-outcomes without relating them to strategies and states of nature—i.e. by considering them as data (which runs into the danger of considering effects without knowledge of what caused them). The complexity of marketing problems does make them difficult to formulate, though new management techniques and the availability of computers should increasingly make marketing decisions more rational than hunch and guesswork have previously permitted.[13]

It seems appropriate that a book on managerial economics should conclude on the subject of marketing, since it is in the market that the success of failure of the business is ultimately decided. But it is here too that many of those intractable problems are evident, with which existing economic and other available techniques are still unable adequately to cope. Marketing decisions, along with other management decisions, however, must always have their economic dimensions. It is thus the continuing task of the economist, with the increasing benefit he now derives from the growth of related disciplines, such as OR, decision theory, social psychology and organization theory, to improve his analytical tools so as to reduce the area of intractability within the whole field of management decision-making.

NOTES

1. Such a concept is used by Alderson, *Marketing Behaviour and Executive Action*, ch. IX. See, however, Chamberlin, 'Monopolistic Competition Revisited', *Economica*, 1951, for a similar model.

2. Chapter 6.

3. op. cit., p. 214.

4. E. H. Chamberlin, *Towards a More General Theory of Value*, p. 107.

5. op. cit., p. 224.

6. Chamberlin, 'The Definition of Selling Costs', *Review of Economic Studies*, vol. XXXI (1), no. 85, January 1964.

7. Quoted in Martin Mayer, *Madison Avenue, USA*, p. 78.

8. Alderson, *Marketing Behaviour and Executive Action*, p. 280.

9. This type of analysis is employed by Chamberlin, *Theory of Monopolistic Competition*, ch. 8.

10. Mayer, p. 318.

11. Dean, *Managerial Economics*, ch. 6.

12. Miller and Starr, *Executive Decisions and Operational Research*, ch. 9, p. 172.

13. Some interesting and fairly technical examples of the application of OR and decision theory techniques to marketing problems, such as brand shares, brand loyalty, media, optimizing message effectiveness, competition from rational opponents, pricing problems, etc., is to be found in Miller and Starr, op. cit., ch. 9, pp. 173–238.

INDEX

Accounting 27, 106, 134
Achievement levels 143
Advertising 91, 211, 218 ff.
Advertising budgets, determination
     of, in practice 221–3
Average fixed cost 104
Average total cost 104
Average variable cost 104

Break-even analysis 114, 197–8
Brookings study of pricing in big
     business 204–7
Budgetary control 136

Capital budgeting. *See*
     Investment policy
Capital structure 67
Cash and investment decisions 50
Competition 81 ff.
  as a dynamic concept 82
  rationale of 81–3
Competitive behaviour 85–6
Consumer acceptance 90, 217–20
Contribution formula 116
Correlation 171 ff.
Cost control 134 ff.
  achievement levels 143
  budgets and standards 136
  error measurement 146
  management 141
  participation 150
  ratio analysis 135
Cost of capital. *See* Investment
     policy
Cost of production 103 ff.
  accounting classification 106
  average fixed 104

average total 104
average variable 104
common costs 119
direct 120
economics classification 103
fixed 106
full 120
inventory 126
marginal 104
operational research and 124
  programming 128
variable 106
Cycle of competitive degeneration.
     See Innovation, pricing for

Decision theory. *See* Game theory
Demand 153 ff.
  curve, explanation of 153–8
  elasticity of 156–8
  elasticity, concepts for
     management purposes 158
  relations, empirical
     determination of 176 ff.
  socio-economic, analysis of 160–2
Demand forecasting 163 ff.
  interview and survey approach
     167 ff.
  projecting past experience as a
     method of 171 ff.
  regression and correlation
     analysis 171 ff.
  role of judgement in 166
Dependence effect 161
Depreciation. *See also* Investment
     policy 28–31
Descriptive approach to pricing
     185, 202 ff.
Direct costs 120

Discounted cash flow techniques
    42 ff.
Diversification 97–101, 212, 214,
    216–17

Earley's study of 'excellently
    managed' firms 18, 203–4
Earnings, costs of 63
Economic and social change 10
Economics cost classification 103
Economics, defined 13
Economic indicators 158–9
Efficiency, economic and
    technological 13, 14
Error measurement in budgeting
    146
Excess Present Value 43

FIFO 31, 32
Firm, economists' theory of 14 ff.
Fixed cost 106
Forecasting. See Demand
    forecasting
Forecasting demand for new
    products 182–3
Full cost 120
Full-cost pricing 198–201

Game theory (and Decision
    theory) 24 fn., 73 ff.
Going rate pricing 201–202
Goodwill 32–34

Holt's method of short-term
    forecasting 181–2

Identification Problem 178–9
Innovation 25, 89–90
    pricing for 194–7
Integration. See also
    diversification 97–101
Internal rate of return. See Yield
Inventory control 126
Inventory valuation 31–2
Investment policy 36 ff.
    accounting systems 37–50
    average cost of capital 66
    business objectives 38
    capital structure 67
    cash movement 50
    cost of capital 59

depreciation 55
discounted cash flow techniques
    42
dividends and earnings 63
life of equipment 55
measurement of opportunities 39
pay-off 42
profit 51–2
replacement of equipment 57
return on original investment 39
taxation 51
uncertainty 72 ff.

Joint costs 119

Kentucky study of pricing in
    small business 207–8

Least squares, curve fitting
    technique 174
LIFO 31–2
Linear programming 128–9
Loan stock, cost of 61
Location 94–7

Management, defined 13
Marginal analysis 15, 17, 188 ff.
Marginal cost 104
Market categories 83–4
Market research 211
Market strategy 210 ff.
    decision theory approach to
        223–4
Mathematical trend curves 180–1
Multiple correlation 175 ff.

Objectives, business 38
Oligopoly 190–2
Oligopoly pricing 190–1, 196–7
Operational research 124
Opportunity cost 14, 30, 70
Oxford study of price theory and
    business behaviour 203

Participation 150
Pay-off 42
Pioneer pricing. See Innovation,
    pricing for
Preference shares 61
Price discrimination 191
Price-minus theory of cost 202

Pricing 86 and generally 185 ff.
Probability and investment
    decisions 75
Product differentiation 87, 213, 214
Product policy generally 210 ff.,
    212–18
Product research 211
Production cost 103
Profit 22 ff., 51–2, 117
    maximization 14 ff., 35
    measurement of 26 ff.
    policy 33–5
    theories of 26
Promotional activity. *See* Sales
    promotion

Quality competition 88

Ratio analysis 135
Regression analysis. *See*
    Correlation
Replacement cost 31
Replacement of equipment 57
Research and development 90,
    100, 214, 215
Return on original investment 39

Sales maximization 192–4
Sales promotion 91–2, 218 ff.
'Satisficing' 18
Science-based industries 10, 90, 214
Scope 97–101
Selective selling. *See* Price
    discrimination
Selling costs. *See* Sales promotion
    marginal analysis of 220–1
Shares, cost of 61
Short-run production cost 103
Size of plant and firm 101–3
Standard costing 136

Taxation and investment
    decisions 51

Uncertainty 18, 23–5, 72
    diversification as a safeguard
        against 101
Unaccounted value changes 32–3

Variable cost 106
Variance analysis 137

Yield rate of return 42